BEYOND I

JOHN DRANE teaches practical theology at the Universi.,
Aberdeen, Scotland.

ROSS CLIFFORD is a former lawyer, a radio presenter, and
Principal of Morling College, Sydney, Australia.

PHILIP JOHNSON coordinates exhibitors' booths in alternative
lifestyle festivals and lectures on the world's religions in Sydney.

Readers can engage in further discussion of the topic addressed
by this book by visiting www.jesus.com.au

BEYOND PREDICTION

The Tarot and Your Spirituality

John Drane, Ross Clifford
and Philip Johnson

A LION BOOK

Published by
Lion Publishing plc
Sandy Lane West, Oxford, England
www.lion-publishing.co.uk
ISBN 0 7459 5035 3

First edition 2001
10 9 8 7 6 5 4 3 2 1 0

Acknowledgments
Extract from 'The Waste Land' by T.S. Eliot from
Selected Poems by T.S. Eliot, published in 1954 by
Faber & Faber Ltd.

Prayer by St Francis of Assisi.

Prayer by Peter Marshall from *The Prayers of Peter
Marshall*, edited by Catherine Marshall, published
in 1955 by Peter Davies.

Illustrations of the Major Arcana from the Rider-Waite
Tarot Deck reproduced by permission of US Games
Systems, Inc., Stamford, CT 06902, USA. Copyright ©
1971 by US Games Systems, Inc. Further reproduction
prohibited. The Rider-Waite Tarot deck is a registered
trademark of US Games Systems Inc. Permission for
the UK is granted by Ebury Press.

Illustrations of the suits of the Minor Arcana taken from
www.arttoday.com

A catalogue record for this book is available
from the British Library

Typeset in 11/14 Baskerville
Printed and bound in Finland

Contents

Introduction

The three of us first started talking about this book in the mid-1990s, at a time when, beginning from different starting points, we had begun to appreciate the vast change that is taking place all over the world in relation to spirituality. Twenty years ago, no one much would have been interested in searching for spiritual answers to life's big questions, and those few who were would have been branded as wacky and marginal. Of course, as long ago as the 1960s, the Beatles had embarked on a very public search for transcendence, and a fair number of stars from the worlds of pop music and movies followed their footsteps in the ensuing decades. They all sensed that the inherited institutions of Western culture had run their course and would not serve us well as guides for the future. But most ordinary people found their lives were still so fully occupied with the everyday business of making a living that few of us could afford the luxury of spending time to speculate about such things – that is, until we started to realize that one of the reasons we find life so tough is because we are often struggling to make it alone, and that without a 'spiritual' grounding it is all too easy to go round in circles.

There have been many definitions of what it might mean to be 'spiritual'. Maybe we don't need to pin it down with any great precision, though the UK government's Department for Education and Employment actually has an official definition of what spirituality is: 'The valuing of the non-material aspects of life, and intimations of an enduring reality'. Many people would be happy with something along those lines. Certainly, everyone who uses the term takes it for granted that, whatever it is, spirituality will be some kind of magical ingredient that adds value to our lives, helping us to be at peace within ourselves, as well as with the wider cosmos, and enabling us to find meaning in the relationships which we enjoy with others as well as living in harmony with the world of nature.

As we have worked together, we have each brought different experiences and concerns to our own search for spiritual meaning in life. We don't even all live within the same cultural context. John lives in the 'old world' (Scotland), while Ross and Philip are firmly planted on the frontiers of the 'new world' (Australia). But that has hardly made any difference, because today's search for truth is a worldwide – even cosmic – endeavour. The one thing we all do have in common, though, is that none of us ever expected to find something as arcane as the Tarot to be a significant guide for our journey. We each have our own story to tell of how we took our first tentative steps to explore what, to start with, was an alien world for us all – and how surprised we were to discover the insights that we now share in this book. We always expected that classic and traditional religious texts would be full of words of wisdom, if only because generations of spiritual searchers before us had found that to be the case. But it was a real revelation – in every sense of that word – to find the wisdom of the ages summarized and presented in such an accessible form in the Tarot.

Of course, it is not the Tarot by itself that has inspired us, so much as the resources to which the cards and their images point. For they direct us beyond themselves into a world where we can begin to explore our own humanity, and where we can experience for ourselves the spiritual wisdom that the creator intended for us to have all along. There was just one thing that might have hindered our search, and that was our own baggage. We could easily have dismissed this message as inconsequential and unhelpful – maybe even something for those who are gullible and easily led astray. It was important to us not to become tangled up in something that had no real wisdom to offer. After all, one of us is a lawyer, and we are all academics! When we started to look beyond the popular image of the Tarot as being only a tool for stargazing and fortune-telling, we discovered things that have not only impacted our own lives, but which have been transformational for many others as we have shared them in many different contexts. For we have all been talking about the hidden secrets of the Tarot for a few years now, in contexts as varied as psychic fairs and traditional churches, and of course on both sides of the world (indeed, John has also shared all this in California, one of the most spiritually aware places in the entire world, to great enthusiasm and acclaim even in that supermarket of faiths).

So we know we are onto something big! That's why, in spite of our own surprise at discovering what we now share with you, we do it with great confidence. For the message of the Tarot regarding our own spirituality really has worked in our own lives, and is transforming the lives of others – not, of course, because we are special in any way, nor because of any magical properties in the cards themselves, but because in the end they point well beyond anything we can see and touch, and control, to the one who is at the bottom of all things, the one whose cosmic wisdom is revealed through foolishness. Who might that be? Well, you don't want the secret to be revealed on the first page, do you? Not if you're a serious searcher for truth, anyway! So read on, be entertained, stimulated, informed, inspired – and in the process we invite you too to explore what that divine one might yet have in store for your empowerment and personal transformation.

John Drane
Ross Clifford
Philip Johnson

Chapter One

SEARCHING FOR OUR SOULS

There was once a tribe who lived in the happiest land you could imagine. Well, perhaps it was not quite a tribe – more an extended family. But its people were certainly happy. Others called them the Barakites, an ancient term that, to those who recognized its secrets, spoke of blessing and contentment. They certainly felt blessed. They loved their home, they cared for one another, and they understood their place in the cosmic scheme of things. Life was not always easy for the Barakites, for though they lived in an attractive place, it was dry, and it was hot. In fact, it was desert. But to its inhabitants it was the most beautiful land imaginable, for the soil was red and the sun was bright, and the land was constantly refreshed by a mighty river.

It was the river that really mattered. As it flowed gracefully across the landscape, it provided life and food to the people who lived along its banks. For as long as anyone could remember, young children had splashed and played in its sparkling waters, while their parents worked long and hard to grow the food that would keep the whole community in good health. It wasn't a particularly easy life, but the Barakites knew they could depend on the river to bring their seeds to life and to mature the harvest. And in any case, they knew they were not alone. The older people of the community were always there to offer advice and encouragement, even if they spent much of their time doing what old people have always done: sitting by the banks of the river, talking about old times and watching their grandchildren with pride. The river spoke eloquently of all the things that mattered most: good health, good food and good relationships. The legends handed on from the ancestors all mentioned the river, and it had certainly been there for longer than anyone now living could remember. In fact, it became a kind of symbol for the good life – rooted in the past, drawing on the wisdom of the many communities through which it passed, and yet constantly moving in new and unexpected directions.

No one could really remember when things had started to change, for it was just here-a-little and there-a-little. The children discovered that the water no longer splashed quite so high. Their parents began to imagine that the fields never seemed quite as green as they remembered them being when they were young. And the old people? Well, they always thought *everything* had been better 50 years ago, and so they didn't notice much either. But eventually everyone could see that the river was beginning to dry up. No one wanted to talk about it at first, because there was still *some* water left. But instead of being lively and bubbling, it was becoming brown and muddy. Instead of tasting fresh and life-giving, it started to smell. Just a little bit at first, but then as time passed there was less water – and more smell. Less water meant fewer crops. The children began to ask what had happened to their beautiful playground. Their parents looked at their bare fields, and wondered if the entire community might one day starve. And the old people? Well, even they began to get just a little bit concerned. But they didn't want to bother themselves too much about it, for what could they do? There had always been plenty of water in the past, and they took it for granted that things were bound to stay the same if only they waited long enough for the river to start flowing again.

Not everyone had that kind of patience, nor did they share the optimism of those who imagined that things would return to normal without somebody doing something about it. And so a small but courageous group determined that they would get to the bottom of things. They were grateful for the way of life that the river had provided for their people from time immemorial, and they were concerned as they saw the waters starting to dry up. What future could there be, not just for the tribe but for the whole of humanity – even for the planet, perhaps – if the river of life disappeared for good? The Barakites loved their people, and they loved this place – and they cared enough to do something about it. They knew that just standing still and accepting things would make no difference: if there was to be a solution, they would need to look for new adventures, explore new territory, perhaps make new friends on the way. And yet... they couldn't get away from the thought that, well, rivers don't just disappear. So the first thing they did was to make for the nearest high hill to get a better view of the landscape. Maybe then they would be able to see what was really happening to their river – and just possibly, things may not be as bad as they imagined.

As the villagers climbed higher and higher, they saw a most amazing sight. For the river hadn't dried up at all. It had been bringing vitality to this land and its people for thousands of years – and it was still flowing as fast as ever, full of sparkling and life-giving water. But it had changed direction, and the Barakites could see that what the people of their village thought was the river was now only a stagnant pool. It would only be a matter of time before it dried up completely – and then what future could there be for any of them?

A few bold souls decided to go closer to the source of the problem, trying to understand just exactly what had taken place. Rivers don't just change direction by themselves, unless something interrupts their flow. And that is precisely what had happened here. As the Barakites journeyed to the place where the river had diverted from its original course, they began to remember some of the stories they had heard from the past, and it all started to make sense. For their grandparents had told them of other, strange people who came to this beautiful land with a different message, and who over the years had captured the imagination of many of their brightest and best young people. These were the Harassenes, and they were well named, for in ancient mythology they had been the destroyers of all good things. The simple life by the river, based on trust and dependency – on the natural world, as well as on one another – was mocked by the incomers as primitive and unsophisticated. By adopting their ways, Harassenes claimed, the next generations could become rich and successful – even conquering the world, perhaps. And just a few of the Barakites had found the temptation too great. They had left their traditional home behind, and gone off in search of fame and fortune, following the guidance of these people who thought they knew best. But in the process they had to learn new ways of doing things. They came to despise the simple homespun wisdom of their forebears, especially about the river. To them, it no longer made sense to think of its waters as the source of life. They were not content to allow the natural currents to flow freely, but insisted that they should be controlled, forced into channels that would, it was thought, be for the greater good of humankind.

The people who had stayed by the river vaguely knew that all this was happening upstream, but never thought to think seriously about it until the water started to dry up. When they realized what was going on, some of them were angry, and all of them were concerned. They brought to mind other ideas that the strangers from afar had introduced to them – ideas about justice, and wrongdoing, and the notion that everyone and everything is working against us, so that life will be a constant struggle for survival. The Barakites had always known that bad things can happen to good people, and that even good people can do bad things. But they also knew that they were loved – by the river itself, as well as by others within the community. As they reflected on their predicament, they knew that it wasn't their fault that the river had dried up in the place where they had lived for generations – though perhaps they should have resisted the ideas of the Harassenes more forcefully, and maybe things wouldn't have ended up like this. But nothing could change the reality: they had a tough choice to make. Either they could stay where they were, in the place where their ancestors had lived happily before them – but which was now only a dry and lifeless shadow – or they could move with the river, and once again find a place where little children could splash and play, where their parents could keep fertile fields, and where the old people could live to a ripe old age.

Rediscovering the wisdom of our past

We don't need to know much about Western history to see the relevance of that traditional aboriginal story to where we find ourselves today. In the course of the last 500 years or so – especially the last 200 – the river of wisdom that once refreshed and inspired our forebears has been gradually blocked up. Some look quite literally at the pollution of our rivers and oceans, and conclude that we might well be witnessing the end of life as we know it. Others, less pessimistic, are happy to acknowledge all the good things that scientific progress has produced, while being realistic about the mess that has been created in the process. We all know that, though we are now able to feed many more people than ever before, that has been achieved only at a price, as the pesticides and fertilizers that have facilitated increased production have also in many places polluted the most basic resource of all, the water supply. Even efficient transportation systems, which have revolutionized all our lives so that we can now reach any part of the world in 24 hours or less, are damaging the atmosphere in such a way that we may all yet be fried alive in our own lifetimes. And though none of us would wish to turn the clock back to the days before the emergence of modern scientific medicine, with its antibiotics and anaesthetics, many are painfully aware of the underlying ideology which can all too easily turn people into machines, and leave even those whose bodies are apparently functioning smoothly with enormous unmet needs for personal healing and wholeness.

In the midst of so much progress, it can often seem as if we have lost our souls, and it is certainly the case that the 20th century was probably one of the most unspiritual periods of recent history, as well as being the most violent century ever. The wisdom of past generations was not only questioned, but rejected, by Western people who increasingly believed in their own capacity to reinvent the world. We did, and the reinvention created a world of such brutality that we were not even shocked by the loss of millions of lives in the First World War (1914–18), but went on to orchestrate another massive conflict 20 years later, this time accompanied by the systematic, industrialized death machine of the Holocaust. By the end of the century, not content with killing one another, we began to realize too late that we were also suffocating the very ecosystems on which we ourselves depend for life. And, in personal terms, that kind of suffering has become reality for very many ordinary people, as relationships crumble and traditional networks of support disintegrate. The very place where we might once have found safety – the family – has for many become a place of abuse and victimization.

It is no wonder that today, with the promise of a new century, so many are looking for answers from a more ancient way of being, exploring different aspects of the wisdom of the ages in the hope of rediscovering ourselves, our purpose, and the truth that lies behind the cosmos. The

Tarot is one of today's most powerful spiritual tools. The very designs of the cards themselves speak to us of a different world, offering a distinctive understanding of life and its meaning. Millions of people, not only in Western countries but throughout South America and Asia, consult these cards every day in the hope of unlocking the secrets of the universe and finding happiness and fulfilment in relationships with others, and within their own inner space. Like all spiritual texts, including the scriptures of major world faiths, the Tarot and its message can be used in many different ways, some helpful and some not so helpful. Our purpose in this book is to explore the cards in the light of questions about personal spirituality. How can I be the best person I can possibly be? How can I find my place in the world? Who am I, and who might I become? Does any of it make sense? And even if it does, who cares anyway? If these are your questions, welcome to the search!

Chapter Two

THE TAROT AND ITS HISTORY

People have been using pictures to give direction to their spirituality since the very dawn of time itself. Such images have not always been in the form of cards, of course; the many elaborate carvings and paintings in the Egyptian pyramids would be an example, while many believe that the complicated architectural designs of the Aztec and Mayan civilizations of South America served a similar purpose. When they see a pack of Tarot cards for the first time, the thing that surprises most people is the way in which their designs seem to transport us into a different atmosphere from the everyday world, evoking images of mystery and wisdom that offer the prospect of connecting with the very foundations of the cosmos itself.

A major reason for the Tarot's continuing popularity is this ability that it has to help us to connect not only with our inner selves, but also with the spiritual understandings of those generations that have gone before us. It is as if the pictures on the cards are speaking of something that is beyond ourselves, and yet which has the power to take us into ever deeper knowledge of who we are, where we have come from and what might yet be in store for us. The fact that the Tarot speaks so easily of the things that concern us today often makes it difficult to get at the history of these cards. For if pictures like this have a universal appeal that addresses the concerns of people without regard for time and place, it is the most natural thing in the world to conclude that they themselves must be of very ancient, if not primal, origin.

The earliest Tarot cards

In fact, the Tarot as we know it today can be traced back only to about the 14th or 15th century. The earliest surviving set of cards consists of an incomplete pack that was hand-painted for Filippo Maria Visconti, Duke of Milan, in 1441. The designs are very typical of the artistic fashions of the day, combining traditional classical themes based on the ancient stories, deities and beliefs of Greece and Rome, which in turn are portrayed in such a way as to make clear references to the lives and times of the rich patrons who were responsible for commissioning them. The earliest written reference to the cards appears in a letter that was sent in 1450 from Duke Francesco Sforza to his treasurer, asking to be sent a pack of Tarot cards. In the letter, he said that if no Tarot cards were available, then a pack of ordinary playing cards would do, something that obviously implies he was intending to use them for playing the kind of games that might be played with any sort of cards. And an official document from the city of Florence dating to that same year (1450) actually lists the game of Tarot (called *trionfo*, or 'trumps' – a reference to the cards of the Major Arcana) as a regular part of city life, along with chess and various other board games. Tarot was a game played for fun, and the cards were created by rich people for their own amusement, and to mark significant events in their lives. Between them, the 15th-century Visconti and Sforza families commissioned at least 11 different sets of cards to commemorate things like weddings, coronations, births and deaths. Of these 11 sets, two survive almost complete and a further four are represented by just a single card each. Since all the earliest references to the Tarot come from Italy, it makes sense to conclude that the cards were invented there; they then later spread throughout Western Europe, and eventually of course to the rest of the world.

In many ways, the Tarot can be seen as a variant of a regular pack of playing cards. The four suits of the Tarot (Wands, Cups, Swords and Pentacles) may look strange to people who expect playing cards to be defined as Hearts, Diamonds, Spades and Clubs, but in fact the original versions of southern European playing cards had the same suits as the Tarot, traditionally referred to as Batons or Staves (the equivalent of Clubs), Cups (= Hearts), Swords (= Spades) and Coins (= Diamonds). According to Joseph Campbell, these suits themselves correspond to the social world that was familiar to the Italian nobles who first created them:

> *What the set of four suits represent are the four estates or classes, of the medieval social order. The Swords signify the nobility; the Cups, suggesting the chalice of the Catholic Mass, are for the clergy; the Coins, for the merchants, or 'third estate', the townsmen, the burghers; while the Staves, Clubs, or Batons, stand for the 'churls', the peasantry and servants.*
>
> JOSEPH CAMPBELL AND RICHARD ROBERTS,
> *TAROT REVELATIONS*, pp. 9–10

It seems that the original Batons and Coins came to be known as Wands and Pentacles only later, when people began to realize how the Tarot might be used to point to deeper spiritual realities about the nature of life and the world. But the most distinctive thing of all about the Tarot is the fact that right from the earliest times it has contained cards with elaborate pictures that belong to none of the four suits. Today there are 22 of these cards, known as the Major Arcana, and regarded as the most powerful of all the cards. The Fool card was even more powerful than the rest of them, which explains why it is numbered zero, while the other 'trumps' have the Latin numbers I to XXI (1–21). The Italian term *tarocchi* (from which the English word Tarot is derived) first seems to have been used in 1516, as a way of referring to these 78 cards with trumps or 'triumphs' (*carte da trionfi*).

Meanings and mythologies

It was not until the 18th century that the Tarot gradually became more widely known among the people of western and northern Europe. This was a period when European people were discovering that the world was much more expansive than they had ever imagined. Part of this was directly linked to the voyages of explorers to lands on the other side of the world. But there was also a growing realization that this was not the only place where secrets about the meaning of life might be unearthed. For alongside the fascination of new cultures (which were, in reality, very old cultures), there was also a growing interest in revisiting the past as a way of discerning new directions for the future. Interest in the historical past of Middle Eastern countries had initially been stirred up at the time of the crusades, but the European Renaissance of the 18th century also created a fresh appreciation for the treasures of ancient Greece and Rome – not to mention Babylon and Egypt. When the French emperor Napoleon (1769–1821) took his armies to Egypt, not only was he impressed by its ancient monuments, but he and others found an endless fascination in speculations about the meaning and significance of structures like the pyramids and the Sphinx, embodied in ancient legends about how they were designed and built, and their alleged role in the future of the world. When they accidentally uncovered the Rosetta Stone, inscribed in three languages, European thinkers for the first time had the key that would enable them to unlock the mysteries of ancient hieroglyphs. Before long, diplomats and explorers were falling over themselves to expand their knowledge of the ancient civilizations not just of Egypt, but also of Mesopotamia and the lands that had witnessed the compilation of the Jewish-Christian sacred writings, which had been so influential in the growth of European civilization.

As long-forgotten texts gave up their secrets, and the story of the spiritual quest of humankind over many centuries was gradually revealed, it seemed to many as if the symbols of the Tarot must have some connection with movements and people going back to a time well before the emergence of life as they knew and experienced it. This was all happening in the context of the European Enlightenment, when scientific knowledge was increasing almost daily, and when it seemed as if there was nothing that humans would not be able to do for themselves, without any aid from anything or anyone beyond themselves. The leading thinkers of the day began to regard everything and everybody as machines, operating mechanically and with predictable precision – a view that has now been discredited, of course, as it led to the spoiling of the natural environment and the alienation of the human spirit that now seems endemic throughout Western culture. Even then, there were those who longed for a more holistic understanding – romantic mystics such as the English poets William Wordsworth (1770–1850) and William Blake (1757–1827), as well as many of the founding fathers of the USA, people like Henry Thoreau (1817–62) and Ralph Waldo Emerson (1803–82). To those who were influenced by these thinkers, and others like them, the Tarot seemed to offer a bridge between their own lives and the emerging world of ancient mysteries.

In this context, many stories began to be told about the Tarot and its 'true' origins. The word 'Tarot' itself gave rise to much speculation as to its ultimate meaning. Some sought to connect it to the *Book of Thoth* (an apparently legendary document referred to in ancient mystical texts from Egypt), arguing that both 'Thoth' and 'Tarot' were derived from a single ancient Egyptian word *taru*, meaning to consult or require an answer of someone. On a similar basis (the sound of the words) others claimed that the Tarot's ultimate origins must have something to do with the name AshTaroth, given to the mother goddess in traditional Mesopotamian and Canaanite mythology. According to Etteilla, an 18th-century French philosopher, both 'AshTaroth' and 'Tarot' were connected to the Egyptian words *tar* (a path) and *ros* (royal), therefore meaning 'the royal path of life'. Linguistically, things are almost certainly much more straightforward, and it seems beyond reasonable doubt that the word 'tarot' was nothing more complicated than being the French version of the Italian *tarocco* (the singular form of *tarocchi*). However, these were not the only mythological associations which came to be attached to the Tarot. Some stories also credit the Romany people of Eastern Europe with preserving secrets from these ancient civilizations through their own spiritual lore, which was handed down from one generation to the next, accompanied by pictorial representations – naturally enough, since these people were largely illiterate. It was even claimed that the common description of Romanies as 'gypsies' was derived from 'Egyptian'.

It was a simple step from such speculations to the conclusion that, when their images were properly interpreted, the Tarot symbols were actually repositories of ancient teachings that had been handed on in a secret form, concealed in these apparently simple pictures, but revealed to those who held the key to knowledge.

Mystical connections

The keys which could unlock this true understanding of the Tarot were identified in many different places. An influential figure in this was the French Protestant pastor Antoine Court de Gebelin, who in 1781 not only made extensive connections between the Tarot and ancient Egyptian mythology but also identified similarities with other spiritual movements in the ancient world. Beginning from the fact that the Major Arcana contains 22 cards, it seemed natural to draw comparisons with the 22 letters of the Hebrew alphabet. A mystical movement within medieval Spanish Judaism had already explored the Hebrew alphabet in this way. The Kabbalah (a Hebrew word meaning 'received wisdom') was based on secret knowledge passed from master to disciple, derived from various mystical perceptions of the different letters. By chanting the letters themselves, it was possible to produce experiences of altered consciousness, and by exploring their numerical equivalences (for each letter was also a number) the sacred Hebrew writings could be interpreted in such a way as to distil 'hidden' meanings that were not otherwise apparent. From as early as the second century there had been Christian movements doing much the same thing in relation to their own sacred scriptures – most notably the Gnostics, whose understanding was also based on the belief that true spirituality could only be discerned by those who knew how to use the keys to mystical knowledge that would enable them to dig deeper than the surface meanings of sacred texts.

An early Gnostic writer had expressed the hope that the human search for wholeness would end with 'the knowledge of who we were, and what we have become, where we were or where we were placed, whither we hasten, from what we are redeemed, what birth is, and what rebirth' (*Excerpta ex Theodoto*, 78.2). That exactly captured the aspirations of a whole generation of Europeans in the late 18th and early 19th centuries, especially people from the upper classes who, following the French revolution, were going through a significant crisis of identity. Their power base in public life was slipping away, and the retreat into secret knowledge (accessible only to those who were in the know) was just one of the ways in which they attempted to reinvent themselves, not now as a group with exclusive political powers but as a spiritual élite. France in particular saw the emergence of many such secret societies, but they had a more general appeal throughout the Western world. Existing movements such as freemasonry and Rosicrucianism saw significant growth, though they were by no means the only ones to begin searching for what Aldous Huxley later called a 'perennial philosophy' (the idea that there was one original religion that could be discovered in its primal form through ancient mysticism, and from which the major world faiths were all derived). It was perhaps inevitable that the Tarot would be seized upon as a useful tool of spiritual discovery in this context. For whatever their origins in the courts of late medieval Italy, once the cards moved west into this kind of cultural ferment those people who were unfamiliar with their Renaissance-inspired classical imagery or with the traditional Italian suit signs naturally found them to be exotic and mysterious. The eventual outcome of all these speculations was that card designs which had once been rooted in a very specific historical context (the Italian courts and their rich patrons) were transformed into mythological symbols, and in effect the Tarot and its meaning was redefined.

Universal archetypes

Arthur Waite was a member of a secret society known as the Hermetic Order of the Golden Dawn, a movement founded in England in 1886. Its members, who included the well-known Irish poet W.B. Yeats (1865–1939), were interested in precisely the kind of ancient spiritual movements mentioned here (the Hermetic literature, from which the group took its name, was a collection of texts claiming to have some historic connections to ancient Gnosticism and to a medieval group known as the Cathars, who had a similar worldview). Within the society the Tarot was identified as giving particular access to the secrets of the universe, and at Arthur Waite's direction a definitive set of cards was drawn by the English artist Pamela Colman Smith. This is what became known as the Rider Waite tarot and is the pack we have used in this book. Waite was concerned that, in his day, there were so many different versions of the Tarot that what he regarded as its 'true' meaning was in danger of becoming lost. In his book *The Key to the Tarot* (1910) he says that he intended 'to introduce a rectified set of Tarot cards and to tell the unadorned truth concerning them' (*The Key to the Tarot*, p. 17). Naturally enough, Waite used the materials that were accessible to him, and that captured his imagination. One of his innovations was to introduce drawings into the cards of the four suits, which before his time had only been designated by numbers. But his major contribution was to the understanding of the 22 cards of the Major Arcana. He was already familiar with the Kabbalah, and connected these cards not only to the letters of the Hebrew alphabet, but also to the Tree of Life which played a central role in Kabbalistic speculation. He therefore found a major source of inspiration in the traditional Jewish scriptures, and many of the images he adopted – and which were subsequently adopted in other Tarot decks – originated there.

The connection of the Tarot images with ancient mythologies and prophecies continues to excite spiritual searchers even today. In his book *Tarot and the Millennium*, mathematical physicist Timothy Betts traces the images of the Major Arcana to an illustrated apocalyptic prophecy that was popular from the 13th century, and was said to be the sequel to the book of Revelation, found in the Christian sacred writings. He goes on to argue that the Tarot contains a secret medieval retelling of the story of the second coming of Jesus Christ. As we will see, some of the cards certainly do seem to point not to the past, though there are many that seem to have a more down-to-earth significance.

The truth is that many of the images on the cards have been used and recycled in all sorts of different contexts since ancient times. This phenomenon itself highlights another major attraction of the Tarot. Arthur Waite had been influenced by a 19th-century French philosopher by the name of Eliphas Lévi, who had claimed in a book written in 1856 that 'an imprisoned person with no other book than the Tarot, if he knew how to use it, could in a few years acquire universal knowledge'. That may sound like an exaggerated claim, but it highlights a major reason for the Tarot's survival, and explains why a game played by medieval Italian gentry is still regarded as more than a quaint historical curiosity. Today, the Tarot is more popular than it has ever been, and the reason for this is simple: it does indeed tell a universal human story. From time immemorial, people have always been interested in the same kind of questions: why am I here, how do I relate to other people, what is my place in the wider scheme of the cosmos, where do I go from here, what is it all about – and how can I live my life so as to be a satisfied person, and truly useful to others?

The images on the Tarot cards are symbolic representations of all these things, and more. As we encounter them, they touch our lives at significant and deep levels. They are, in effect, what the Swiss psychiatrist Carl Gustav Jung (1875–1961) identified as universal archetypes – that is, they provide us with a unique mirror into our inner beings, while also offering us possibilities for transformation as we seek wholeness and purpose. They connect with the same symbolic world that we find in the writings of novelists such as C.S. Lewis or J.R.R. Tolkien, a connection which was made quite explicit by Charles Williams in his novel *The Greater Trumps*. Moreover, this imaginary – and imaginative – way of looking at things still has enormous appeal, as can be seen in the popularity of J.K. Rowling's character, Harry Potter. A key reason for this is the obvious fact that it is at one and the same time not our world (for it is full of strange mythological beasts and unexpected happenings) – and yet it *is* our world, closer to us than anything else we could imagine. For this is the world in which we as individuals stand alone, struggling to be human, wrestling with forces that seem as if they have the power either to destroy us or to bring wonderful transformation to our lives. In other words, the Tarot has within it the power to connect us with the deep secrets of life itself. In her book *The Illustrated Guide to the Tarot*, Naomi Ozaniec captures this sense of power and vulnerability exactly:

> *The Tarot offers a spiritual philosophy to a Western generation looking for meaning. Meaning is healing. To live without meaning is soul-destroying. The Tarot affirms our worth. It affirms the value of our journey. It affirms our place in relation to a greater whole. We are the products of a generation that has been educated from the head, taught to think logically and rationally, not subjectively, and certainly not imaginatively. Cerebral thinking is a fair tool, but a poor master. The Tarot reminds us how to think symbolically. This is a whole way of responding that includes the imagination and touches our sense of connection to everything. This is the seed of heart thinking. This is the seed of living holistically. This is the seed of a way of life that heals.*
>
> THE ILLUSTRATED GUIDE TO THE TAROT, p. 127

In light of this, we need not be surprised to find connections between the images on today's Tarot cards and the symbolic depictions of life and its meaning in many ancient cultural contexts. The illustrations used in the Rider Waite Tarot certainly have similarities to some paintings found in the pyramids, while there are obvious connections with episodes from Greek and Roman mythology as well as many references to stories and people who appear in the Jewish-Christian sacred writings and in Kabbalistic speculations based on them. But they also have connections to other contexts, and anyone familiar with, for example, the woodcuts of Albrecht Dürer (1471–1528) will notice some striking similarities. But this diversity of inspiration and artistic expression only adds to the usefulness and universal appeal of the cards.

Some question the usefulness of the Tarot, observing that it has sometimes found its greatest popularity among clairvoyants and occultists. The medieval church denounced the Tarot as 'the devil's picture book', not so much because of any supposed occult connections but because the games that rich Italians played with it were often accompanied by a lot of gambling. In his famous poem 'The Waste Land', written in 1922, T.S. Eliot perpetuated a slightly different image, referring to:

Madame Sosostris, famous clairvoyante…
the wisest woman in Europe,
With a wicked pack of cards.

This 'pack' was, of course, the Tarot. Eliot was not the first to suppose that the Tarot's sole purpose was to serve as a vehicle for fortune-telling, nor will he be the last, but he was at least honest enough to admit in his own notes on the poem that 'I am not familiar with the exact constitution of the Tarot pack of cards, from which I have obviously departed to suit my own convenience.' Actually, the way in which he did refer to them in the poem was very much in line with the kind of wisdom that many people today are seeking, for he used them as a way of making connections with our own innermost thoughts and exploring the deeper realities of life.

By encouraging us to tune in to a different world than the one we experience and know in everyday life, the cards draw our attention to the underlying truths that govern the universe, and our place within it. They invite us to broaden our horizons beyond our consciousness of the mundane material world, and to discover the underlying purpose of things as we reconnect our souls to the divine source of all life. This is the journey on which we invite you to come, in the remaining chapters of this book.

Chapter Three

THE HEALING POWER
OF MYTH AND SYMBOL

The word 'myth' can be understood in many different ways. A hundred years ago, it would have been commonplace for people to contrast 'myth' with 'reality', implying that the one was fictional whereas the other was true. But we can now see that truth comes in many different forms, and the very deepest and most important truths about personality and relationships simply cannot be expressed in the measured language of scientific discourse. We actually *need* stories and pictures to help us deal with our innermost beings. The ancients got some things right, after all, and we now value myth and symbol (two of the major categories of knowledge used by past generations) as catalysts for personal healing and spiritual nourishment. Many Tarot interpreters, such as Sallie Nichols and Carl Sargent, relate its images to the quest for myths and symbols that will facilitate psychotherapeutic growth. Their inspiration for making such links is Carl Gustav Jung. He is undoubtedly the single most influential figure for the renaissance of myth, and indirectly for the interest in Tarot as a tool for healing and growth.

Jung reshaped the way we define personality types and gave us jargon with which to describe the human condition –

terms such as 'archetype', 'individuation' and 'the collective unconscious'. He accepted the reality of the soul and made strong connections between psychology, myth and religion. Jung's researches led him to study dreams, fairy tales, folklore, legends, myths and religious stories. As we briefly noted in the previous chapter, Jung believed that we all carry within us images or symbols that relate to fundamental themes of life. Moreover, he found that these inborn images or archetypes were common to all human beings and cultures; and since these symbols were universally experienced across cultures he referred to this common fund of motifs as the archetypes of the collective unconscious – archetypes which, being embedded within us, are hidden or masked until we come into direct contact with the symbols themselves.

Jung believed that every culture offers a filter or matrix in which the archetypes are passed through stories and folklore from person to person and across the generations. Sometimes these archetypes appear to emerge from the subconscious into our dreams. Jung drew attention to the way in which these apparently diverse stories regularly focus on images or motifs of legendary figures, which can then be distilled into several universal categories. Such distilled figures would include the wise old man, the trickster, the great earth mother and the universal hero, and it is certainly striking how these themes can be found running like golden threads through the stories of many cultures. For example, Jung found the 'universal hero' in the stories of King Arthur, Homer's Odysseus, Rama, King David and Columbus. These universal archetypes represent the potential within us to grow and find healing. Not surprisingly, perhaps, very similar themes can be traced in many of the world's classic religious traditions, and on the basis of his research in this area the religion scholar Mircea Eliade came up with a checklist that has remarkable similarities to Jung's conclusions.

Jung's ideas about myth and personal growth have

inspired many people who are part of today's new spiritual search. Joseph Campbell's television series *The Power of Myth* and the books that accompanied the series have helped many people to appreciate what Jung was saying. In discussing Jung's ideas, Campbell himself once remarked, 'I began to read American Indian myths, and it wasn't long before I found the same motifs in the American Indian stories that I was being taught by the nuns at school' (*The Power of Myth*, p. 10). Jung felt that myths and religious statements could tutor our souls on the path to growth and healing. This is the sense in which increasing numbers of people now believe that the Tarot can act as our tutor and guide along the way.

Modern myth making

The desire to find meaning and develop an authentic spiritual life through myth is reflected wherever we look in today's culture. Think, for instance, of the popularity of the burgeoning genre of fantasy novels, or our fascination with fantasy-role-playing games and books. The success of the stories of Harry Potter's adventures (against all the expectations of educationists) shows how popular myth still is with children. But myth is also important among adult readers. At the end of the 20th century Waterstones bookshops in Britain, Amazon Books in the USA, and Angus & Robertson in Australia polled their customers to find out what were the most popular books of the century. In each of these polls J.R.R. Tolkien's *The Lord of the Rings* was voted number one. Tolkien's mythology about middle earth includes a cast of mythic characters, from the diminutive yet heroic hobbits, to the stately King Aragorn and the awesome wizard Gandalf. We all find ourselves sometimes wishing we could be befriended by characters like those in Tolkien's world. Could it be that looking at the world this way is somehow part of what it means to be human – a primal way of coming to terms with who we are, what the world is, and who we might yet become?

Myth making is not just the special province of fantasy novelists. It is also at the heart of storytelling more generally. John Warwick Montgomery, who has had a significant impact on our own thinking, has inspired us to begin exploring the archetypal connections both in literature and also in the Tarot (see his history of the occult, *Principalities and Powers* as well as his provocative work *Myth, Allegory and Gospel*). The kind of archetypal connections which Montgomery has highlighted can be illustrated as follows. Our common frailty and angst is reflected in Albert Camus' *The Plague*, which depicts in graphic detail a city in the grip of the plague, and for which there was no hope or prospect of cure. Camus used that image to portray the human condition, which also seems to be mortally diseased and incapable of being cured. George Orwell's novel *1984* uses similar kinds of archetypal imagery to depict the consequences of the human capacity for nasty and brutish life. John Le Carre's novels deal with similar issues, as they plumb the depths of human treachery and betrayal. These familiar themes are all well reflected on the Tower and Devil cards in the Tarot deck. Franz Kafka's *The Trial* depicts the universal human being judged, a theme which also features in the Tarot on the Judgment and Justice cards. Then there is the hero – the Christ-figure, if you like – who is represented on the Fool and Chariot cards and who surfaces in such classics as Dostoyevsky's *The Idiot*, Jerzy Kosinski's *Being There*, Conrad's *Lord Jim*, Scott Fitzgerald's *The Great Gatsby*, John Steinbeck's *Grapes of Wrath* and Ernest Hemingway's *The Old Man and the Sea*, among many others. In the book *Tarot Revelations*, co-authored with Richard Roberts, Joseph Campbell claimed to be able to trace direct connections between the images on the Tarot cards with themes and symbols that occur in the work of medieval Italian poet Alighieri Dante (1265–1321), most notably in his *Divina Commedia*, published about 1307, which explored the meaning of life through a sometimes lurid journey through purgatory and hell, thence to paradise, illuminated not only by traditional Judeo-Christian concepts, but also using the works of various classical authors of ancient Greece and Rome. That is certainly a plausible suggestion, given the fact that the Tarot cards seem to have been invented in Italy not so very long after Dante's lifetime.

You don't have to be a bookish kind of person (or a historian) to come across such ideas, for all these motifs can just as easily be found in Hollywood films. Dr George Miller is the award-winning director of the *Mad Max* movies, the co-producer and co-writer of *Babe*, and he too has picked up on Jung's theories about the inner psychic life, believing that we all carry within ourselves narratives or myths that make up the mosaic of who we are and what we believe. Sometimes these stories that we each cherish turn out to be universal – in other words, we all respond and relate to them, because they address basic human needs and concerns.

Miller has no doubt that this is a key element explaining the success of his *Mad Max* movies: they have a natural, universal mythic appeal. When the films were screened in different countries, both the stories and the character of Max resonated from culture to culture. In Japan, Max was understood as an outlawed Samurai; in Scandinavia, he became a lone Viking warrior. When Miller wanted to shoot some scenes on the sacred lands of the aboriginal people living in the central Australian desert, he realized he would need to gain their support for his venture. So he went and read the story to them as a way of asking their permission. Their response? They danced! Why were they so excited? Well, because they had heard the Mad Max story before. Its motifs and symbols corresponded to some of their own traditional narratives. Little wonder, then, that Miller concluded that Max was tapping into the myth of the universal hero – the dream of a superman or superwoman who will come to rescue and renew us.

As we will discover in the following chapters on the cards, and then in the exercises that follow, these kinds of archetypal insights run right through the Tarot and the Jewish-Christian sacred writings. Generations of spiritual searchers before us have discovered that the healing journey can really begin once we become conscious of these archetypes and cultivate them into our own being. It is not enough for us just to acknowledge their existence intellectually: we must be courageous and 'own' these myths. In his book *The Secret of Shambhala*, novelist James Redfield encourages his central character to move into these archetypal ways of being as a beginning of the journey towards transformation: 'I'm not telling you how to be an ordinary human being. I'm telling you how to be at the edge of evolution. I'm telling you how to be a hero' (*The Secret of Shambhala*, p. 71).

The Tarot in myth

Subsequent writers like Sallie Nichols, Carl Sargent and Edward Aviza have independently acknowledged the relation-ship between archetypes, myth and Tarot that for us was first highlighted by Montgomery. These latter writers emphasize that the real purpose of the Tarot is not for predictive readings or fortune telling. Instead the Tarot consists of fundamental archetypes that point us to the universal search for spiritual meaning and healing. We are increasingly finding Tarot readers who acknowledge the mythic archetypes and offer their services as counsellors rather than as diviners of the future. Some even go so far as to say that their sessions with clients are like the old priests' confessionals.

Tarot symbolism is not just aesthetically pleasing but it is also spiritually potent. Visual contact with the archetypes of the deck intuitively impacts on the deepest recesses of our being. Jung was right when he suggested that the archetypes are already hidden within us. So when the external symbols of the cards match up with what is going on inside us, we have to ask ourselves if we are willing to be spiritually transparent. It is one thing to acknowledge our pain and desire for healing, and it is another to be bold enough to tread the pathway to holistic healing. Yet it is only when the archetypes are aroused within us that the highest and deepest understanding of the Tarot can be unlocked. The Tarot symbols urge us to pursue ultimate healing. Card by card we are confronted with positive and negative energies that can be found inside us, as well as in the external world. These powerful symbols take us on an intimate and ultimate spiritual journey.

As we explore our personal spirituality, the Tarot's symbols evoke some powerful questions which were briefly mentioned in earlier chapters, questions such as: How can I be the best person I can possibly be? How can I find my place in the world? Who am I anyway, and who might I become? How can I reconnect my soul to the divine source of all life? Charles Williams connected these spiritually potent questions with the Tarot in a way that makes our intimate and ultimate journey crystal clear. Williams was a playwright and novelist, and is best remembered for his friendship with the Oxford scholars C.S. Lewis and J.R.R. Tolkien. Lewis is best known for his children's stories *The Chronicles of Narnia* and the tensions of pain and ecstasy that he faced through his late-in-life marriage to Joy Davidman (a story dramatically portrayed by Anthony Hopkins in the film *Shadowlands*). Lewis formed a circle of literary friends that met on Thursday evenings known as The Inklings, who would gather both for social chit-chat and also to read to one another the books they were writing at the time. Tolkien and Williams were both key players in this group, and in addition to meetings of the group the three of them – Lewis, Tolkien and Williams – met regularly on a Tuesday at the Eagle and Child pub in Oxford to talk about their common interest in myth, symbol and archetypes, as well as to enjoy one another's company. Not many scholars would have the leisure for that nowadays! But as novelists, each in their own way wrote tales and myths that drew on the universal archetypes that Jung had spoken of. For Lewis, Aslan the Lion is the universal hero, the Christ-figure in the *Narnia* stories, and in Tolkien's *Lord of the Rings* Gandalf the wizard also evokes the same image when he dies and rises again, while King Aragorn also reflects the universal hero. Williams, however, did not create mythical worlds in his novels, but instead wrote about ordinary people living their regular lives, and experiencing sudden eruptions of the spiritual realm into their daily routines. He saw the spiritual realm as impinging on our mundane realm in much the same way as the law of gravity affects us. Williams picked up the universal archetypes in several of his novels, but his most striking use of the archetypes occurs in his novel about the Tarot, *The Greater Trumps*.

In Williams's story the original Tarot deck has been bequeathed to a civil servant, Lothair Coningsby, whose daughter Nancy is engaged to a gypsy lawyer Henry, who in turn recognizes the deck's true value. Henry's grandfather possesses a curious set of dancing figurines that seem to be in perpetual motion, and which turn out to be sculptures depicting the symbols of the Major Arcana. Both Henry and his grandfather believe that the power to create and control will be theirs if only they can bring the cards and the figurines together. There is just one problem, of course: they are not theirs. But that doesn't deter them in their lust for power, though as they plot to seize them and murder Mr Coningsby, Nancy intervenes in an act of unconditional substitutionary love. The central archetype of this particular story is the Fool. When the main characters view the dancing figurines it appears that the Fool is stationary while all the other figures dance around it. The only character who cannot see the Fool being stationary is Mr Coningsby's sister Sybil. She is a person who is spiritually contented, in sharp contrast to the other characters, and who assures them that the Fool is actually darting in and out so swiftly that he is hard to see.

Williams uses the motif of the dancing figures as a metaphor for our own journey through life. There is a divine dance, and each one of us must move in rhythm with the Fool – and so Williams invites his readers to join this dance, and let the Fool be our partner. The way to join that dance is set out in our remaining chapters, where we uniquely explore the relationship of the Tarot to the Jewish-Christian scriptures, and the journey that we all must take, from birth, to death – to new life.

Chapter Four

AWAKENING THE MAJOR ARCANA

The Tarot deck consists of 78 cards subdivided into two parts: the Major Arcana and the Minor Arcana. The word 'arcana' means 'secret'. The Major Arcana consists of 22 cards and is considered to be the most powerful part of the deck. The cards comprise images of significant figures or cosmic symbols. The Minor Arcana will be examined in the next chapter.

The Major Arcana cards describe our universal longings or what Jung calls our common archetypes. It addresses the macro-questions of who are we, what are we here for, where are we going, and how we can find happiness and purpose for living. We naturally focus on this arcana.

Finding ourselves through the Major Arcana
As we look at the cards in the Major Arcana we will discover very powerful symbols of our common human story.

Magician Card

Spiritual key
With our eyes wide open we experience grace. At the heart of this is the Magician.

General meaning

The Magician card – along with the Fool – is the most powerful and positive card of the entire pack. The Magician is the infinite source of all being, the spiritual master who suffuses the cosmos. He stands with arms outstretched connecting the spiritual realm with our earthly realm. There is vibrant life. We are invited to celebrate the divine and natural powers and through the Tarot to rediscover the image of the divine that has been forgotten.

The Magician is more than the Jungian archetype of the Wise Man, the herald and guide of the deepest mysteries. For above his head is the symbol for infinity,

THE MAGICIAN.

which the seminal Tarot specialist A.E. Waite identifies as God the Holy Spirit (*The Pictorial Key to the Tarot*). It also indicates that his knowledge and wisdom is without beginning or end. His belt is a serpent swallowing its tail. This is a classical representation of eternity, and Waite suggests that it further signifies eternal spiritual attainment. In his upraised hand is a white wand, which is a widely known symbol for divine grace. This grace is in the spiritual realm. The Magician's other hand is pointing down to our realm, indicating that grace must be brought here.

What is grace? Grace is an unmerited good gift given freely that enhances the state of the recipient. As the well-loved song says, 'Amazing Grace' liberates.

On the table before the Magician lie four tools: pentacle, sword, staff and cup. These relate to the four suits of the Minor Arcana. They stand for the four classic elements of nature: earth, air, fire and water. On a personal level they represent the combination of practical living, clear plan, enthusiasm and right motive. These tools are on the table in submission to the Magician who created them, and they await his energizing power. Around the card's border are red roses and white lilies. The flowers disclose a harmonious rich relationship with the divine that is available to us all. For most of us, the red rose stands for love, but it also speaks of the renewal that bursts forth within us when we are touched by the Magician. The white lilies are a sign of the purity that ideally permeates all things. The Magician's robes are red and white, emphasizing these very same qualities.

Positive and negative outcomes:
As we have said, this is a powerful card to focus on. It discloses the presence of the divine grace throughout the universe. It is a grace that, when we receive it, empowers our daily living, clarifies our plans, activates our enthusiasm, purifies our motives and unifies all things. When the Major Arcana cards are linked in a seamless story we discover this empowering grace is fundamental to eternity. In earlier chapters we talked about our search for healing and wholeness, and grace is the key: we are healed, restored and transformed when we embrace the gift of the Magician.

The worst outcome for any of us would be to dismiss or

decline the card. If we are going to progress in the journey of the cards, we need to take hold of grace. This is the opportunity to reflect. Where am I without grace? Am I willing to step forward and receive it?

Intuition
Your thoughts of love are so many that my mind never gets away from them, they surround me at all hours. I go to my bed, and God is my last thought; and when I awake I find my mind still hovering above your palace gates. God is ever with me, and I am ever with you Lord. This is life indeed.
  CHARLES SPURGEON IN ANN SPANGLER, *DREAMS*

High Priestess Card

Spiritual key
We are chosen to be the vessels of divine grace and power. At the heart of this is our spiritual attainment.

General meaning
The High Priestess depicts a woman who is open to her spiritual potential. She is at peace in the presence of divinity. She is the end point of our spiritual journey.

The High Priestess is seated in a temple and enfolded in sacred robes. Upon her head is a horned diadem, and she clasps a partly unfurled scroll. On her chest is a white cross. She is surrounded by pomegranates and palm leaves. At her feet is a crescent moon. On either side of her we see the pillars labelled 'B' and 'J'.

This card is rich in symbolism that when unpacked is patently obvious and simple. The woman is easily recognizable as a High Priestess because she is enthroned in royal garments and wears the diadem. The garments are not just regal robes but are spiritual apparel because she is in a holy temple. Her crown is worn here because this is her coronation. How is it that she is being crowned? The keys to this happening are the symbols that she embraces on this card.

One symbol is the scroll. It is inscribed with a Hebrew word 'Tora'. The 'Tora' is the divine law, which comprises the first five books of the Jewish sacred writings. Yet the scroll is only partly opened. Why? We are being encouraged to move on from the universal moral guidance, such as is found in the ten commandments, to the Christian scriptures and the New Testament. To find the complete message the entire Bible must be opened and read.

It is appropriate that we now turn to the symbol of

THE HIGH PRIESTESS

the solar cross, which is actually at the heart of the scroll. The cross, as the Judgment card shows, is a symbol of healing, a bringing together of the vertical (spiritual plane) and horizontal (earthly plane) dimensions in unity. A guide whom we shall encounter later in the Major Arcana accomplishes this. The moon reflects the light of the scroll and the cross, which are permanent guides on the journey to coronation.

We also find the

symbols of the temple. This temple was built thousands of years ago in the reign of King Solomon. It had pillars named 'Boaz' and 'Jachin' (two people of renown in ancient Judaism), representing the masculine and feminine elements and identified on the card as 'B' and 'J'. The pillars are black and white, thereby concretely portraying the complexity of our inner being. The real meaning of the pillars lies in the Hebrew names. Jachin means 'Yahweh [God] shall establish' while Boaz means 'in the strength of'. The temple is founded and sustained by the Almighty.

Behind the High Priestess is the veil with the pomegranates and palm leaves. Both items were used in ancient Hebrew culture to celebrate a person of honour. The pomegranates were on the High Priest's garments. The palm leaves, as in the case of Jesus, were thrown down like a red carpet to tread upon. The High Priestess is truly revered because of her reliance on the above symbols.

Who is the High Priestess? Some say she is the Virgin Mary, others say the goddess Isis. Waite identifies that she is really the secret church. For some, the word 'church' conjures up a temple of God made of bricks and mortar. It is a 'secret' because many have fallen for this fallacy. However, the card shows that while the temple building has a symbolic place, it is really the High Priestess who is significant. People matter more than bricks and mortar. No doubt Waite had in mind the insight from Paul the apostle, 'we are the temple of the living God'.

Positive and negative outcomes

The positive aspect of this card is that it shows us how we can take the journey. We do not have to rely on institutions, temples or objects. Rather we find we partake of the divine nature by hearing the whispers of the Tora and the cross.

The negative aspect of this card is its own simplicity.

Isn't it easier to rely on temples and others rather than our own discoveries?

Intuition

On the high plane of divinity or God-Consciousness, the High Priestess denotes the Glory of Shekinah, the manifested presence of God as she begins to reveal Herself to her children, the Initiates.

CORINNE HELINE, *THE BIBLE AND THE TAROT*

Empress Card

Spiritual key

To understand ourselves, we must understand our feminine potential. At the heart of this is nurture.

General meaning

The Empress is the feminine principle in all of us, seated and grounded in the celebration of creativity.

She wears a 12-star crown, and her robe is adorned with pomegranates. Life, verdant lawn, trees, corn and flowing water surround the Empress, suggesting fertility. She has a heart-shaped shield on which is the symbol of Venus. Truly she is a feminine figure.

One of the secrets of the Tarot is how the cards are linked. The Empress is in tune with the teaching of the Hierophant as witnessed by her also wearing a triple crown that symbolizes the unity of God (Father, Son and Holy Spirit). She is also connected to the High Priestess with the pomegranates. In her openness to spirituality in the world, the Empress seeks to fulfil her feminine potential as envisaged in the High Priestess.

The heart bears the sign of the cross as a component of the Venus symbol. Venus is the symbol for love and she is also known as the 'bright and morning star'. The strongest Christian symbol is the cross, a sign of God's gift to the world through the beloved Son. The flowing water is the symbol for life and for the divine spirit who fills us up and flows through us. The Empress is surrounded by elements of nature that are brimming with life and fertility. Her love is nurtured and nurturing, strengthened and out-giving. The sceptre she holds is a sign of her authority. She is poised to govern in tough love. These 'masculine' traits prefigure the Strength card, which shows how the feminine aspect of the Empress and the masculine aspect of the Emperor card need to be in harmony.

Positive and negative outcomes

The positive outcome is that we can all be like the Empress. To love and be loved is the core of the human journey. Those of us who are in positions of 'authority' – parents, teachers, employers, community leaders – excel when our leadership is one of servanthood love. Those around us are nurtured when they share in that abundant love. When we are feeling drained we need to drink from the flowing water.

Our capacity to love can also be renewed by taking a break in the countryside and reconnecting with the sphere of the natural world portrayed on the card. Nature can be reinvigorating because it is energized with the creator's love.

The negative outcome is to miss seeing this side of who we are. A loveless time is barren and dysfunctional.

Intuition

There are three things that will endure – faith, hope and love – and the greatest of these is love.

PAUL, 1 CORINTHIANS 13:13

Emperor Card

Spiritual key

To understand ourselves, we must understand our masculine potential. At the heart of this is a warrior.

General meaning

The Emperor is a mountain man, enthroned. The card presents a person of authority, who on the surface appears to be forceful and dogmatic. Yet the Emperor represents the archetypal father, a spirit common to all those who are committed to the discipline of spiritual maturity.

The Emperor wears a red robe and a jewelled crown. In his right hand he grips the sceptre and in the other hand he holds an orb. On the four corners of his throne are ram's heads. His stern countenance contrasts with that of the Empress, suggestive of one who metes out judgments. He is sure-footed as one who has scaled the craggy heights of the mountains and attained great strength and wisdom. In Tarot parlance, the ram's heads represent his intellectual attainments. The sceptre is an ankh, or ansate cross, which appears in ancient Egyptian art as a symbol of life, and consists of a T-shaped cross with a loop at the top.

In an age where a deeper life is primarily associated with the lost non-patriarchal spiritual disciplines, this card brings into focus our holistic self. It is a mirror for those who have found the feminine, inviting them now to capture and own the authentic masculine side. Freud held that we all project a need for a positive father figure. The ram's heads point to the left brain, and its intellectual attainments. The throne tells us that the Emperor is one who disciplines and judges conduct. His red robe is regal and likewise emphasizes that he judges. The footwear is of the warrior ready to go into battle for family, for indigenous peoples, and for the down-trodden, should the need arise.

Positive and negative outcomes

The card is a good balance with the Empress. At times it encourages the parent, the judge, the policewoman, the employer, to discipline and lead. The ankh is an Egyptian symbol of eternal life, and also stands for the feminine and masculine principles held in balance. The fact that the Emperor holds the ankh indicates how he understands that the state of the High Priestess can only be reached by those who embrace both the Empress and the Emperor.

The negative side of the card is legendary. We have lived in a time of patriarchal abuse where Emperor figures have used their warrior status to exploit women, the employee, the powerless, and the gentle. When selected and viewed properly, this card should always challenge that aspect of our being. In a 'negative' way the card can bring to recall those suppressed memories of pain when we have been recipients of abusive behaviour. The path to healing involves owning this, but the deck moves us forward.

Intuition

The adult warrior inside both men and women, when trained, can receive a blow without sulking or collapsing, knows how to fight for limited goals, keeps the rules of combat in mind, and in general is able to keep the fighting clean and to establish limits.

ROBERT BLY, *IRON JOHN*

Hierophant Card

Spiritual key

We gain from a guide. At the heart of this is a spiritual mentor.

General meaning

The figure of the pope is enthroned, and blessing those who seek the keys to the kingdom. He offers himself as the guide who can lead us to the divine. He is a welcoming teacher who is keen for us to grow in knowledge and understanding.

The Hierophant, like the High Priestess, is seated

between two pillars. In his left hand he clasps a sceptre capped off with a triple cross. His right hand is raised in a traditional sign of threefold blessing. He wears a golden triple crown, and down the centre of his vestment there are three crosses. Both of his sandals are marked by a cross. His robes are red and his tunic is white (the same colours worn by the Magician). At his feet are two crossed keys, representing the keys to the heavenly kingdom. Kneeling before him are two disciples. The disciple on the right wears a robe adorned with white lilies, while the one on the left has a robe adorned with red roses. The symbols adorning the disciples' robes, the roses and lilies, are also found on the Magician card, and indicate that the disciples are experiencing abundant life.

The Hierophant is one who can teach us. He stands out from the crowd as one of those who have given themselves over to the pursuit of wisdom. At different stages of life there are times when we need to listen to a trusted guide and friend, one who knows what it is to travel spiritually and has gained understanding. The teacher is one who is willing to take us by the hand and share out of the abundance of his or her sojourn and study.

The power of the teacher is shown in the Blake Prize for Religious Art. A recent award was made to the artist and photographer George Gittoes, who was stationed in Rwanda with the United Nations' medical team during the civil war. The group were in the village of Kibeho when news came of impending doom: another tribal group with swords and guns were coming to massacre the villagers. The medical team were helpless and were in the process of leaving when a man stood up and just began 'giving this sermon in one of those beautiful melodious African voices, mingling English and French and Rwandan, quoting sections of the New Testament, those bits which give hope'. Gittoes took a photo of the preacher but never saw him again, assuming he had been murdered. Gittoes painted from the photo and said that the preacher as a teacher and guide 'represents what I think religion should do, raise people up, make people feel human and spiritually alive and give them courage and faith'. A good teacher equips and encourages in all circumstances.

How is the Hierophant found? The key is on the card. This symbolic figure is spiritually connected. The triune symbols of his crown, sceptre and upraised hand, and on his vestment, point us to the unity of the divine. The Hierophant points beyond himself, directing our attention to God. The pathway he brings into focus is the same cross-like one found portrayed on the Hanged Man card.

The stone pillars behind him are a dull grey, indicating we should not be averse to finding the Hierophant within the walls of traditional faith.

Positive and negative outcomes

It is a rare bird that can walk this pathway in life without seeking instruction and guidance. The Hierophant reminds us it is there, and for some it will be found in unexpected quarters. To be mentored is a privilege and an enriching experience. Let's not only find a mentor, but also develop our wisdom and understanding so that we might act as the Hierophant to others.

The downside is allowing the Hierophant to be an authoritarian figure in our life. That happens when a mentor takes over our mind and heart and manipulates us into his or her own suspect agenda. Dangerous persuaders dominated the 20th-century landscape in politics and religion. Jim Jones, David Koresh, and Shoko Asahara represent the political Hitlers in traditional and non-traditional faiths. When sitting at the feet of an inspired one we should not forget the personal warning of Socrates: 'The unexamined life is not worth living.'

Intuition
If you encounter the Hierophant, you may need to examine your spiritual life, particularly in terms of the communal expression of that spirituality. Perhaps there is a need to return to our spiritual roots and explore forgotten traditions.

EDWARD AVIZA, *THINKING TAROT*

Lovers Card

Spiritual key
We were born for harmony with each other, the world and the divine. At the heart of this is love.

General meaning
The Lovers show a woman and a man who are totally open to each other, with nothing to hide. They are at peace with their environment. Here is the innocence of the newborn child. The natural and spiritual world is alive and harmonious.

This card contains archetypal symbols. As we noted in a

previous chapter, an archetype is a universal religious motif or symbol that addresses some aspect of our spiritual and biological make-up. The Lovers represent the primordial humans, Adam and Eve, that we all aspire to be. In this ideal state these two bear unblemished in their being the very image and likeness of the radically perfect creator. This image is also seen on the Magician card. The paradise they are in is the Garden of Eden. The mountain in the background stands for one of the meeting places between humans and the divine. Mountains are represented throughout the Bible in the stories of Noah's survival from the flood, Moses receiving the divine principles for living, Jesus' teaching on the Mount, and the time when he was transfigured into his eternal appearance before his disciples. For a Jungian, mountains can be a symbol of ascent to greatness.

The cloud is a symbol for God's presence, and is known in Hebrew wisdom as the Shekinah glory. This same cloud was with Moses as he meditated on the mountain, led the people of Israel out of their bondage and slavery, and engulfed Jesus at the time of his ascension. Notice the nearness of the cloud to the couple. It represents the immanence of the Holy Spirit in their spiritual experiences and journeys. Observe how they are responding to this holistic scene by being completely transparent before God and each other.

The angel, possibly Michael the archangel, who rides upon the cloud, has his hands outstretched pouring down blessings on the couple. The sun above him shines brightly, indicating that all is well. Behind the couple stand two trees. These trees, which are known as the Tree of Life and the Tree of the Knowledge of Good and Evil, represent two spiritual realities. The Tree of Life signifies the choice of continuing to live and share in physical, emotional and spiritual harmony. It bears the 12 fruits found in the book of Revelation and presents a spiritually potent number that recurs throughout the deck. The Tree of the Knowledge of Good and Evil offers another tantalizing pathway where we can opt to explore life using principles not commended by the divine. Around the tree a serpent is entwined. The serpent, who is in disguise (see the Devil card), symbolizes the one who invites us to travel down this route.

Positive and negative outcomes

The inspiring focus of the Lovers is that whenever we feel down, because of our fractured personal relationships, our concern about the environment, and our lack of spiritual

spark, this couple remind us that this is not the way we are meant to be. It speaks to us of what we can be and instils in us hope for renewal. This is for us both the beginning and potentially the ending of our journey.

The negative sense here is the presence of deception to blind us from being true to ourselves and to the divine. Sadly, the alluring choices suggested by the serpent are universally explored and experienced. We are no longer the Lovers in this card.

Intuition

The figures (the Lovers) suggest youth, virginity, innocence and love before it is contaminated by gross material desire.

A.E. WAITE, *THE PICTORIAL KEY TO THE TAROT*

Chariot Card

Spiritual key
We understand our future when we recognize the rider in the Chariot. At the heart of this is the eye of faith.

General meaning
A prince who wears a crown and holds a wand drives the Chariot. On his shoulders are epaulettes of crescent moons. Two sphinxes pull the chariot.

Who is the prince? His crown gives us a clue. It has an eight-pointed star and shows he fulfils all that is spoken of in the Star card. Waite notes that the figure 8 when turned on its side is the symbol of infinity, and that infinity reminds us of the eternal realm. As Tarot interpreters usually note, the prince's belt displays the signs of the zodiac. The prince is lord of the cosmos, and the wand he holds is the vehicle of grace offered on both the Magician and Fool cards.

The Chariot rests on both water and land and behind it is the celestial city bathed in sunshine. These symbols come from the Death card, and here indicate that the Chariot is the ferry that takes us across to the celestial city. The winged disc is the symbol of Isis, the goddess of magic and compassion.

All mystery and love is bound up with the rider. This princely rider embraces all earthly wisdom: he has clearly answered the classic riddle posed by the sphinxes because they now serve him. In Greek mythology the riddle of the sphinx was a test of true wisdom. The riddle posed was,

'What creature in its infancy goes about on four legs, as an adult goes on two legs and when elderly goes on three legs?' The answer is 'a human being'. The epaulettes on the rider's shoulders are two crescent moons, which depict two stones worn by a Jewish high priest. These two stones represent spiritual wisdom. In the right hands, the High Priest could use them for 'yes' and 'no' decisions. As the prince now possesses these on his uniform he also holds spiritual wisdom. From these motifs we can see that the rider fully identifies with us because he has been one of us. Yet he is also more than us.

The Chariot is a classic vehicle to drive in a victorious race. It is common in the Bible, and many legends and stories. Only triumphant figures are qualified to ride in a chariot. In the book of the prophet Ezekiel, when the chariot appears God's message is given, and even today in UFO accounts the chariot is a sign of supernormal encounters. Another sign of victory is the Chariot standing over the river. In ancient myths the rivers were evil deities whose power in nature could threaten the agricultural cycle. Such deities had to be subdued, and other deities like Baal were looked to for victory. Here the rider's Chariot has conquered whatever the river may hold. With this rider one need not fear evil.

Those who search for a triumphal life will find hope in the strength of the Chariot.

Positive and negative outcomes

This is an appealing card when drawn because it teleports us out of the mundane and into another realm which is a world of both earthly and spiritual victory, wisdom and expectation. In a world that's been locked into agnostic science and technology, divorced from spirituality, here is a card of re-enchantment for those who know the prince.

For those who do not recognize the rider there lies the possibility of the Chariot being unattainable. At times the themes of the Chariot are remote and we can settle for the mundane.

Intuition

You make the clouds your chariot, you ride on the wings of the wind, you make the winds your messengers.

PSALM 104:3–4

Strength Card

Spiritual key

We can tap into bi-polar strength. At the heart of this is confidence.

General meaning

A woman subdues a male lion. Above her head is the sign of infinity. She is garlanded with flowers. In the background is the mountain, with the woman and lion on open level ground.

The woman represents the feminine aspect of Strength. It is not by violence that she shuts the jaws of the lion. It is by her inner peace, assurance and fortitude. She is clothed in a white robe, symbolizing purity. She is a maiden. By contrast the lion stands for the masculine aspect of Strength, the warrior. This warrior nature is found in Jesus as the lion of the tribe of Judah. The maiden and lion are joined together by a chain of flowers. On other Major Arcana cards, flowers signify that all is well, so we can appropriate both the woman and the lion, provided that the feminine aspect tempers the masculine.

In Tarot parlance the maiden also signifies Virgo, while the Lion is Leo. The astrological sign of Virgo is connected to the Virgin Mary, the one who had the inner strength to bear the Christ-child as an unwed mother. Paul Fenton-Smith says of Leos that they 'can sometimes put great effort into projecting a strong, confident persona, while feeling inadequate underneath' (*The Tarot Revealed*, p. 183). To be authentically strong on the outside we need the inner strength of the maiden.

The symbols of the mountain and infinity (the reversed 8) reappear on this card. Both remind us of the divine source of everlasting Strength. The open field indicates this is Strength not for things done in seclusion but in the playing field of life.

The Strength card draws our attention to the concept of balancing seemingly opposite principles, be they right-brain/left-brain, yin/yang, male/female. In this case it is a 'both/and' of masculine and feminine characteristics. S/he who is strong has a quiet as well as a courageous strength. This is seen in the life of Jesus, who slept on a boat in a storm while his male followers were terrified. Yet he is also the one who threw out the obnoxious money-changers who corrupted the temple. New Age writer, Corinne Heline, in her book *The Bible and the*

Tarot, points to the feminine aspect of Jesus when he wept over Jerusalem. Jesus' pain and love is likened to the protective care of a mother hen that gathers in her chicks.

Frederick Buechner wrote, 'There is a female element in every male, just as there is a male element in every female, and most people if they're honest will acknowledge having been at one time or another attracted to both' (*Whistling in the Dark*, p. 86).

Positive and negative outcomes
This card draws us to the source of true Strength. It is a fruit of the Holy Spirit. It is grace. It calls us to allow

this fruit to balance the bi-polar aspects so that we may possess true Strength. This is a card of inspiration and of instruction. Strength for living is probably the most often sought ingredient.

The flip side is that this card can destabilize our commitment to pursue personal growth and deeds. Why bother unless lightning strikes? This is to misunderstand the card's positive message of capitalizing on our good intentions.

Intuition
The card has nothing to do with self-confidence in the ordinary sense, though this has been suggested – but it concerns the confidence of those whose strength is God, who have found their refuge in Him.

A.E. WAITE, *THE PICTORIAL KEY TO THE TAROT*

Hermit Card

Spiritual key
We are called to meditate. At the heart of this is the divine light.

General meaning
The Hermit is the universal human, an archetype of every woman and man who seeks meaning and truth. He is on a journey carrying spiritual tools for guidance and direction.

The Hermit is dressed in a monk's cassock, suggesting one who is an earnest searcher for authentic spirituality. Often we might think of a monk as one who has renounced society and gone into spiritual isolation. While that portrait can be true in some religious orders, the fact is that we can all be monks and yet remain involved in the hurly-burly of daily living. As pilgrims we still participate in the nine-to-five grind, but can take time out to reflect and recharge. There are times when we need room to breathe and create some sacred space. Solitude for meditation can be valuable.

The Hermit card gives us the keys to meditation. The Hermit stands on top of a mountain. We have talked about the importance of mountains in the Lovers card. This is one of the meeting points between the divine and us. So we need to have an open heart and mind to the presence of the spirit. The lantern shines forth spiritual light for the Hermit to travel along life's paths. Notice that this light is external to the Hermit and is not inside. It is shaped as a six-pointed star, which in Jewish tradition is called the star of David. The star's light points upwards, downwards and outwards in all directions. The uppermost point indicates that true spiritual light comes from beyond us. We are able to connect with this divine light by seeing God around us, and by listening to the divine voice. When we do this the divine light and voice then speaks to our inner being where the image of the creator is yearning to find wholeness and healing.

The staff is a shepherd's crook and reminds us that we long for a guide who can lead us in our meditation. We are like sheep who have gone astray. In the Major Arcana the Fool is the one who holds the shepherd's crook and helps the Hermit with good directions to take. Here we peer further into the mystery of the Tarot as more of its message to us is now unfolding.

Positive and negative outcomes

In an age of spiritual questing the card opens the door to meaningful meditation and prayer. The spiritual resources of light and guidance are within easy reach and do not require us to travel to enchanting sites of religious renown or open our pockets. The beauty of the cards is that although they are surrounded in mystery, as we unpack them one by one we discover the simplicity and accessibility of their message.

The negative outcome of the Hermit card is that it shakes up our sophisticated pretensions to keep all our books and courses on the inner life. Useful as they may be, they can clutter us up. The Hermit is prepared for the journey through the call to simplicity. As Waite states, 'His beacon intimates that, "where I am, you also may be".'

Intuition
All I really need to know about how to live and what to do and how to be I learned in kindergarten. Wisdom was not at the top of the graduate-school mountain, but there in the sandpile at Sunday School.

ROBERT FULGHUM, *ALL I REALLY NEED TO KNOW I LEARNED IN KINDERGARTEN*

Wheel of Fortune Card

Spiritual key
We must accept that life is a roller coaster. At the heart of this is providence.

General meaning
At the card's centre is a wheel, which has inscribed on it the divine name of God and the letters 'taro'. Appearing with the wheel are several symbols that recur in the deck: the four creatures, the cloud, the sphinx and the serpent.

The turning wheel represents the cycle of life with its ups and downs. It is constantly in motion experiencing good and bad periods. The letters 'taro' are inscribed around the circumference of the wheel and when we read them clockwise we find the word 'Tarot'. This shows that all the good and bad experiences of the Major Arcana cards, such as the Lovers and the Tower, go with us. The good seen is that God is clearly present in our lives, as signified by the cloud and the divine name in the Hebrew letters, YHWH (Yahweh). The name reappears in the Judgment card. The cloud represents the divine presence in the world, as on the Lovers card.

The serpent, the master of temptation, signifies evil. The jackal Anubis can also be interpreted as a devilish character. Edward Aviza says, 'The devil at the bottom of the wheel is there to keep us alert, to help make us aware that all things are subject to change' (*Thinking Tarot*, p. 75). Other readers assign a more positive role to Anubis. Although he is a dark figure he is rising with the wheel, and this indicates the hope of new life for those who understand the cycles of the wheel.

The sphinx rides atop the wheel and has been identified in the Chariot card as the test of earthly wisdom. The key to riding the Wheel of Fortune is equilibrium, not being phased by the passages of life.

It is not surprising that the four creatures appear on this card. Waite says that they spring from the vision of Ezekiel who saw a heavenly chariot with many wheels and within it were these same four creatures. Notice that each of them has an open book; they are declaring the word of God. In religious art these same characters are portrayed as the four gospel writers, Matthew, Mark, Luke and John.

What comfort is furnished by having this word of God spoken to us? The word is filled with promise and is practical. 'I am with you always'; 'All things work together for good'; 'Do not worry about tomorrow, for today has sufficient worries of its own.' The sphinx clasps a sword, which is a common symbol for the word. He is riding the roller coaster, with the promise that he is not alone when facing the valley and mountain-top experiences.

Yet the symbols at the wheel's centre take us to an even deeper awareness. The eight spokes stand for the eight points of the compass, reminding us that no matter where we are and no matter what happens, God's providential care is always with us. On the vertical spoke there are two astrological signs. Underneath the letter 'T' we have the ram, which represents Aries. Above the letter 'R' we have the water, which represents Aquarius. The ram of Aries commences the astrological year, and in the divine word a sacrificial ram begins the process of forgiveness. The ram is one who gives up life so that others may receive life. We find this reiterated in the message of the Hanged Man card. The water of Aquarius points us to the culmination of the world's purpose in a renewed age of Aquarius.

This is reinforced in the World card. Providence guides us through each phase of the zodiac.

Positive and negative outcomes

This card tells us how life is. It is not a merry-go-round, but a roller coaster. It encourages us to realize that there is a purpose and equilibrium to it. We do not walk alone. There are tools to help us on the journey.

The negative side

is a jolt. In the uncertainties of life it can be a despairing card. No matter how well we are doing, the next stage of life may very well yield bankruptcy, ill health and discouragement.

Intuition
In the mundane world the Wheel of Fortune points to the laws that govern life and death – the principle of change within which nothing is constant, nothing can be grasped and held with certainty. The only freedom from the wheel possible while on earth comes through accepting its motion and living in harmony with it.
        ALFRED DOUGLAS, *THE TAROT*

Justice Card

Spiritual key
In this realm we need to uphold fair mindedness and fair play. At the heart of this is justice.

General meaning
The Justice card brings to mind a universal understanding of virtue that can be traced to Philo's four cardinal traits: temperance, wisdom, courage and justice. Two of these virtues are specific cards – Justice and Temperance – while the other two are reflected throughout the deck. The Tarot is a mirror of the universal human journey.

A woman, wearing red robes, is enthroned between two pillars just like the High Priestess and Hierophant. Strung between the two pillars is a red sheet or veil. The woman wears a golden crown and above her is a golden sky. In her right hand she holds an upright sword, and in the other hand the scales.

The scales classically represent the courts of justice. We likewise must be pursuers of justice. The upright sword represents the dual aspect of life – of right and wrong, positive and negative, yin and yang. Justice therefore deals with determinations about what is right and wrong. In royal courts the sword would be brought down once a decision had been made. The red robe worn, together with the crown, evokes a regal image, as in olden times royal figures were responsible for making judgments. Above is the golden sky, which is an image for the transcendent realm, and ethics here are sourced from a higher realm. As Rousseau said, 'It would take gods to give us laws.' This golden sky fully appears on the Magician, Lovers and Fool cards.

The two pillars and red veil suggest that there is a

doorway hidden behind them. Again we have the same theme of a deeper insight. Yet once the veil is removed we discover, as we see in the Magician's card, that a spiritual gift is available for higher things. The gift is grace.

Positive and negative outcomes
There are some 45 million people around the world who are blind. Of these some 20 million are blind owing only to cataracts that can be surgically removed. For the price

of $30 in a 15-minute consultation, those who are blind could see again. Does not this card exhort us to enact justice in our world and to expect others to act justly towards us?

The downside is to fall for the trap that our works alone will save us. A virtuous person, unless energized by the things of the spirit, is an inadequate model to follow.

Intuition
Because the primary ethical challenge of our day-to-day lives is not usually a matter of knowing what is right and good but of having the character to do what is right and good, the all-important, destiny-determining question for us will largely be one of how to develop character that does what is right and good.

RUSSELL GOUGH, *CHARACTER IS DESTINY*

Hanged Man Card

Spiritual key
We come to the Living Tree to understand what is the authentic model of living. At the heart of this is self-sacrifice.

General meaning
The Hanged Man is upside down, dying on a living tree. Around his head is a golden halo or aura. His face is serene. One leg is bent at the knee and folded across his straightened leg to form a symbolic cross.

The symbols on this card evoke a universal myth. To understand this myth we must explore what these symbols stand for. At first glance this card might give us the sense of how pathetic the Hanged Man appears. To be crucified upside down is hardly what anyone would want. He seems so helpless and hopeless. Yet the halo and the flowering cross suggest there is more to this card than initially meets the eye.

The myth is that of the dying–resurrected hero. In ancient mythology we find the Phoenix, Osiris and Balder. According to the most common version of this story, when the mythical Phoenix felt death approaching the bird flew to Heliopolis and there burned itself to ashes. From the ashes the Phoenix rose once again, more radiant than before. In Egyptian mythology the god Osiris dies, travels the underworld and rises from the dead. A similar story is found about the Norse figure Balder. In contemporary cinema the same myth is constantly played. In *The Matrix* Keanu Reeves takes the part of Neo, the one who will save humanity, and in the course of his mission he fulfils the oracle's prediction that he must first die in order to be the resurrected hero. The powerful stories of Tolkien's *Lord of the Rings* and C.S. Lewis's *Narnia* both have the universal hero who dies and rises again. For Tolkien it is the wizard Gandalf who sacrifices himself on behalf of the hobbits. For Lewis it is the lion Aslan who dies on behalf of the children and the Narnians before he can lead them into their true land. Both characters conquer the experience of death by rising again. Waite suggests that this card cannot be understood without appreciating the significance of this myth.

The key to grasping the meaning of the Hanged Man card can be stated as: 'I cannot have a risen powerful life without first of all dying to self.' The card cuts across materialism, hedonism, selfishness and the gods of Western culture. It offers us a paradox. Dying is not weakness, but rather through it we are strengthened. In our relationships, work situations and social interactions, the truly great people are those who consider others and put the care of others before their own interests. In loving others one enriches oneself. It is the golden rule of all religions. Let us love one another as we would love ourselves.

All Tarot readers concur that this card represents the disciple Peter, a great example of humility. An old story describes how when Peter was executed he requested to be crucified upside down. The reason for this request was that he did not feel himself worthy to be impaled in the same position as his master Jesus. So although he was an exemplary model, Peter pointed beyond himself to Jesus. As Waite indicates, the living tree on which the Hanged Man is affixed is a tau cross. The crossed legs form a fylfot, which is a swastika. The swastika is an ancient symbol for eternal life, brutally perverted by Nazism. The Hanged Man's

crossed legs point to another cross on which one died who was the archetypal servant and who experienced and bestows the resurrected life.

Positive and negative outcomes

The positive aspect here is that the Hanged Man affirms what both our inner being and our culture really admires and values the best. Love for others is paramount. Contrary to expectations it is a good card with which to begin each day.

The card, if taken on superficial appearances, is quite disturbing and defeating, causing us to be bleak and dour about life.

Intuition

I am no lofty abstract philosopher, nor could I ever be described as a humbly peaceful Silent One. I am deeply involved in intensely intimate relationships, a singer of songs, a teller of tales, and easily given over to fighting the good fight.

SHELDON KOPP, *THE HANGED MAN*

Death Card

Spiritual key

We must all die, but there is eternity. At the heart of this is a promise.

General meaning

The Death card confronts us with the Grim Reaper. He appears to be victorious but this is not necessarily so. Issues of life and death are being raised constantly not just when we take our last breath.

The Grim Reaper rides forth on a white horse, weaponless and carrying a black banner. On the banner is a white rose. In front of the Grim Reaper we see a woman, man and child falling down, succumbing to his presence. The dead man was a king, signified by his crown and sceptre beside him on the ground. Standing before the horse is a pope, awaiting death, with his hands in a prayer posture. In the background there is a river, and upon it is a ferry. The river separates this realm from another one. The other realm is seen in the top right-hand corner of the card. There are two pillars to a great city, from which bright sunlight shines.

There are two dimensions to this card. The first concerns the experience of physical death. No one can escape the Grim Reaper! Irrespective of our status the old saying rings true: the two certainties in life are death and taxes. Although this is distressing, there is a glimmer of hope on the card. This is found in the city where the light shines. To reach the city one has to cross the river on the ferry.

However, if we are going to ride on the ferry we must pay for a ticket. Nobody is on board the ferry because the cost of the ticket is very high. The price of the ticket has to be paid to the Grim Reaper. His authority to demand payment is symbolized by the white rose on his banner. The white rose stands for true spiritual life. As the Lovers card showed us, the primordial humans once enjoyed life without the presence of death. Through their choosing a pathway not endorsed by the divine creator, death has become a reality for everyone. We have forfeited our true spiritual life to the Grim Reaper. So to reach the city beyond we must have a ticket and yet nobody can afford the price.

Even so, all is neither lost nor futile. The fact that there is a city beyond, where we can live again, suggests that if we cannot buy a ticket then maybe someone more powerful than us can help us out. This is where the promise is indicated. The divine creator has made arrangements to purchase our ticket. The white rose, which here is possessed by the Grim Reaper, on the Fool card is owned by another. The gift of true spiritual life is found in the Fool.

The second dimension is at a day-to-day level of experience. We face difficult decisions that are painful, that may impact our relationships, livelihood and well-being. Being stuck in old habits may seem comfortable, but sometimes we need to change. A fear of change can at times be almost as strong as the fear of physical death itself. It may involve a major loss of some kind. The card points to the universal nature of these experiences. Although we can glimpse the hope lying beyond the change needed, the real struggle is finding the wherewithal to implement it. Where will we find someone or something to empower us with a white rose? To remain fixed is to wither.

Positive and negative outcomes

This card is not just about doom and gloom. Deep down we all intuit that there is a promise or hope of life beyond the grave. The card directs us to be eternity-focused. It encourages us to explore how our inner hope will be fulfilled. In some sense this is a joke card: the Grim Reaper may seem to reign supreme but really he does not. In our day-to-day life the card motivates us to identify what is 'dead' in our lives and to move on.

The negative side is the darkness of death. It is a sad experience to lose loved ones and at such times death appears eternal. Also, for some, death is a snare that captures their thoughts and emotions. They live and breathe death. The card reminds us that we often don't prepare ourselves for life's ultimate encounter. Another factor in daily life is that it is often more pleasant to live life navigating around those things that need change. Such attitudes are challenged by the realities portrayed on the card.

Intuition
In a world where we are surrounded by death on all sides, we continue to be a being who says 'no!' to death – and through this 'no!' is brought to faith in another world.

       PETER BERGER, *A RUMOUR OF ANGELS*

Temperance Card

Spiritual key
We can attain inner harmony. At the heart of this is a synthesis.

General meaning
An angel stands with one foot on land and the other in water. The angel holds a chalice in each hand pouring fluid from one into the other, and that represents the harmony of an in-tune person.

    This card discloses another member of the angelic court who is different from those found in the Lovers and Judgment cards. What distinguishes this angel is found with the symbols on its forehead and chest. On the angel's forehead is the symbol of the sun, which is like a bright crown. On its chest we find the Hebrew letters for Yahweh, the God of Israel. Also there is a triangle, symbolic of the three persons of the Godhead (Father, Son and Spirit). The Temperance card has for some people evoked a negative, weak image. However, this is misleading because the angel is a good figure, one who is strongly and closely associated with God. Rather than being a figure of weakness, the angel exudes spiritual strength.

In the background of the card we see a road trailing towards mountains in the distance, above which is a shining light through which a crown can just be seen. The road represents the path of wisdom that takes us to the mountains. The mountains, as we have seen before, are a meeting place between God and us. One sign that we are ascending the mountain is the discovery of inner harmony. On the mountain's peak lies the forfeited crown of the upcoming Tower card.

On this card the pouring of the liquid from one chalice to the other represents the need for the contrasting principles or energies inside us to be brought into harmony. Classically the contrasting principles within us refer to things like the masculine/feminine side as seen in the Strength card. They also refer to the light/shadow of Jung, positive/negative energies, Freud's libido/mortido (life/death urge). The card helps people to deal with these aspects. For the one in anger it draws them to the serene side, the lustful find themselves on the giving side, the one entrapped in the negative extremes of a Myers–Briggs or Enneagram category owns their positive personality opposites. Jung spoke of a synthesis of these contrasts in terms of inner healing via the individuation (integration) process.

Ultimately to experience this synthesis of inner healing we really must be reconnected with the divine creator. It is remarkable that alchemists draw us to this even deeper understanding of the liquid by saying that it also represents the elixir of life. The elixir of life is the alchemical substance which transforms our human dross into gold. Notice that Temperance is placed in between the Death and Devil cards. The agony of these twin cards of seeming doom can be tempered by the positive message of Temperance. And it's the Fool who is the elixir and who, through this trilogy of Death, Temperance and Devil, will bestow healing on those open to seeking new life.

Finally, there is an interesting spin on the card's symbols. The portrait of the angel standing on both sea and land, pouring out water, can be traced to the book of Revelation. In that book we have the cosmic drama of good versus evil, and in one high episode an angel stands on the sea and land pouring out divine judgment on evil. This explanation dictates that some things cannot be reconciled and must be excised if we are to be healed.

Positive and negative outcomes

This card is invigorating, as it reminds us of our opposite sides and that we function best when these are harmonized. Even in our bleakest moments, when the negative side comes to the fore, this card reminds us that at a brighter time we can find inner renewal.

The negative aspect is that we can be enslaved to frustration, held back by repressed attitudes or circumstances. The card reminds us of what we are not.

Intuition

By getting in touch with all the different sides of yourself, you can learn that one side of you doesn't make another side invalid. A loving parent, child or spouse can also be angry and resentful at times. A creative or highly intelligent person may have to struggle in certain areas.

JOAN HARVEY AND CYNTHIA KATZ, *IF I'M SO SUCCESSFUL, WHY DO I FEEL LIKE A FAKE?*

Devil Card

Spiritual key

We cannot avoid the Devil, but woe betide those who cannot see hope. At the heart of this is deception.

General meaning

The Devil sits on his throne, with one hand upraised and the other holding a flaming sceptre. At his feet we find a naked woman and man in chains to each other and chained to his throne. They have acquired the horns and tail of the Devil.

This card is in total contrast to the Lovers card. Adam and Eve are no longer in paradise but are subservient and in chains to the Devil. This has come about because they have gone the way of the Tower card. When we come to the Tower card we discover how the Lovers have fallen for the alluring choices of the serpent that are contrary to the divine purpose. They have also supplanted the divine spirit by inventing their own spiritual paths and truths.

The Devil is one of the most potent archetypes in the deck. As we have seen in our previous chapter, an archetype is a universal motif or symbol that addresses some aspect of our spiritual and biological make-up. The Devil archetype can be found in diverse forms as the horned goat, the tempter, the trickster and the evil spirit in many different religious traditions. In literature he is encountered as the dark lord in Tolkien's *Lord of the Rings*. He has also been translated archetypally in the world of film, for example in the characters played by Jack Nicholson in John Updike's *Witches of Eastwick* and Al Pacino in *The Devil's Advocate*, and – as Joseph Campbell affirmed – in the sci-fi figure of Darth Vader in *Star Wars*. Jung posited that this archetype, which recurs in our dreams and our psychic life, bubbles up from the collective unconscious. He described his own contact with disembodied entities in altered states of consciousness. He further taught that every individual encounters his/her own 'shadow': that is, the dark side of our natures. For Jung

the shadow is not an actual being external to us, but rather a malevolent side inherent in us. He believed that to find growth or healing we had to 'own' the shadow.

Although we can surely learn from Jung, the archetype on the card is something more than this. Here the archetype is not an impersonal or abstract concept, but embodied in a real being who is external to the human race. Upon his head we see an inverted five-pointed star or pentacle, which is his distinguishing star symbol. It classically indicates from an occult stance the reality of evil. In contrast to the angel on the Lovers card who had open-palmed hands showering down blessings, here the Devil raises one hand over them as a sign of his rulership. In the other hand the burning sceptre points down as a sign of the spiritual oppression he brings upon the Lovers.

The Lovers now have miniature horns to show that they have acquired in some measure the same dark spiritual qualities as the Devil. They have also grown tails. The tails have two sides to them. First, they have grown tails in imitation of their new master. However, in contrast to his, their tails consist of the fruits from the two trees found on the Lovers card. This means that although their natures have been perverted, they still retain something of their original being from paradise. The image of the creator is borne inside their being, but is now fractured and confused. The subjugated Lovers now represent a paradox: originally made for greatness, they are now spoiled by evil. The chains around them reinforce how oppressive this experience is and how they are seemingly helpless to be free from the Devil's power.

Why does this card still appear in our contemporary, 'enlightened' culture? Alfred Douglas, in *The Tarot*, suggests that the cards are connected with the Gnostic group the Cathars, who saw the Devil as being the vengeful god of the Hebrew Bible and Jesus as bringing us to the superior loving God of the Christian scriptures. This approach moves us from a deficient deity to an empowering one, and the card can act as a catalyst for this. While that is one view, it simply does not adequately explain why the card has been universally retained. Another possibility is that such an archetype cannot be dispensed with. To make sense of all the evils and misfortunes of the world and our own personal darkness, we are forced to face the card.

Positive and negative outcomes

The card keeps us honest about our propensity to do evil, personal or social, individually or corporately. Jung reminds us that we take responsibility for our own shadow. The card also urges us not to dismiss the dark forces around us. The Lovers' tails give an inkling of hope that elsewhere in the Tarot we will break the chains of the Devil.

The downside is that we can become enveloped by our own shadow. We become brainwashed by our negatively programmed thoughts about our world and ourselves. Our original goodness is soured and we become like Darth Vader even to those we love.

Intuition

The line dividing good and evil cuts through the heart of every human being. And who is willing to destroy a piece of his/her own heart?

ALEXANDER SOLZHENITSYN, *GULAG ARCHIPELAGO*

Tower Card

Spiritual key

We were made for greatness, but have experienced the opposite. At the heart of this is frustration.

General meaning

The Tower shows a woman and a man falling away from each other and into utter chaos. Here they are not at peace. They are descending from the source of all inspiration and harmony. There is a loss of innocence.

The Tower has two stories that are not dissimilar. The first story concerns the primordial couple of the Lovers card after they have sampled the alluring choices of the serpent that are contrary to the divine purpose. Scott Peck, in tune with the sacred writings, says, 'We cannot not sin. There are a number of possible definitions of sin, but the most common is simply missing the mark, failing to hit the bull's-eye every time. And there's no way we can hit the bull's-eye every time' (*Further Along the Road Less Travelled*, 1993, p. 157).

As a consequence of their actions, the couple are being ousted from paradise. The crowns they once wore, which signified they were king and queen of creation, are being forfeited. The man has already lost his crown, while the woman is tumbling with hers about to drop off. The parted Lovers have lost their naked innocence, which is symbolized by their now wearing garments. They appear

helpless without direction or purpose. It is something we can all identify with because we feel the pain of significant wrong choices.

The Tower card also stands for the Lovers' good handiwork in the Garden. It is falling into ruin as we witness its crown being dislodged by the lightning bolt from the sky. It was built upon the Lovers' mountain but is now perched on a rugged cliff-face that is beyond the capacity of anyone to climb.

The flames within the Tower are consuming the goodness that was once there. Surrounding the Tower are storm clouds which complete the picture of disharmony at all levels: in relationships, in nature and in spiritual connections. The darkness in the backdrop shows that the light in the creation has been blotted out. This represents what is known in both mythology and the sacred writings as the fall of humanity.

The second story unfolded by the Tower concerns our arrogance, ego and rationality. It is the story preferred by Waite. This is where we create our own idols and falsehood. We supplant the divine spirit by inventing our own spiritual paths and truths, a pattern which finds its depiction in the story of the Tower of Babel. There humankind was scattered after striving to scale the tower of enlightenment without reliance on the enlightened one. The lightning represents judgment on our pretensions, and all our efforts are destroyed. As seekers we all yearn for divine wisdom, but how easy it is at times to fall in love with some of our own spiritual utterances that are rubble.

Positive and negative outcomes
This card can be a reality check because it helps us to face up to who we are. We can be deceived, get carried away with our own importance, and seek transformation beyond grace. The Tower can direct us back into the rhythms of life and away from the repression represented by the Devil card. In the world's mythology we encounter both the collective and personal archetypes of darkness or shadow. With the Tower we have both archetypes. Through the card we encounter this most feared part of ourselves. We are stripped away to join the Jungian search for transformation.

This card can be depressing because it shakes our sense of well-being. For those on the downward spiral it can cement us to the experience of the dark night of the soul. The card can also be frustrating because it does not give

us the direction we need for liberation from its message. It is clear that we cannot return to the Tower on our own merits.

Intuition

It illustrates in the most comprehensive way the old truth that 'except the Lord build the house, they labour in vain that build it'.

A.E. WAITE, *THE PICTORIAL KEY TO THE TAROT*

Star Card

Spiritual key

The Star unfolds the potentiality that follows the Tower and the Devil. At the heart of this is the meaning of the Star.

THE STAR .

General meaning

This card offers us a portrait of a naked woman pouring water from two jugs, and above her are eight stars in the sky. There is also a bird perched on a tree. The card in the modern deck is captivating.

The contemporary reading of the card is

of the peace that can come after the experience of the Devil and Tower cards. Once we have resolved the issues they raise we come to a threshold of emotional well-being. In this interpretation the land is the material world and the water the spiritual realm, and the water of life pours into both, bringing fertility and nourishment. The water of life is an expression used by Jesus to speak about himself as a healer. The dove perched on the tree represents the divine spirit. All this takes place in the presence of the guiding, energizing stars.

There is an alternative interpretation. In medieval and Renaissance times the prototype of the card shows poisoned water, and the stars are associated with the opening of the sixth seal of the apocalypse found in the book of Revelation. In this 'end times' vision the stars are falling from the sky and the angel pours forth the vial of judgment on land and sea. Nothing escapes. Those who have struggled to respond to the Tower and Devil cards are further motivated by this dark aura.

The cards are a mirror of who we are and our spiritual state at any one time.

Positive and negative outcomes

The positive aspect is that this can be a card of hope. To have selected this one suggests that our lives need not be controlled by what is portrayed on the Tower and Devil cards.

The alternative is to allow the ancient reading of the card: we are ruled and stultified, and so stay in the grips of dark energy.

Intuition

It has been said truly that the mottoes of this card are 'Waters of life freely' and 'Gifts of the spirit'. The summary of several tawdry explanations says that it is a card of hope.

A.E. WAITE, *THE PICTORIAL KEY TO THE TAROT*

Moon Card

Spiritual key

Life has periodic cycles of negative energies. At the heart of this are our unconscious fears.

General meaning

The barren Moon card is one of the most negative in the entire pack. It seethes with desolation. There is no positive presence or life to be found here. It is obviously associated with the other negative cards, such as the Devil.

The Moon has several large and lesser rays bearing down on the landscape. In the foreground is a stagnant pool, from which the crayfish emerges. From the pool is a winding path that leads to the desolate mountains in the background. In the middle a dog and wolf are fighting. Behind them are twin pillars or gates that open onto the stark wilderness.

This card truly portrays our worst nightmare. The Moon does not have light in itself, but can only reflect what is shone on it. Classically the Moon has symbolized a dark spiritual realm. It was known in ancient times as the abode of dead souls. In its most negative aspect the Moon was a symbol for Hecate, the guardian of the gates of Hades. She was a dark goddess who brought lunacy.

Alfred Douglas notes: 'The dark realm of Hecate is illustrated here. At the foot of the card is a crayfish, symbol of the primitive devouring forces of the unconscious which have to be overcome. In the middle distance are the wolf and dog, guides to the land of the dead, who are also unstable and not to be trusted. Behind them are the pylons of the gateway into Hades, the portal of the dark womb, whilst above all hangs the moon itself, drawing souls to it with its irresistible magic power' (*The Tarot*, p. 106).

This card thrusts before us our unconscious fears of our own darkness and unworthiness. The crayfish is drawing us past the animals towards the gates of Hades, with no turning back. The film *The Exorcist* plays on the card's symbolism of the wolf and dog fighting, and early in the story this image represents demonic powers and possession.

Further, Timothy Betts in *Tarot and the Millennium* links the Moon card to the apocalypse. In the book of Revelation the seventh seal is opened and a vial of judgment is poured out. An outcome of this is found in Revelation 8:12 where a third part of the Moon is darkened.

Wiccans, whose spirituality is based on reverence for

the workings of the natural world, have another view. They see the Moon card in a positive way, linking the monthly cycle of the Moon to the menstrual cycle. For them the Moon is a symbol of empowerment, celebrating fertility.

Positive and negative outcomes

The positive aspect of the Moon card is that we are reminded about what Jung called the dark shadow within us. To be genuinely in touch we must acknowledge and confront the shadow, this Jungian message we found on the Devil card. Scott Peck's writings resonate with this truth, as we saw on the Tower card. The Wiccans are also positively teaching that even darkness can be turned to light.

The negative aspect is that those who fit the 'unlucky number' personality syndrome and draw this card may continue to be engulfed by 'woe is me' statements of their own unworthiness. People of that personality type need to be cautious. The ultimate negative feature is to deny the message of this card.

Intuition

Chuang Tzu said that he once dreamt that he was a butterfly. That dream left him puzzling ever after whether he was a man who dreamt he was a butterfly or whether he was a butterfly who dreamt that he was a man.

FRASER BOA, *THE WAY OF THE DREAM: CONVERSATIONS ON JUNGIAN DREAM INTERPRETATION*

Sun Card

Spiritual key

We are invited to embrace spiritual simplicity. At the heart of this is the faith of a child.

General meaning

This card represents optimism and joy, which is to be gratefully received. A naked child holding a red banner is riding a white horse, clearly free of any inhibition. Red, as we have seen, is the colour of primal love and the spirit of renewal. Behind are sunflowers and a wall, and, above it all, the golden sunlight shines down. This is a scene of peace and contentment.

The Sun card illustrates our inner self at its best – confident, free and at ease. It is about finding the healthy child within. There is a concern in many quarters today that we should learn how to uncover the child within ourselves. This motif is a call to us to realize the passionate simplicity of the unfettered child. It is a reminder to laugh, to play and to love more. This card shows us at our happiest and seen at our most natural with others. Notice how the sunflower finds its energy and life from turning to the light: the way of discovering the child is to live under the embrace of the sun. The white horse reminds us of the need for purity in spirit.

Positive and negative outcomes

This card reminds us of the times when we are at our happiest. It brings us back to the basics. It allows us simply to feel good.

The only negative feature is that when we are the laughing child we do not see, or we forget, the adversity and suffering of others.

Intuition

Let the children come to me and do not stop them, because the Kingdom of God belongs to such as these. I assure you that

*whoever does not receive the Kingdom of God like a child will
never enter it.*

MARK 10:14–15

Judgment Card

Spiritual key
We have to face up to who we are, as an aspect of our
maturity. At the heart of this is growth through personal
confrontation.

General meaning
On this card we see the archangel blowing a trumpet,
summoning the dead from their tombs. Attached to
the trumpet is a flying pennant. The archangel rides on
a cloud and in previous cards we have noted how this
represents the presence of the divine. In the foreground a
woman, a man and a child are rising up from their graves.

Usually when we think of Judgment dire images form
in our minds of condemnation, punishment and despair,
an aspect of the card that is common to many religions.
Judgment is also a familiar motif in dreams and myths
about the 'great mother', who can offer both a fruitful
womb and potential to be a devouring destroyer, and the
'great father', who may be both a wise old man and a
wrathful judge. The card plays on images found in the
Christian scriptures of the New Testament. There we read
about the last days when God brings time to an end and
judges the world. We read of the last trumpet blast by the
archangel, followed by the dead rising from their graves.

Surprisingly, card 20 is full of hope and life. It is
replete in joyous apocalyptic symbolism. On the pennant
there is a red cross, which is a universal symbol of healing.
Of course it is the very symbol of the organization the

International Red Cross. Paul Fenton-Smith comments that 'the cross on the flag represents the meeting of universal time [the vertical] and linear time [the horizontal], suggesting on some level you have already arrived at your destination, but while you believe in linear time (as you must to exist on the physical plane), you are still progressing toward your clarity of judgement' (*The Tarot Revealed*, p. 217). So judgment is a means of healing both now and in the future. The red cross also stands for the one who will bring healing and transformation to us.

In Tarot readings we often focus only on the present aspect of this card. All of us need to come to grips with who we are and what we've done. It is an inner awakening to lay before ourselves and others our past actions, mistakes and experiences that often live on into the present. Often in our own misdeeds we hide behind bitterness and hate towards others. The card helps liberate those who own up to their own actions or indifference.

An affirmation of the card is the oft-neglected future judgment. Shortly before he was assassinated Martin Luther King prophetically declared that he had seen the Promised Land, he was unsure that he would be there with his hearers – but he'd seen the coming of the king. He was encouraging his African-American audience to keep the vision of the day of universal sisterhood and brotherhood, as it was approaching. It was a day that clearly could not arrive until America faced up to and judged its past. The card likewise points to a Promised Land that we see approaching. It can only be truly entered in hope for those who are honest enough to face up to themselves. There is a future cosmic day where entry into the celestial city on the Death card is for those who prepare for judgment now.

In the card's foreground the people who are rising in joy are the same ones who succumbed to the Grim Reaper on the Death card. So it is a card of resurrection hope.

O grave where is your victory?
O death where is your sting?

Positive and negative outcomes
The positive aspect is that we don't have to be afraid
of judgment both now and in the future. To personally
evaluate one's life is a healing process. God is calling us
home to be in the divine presence, but also asking us to be
prepared for the future judgment. Waite says it has truly
been called a card of eternal life.

The negative aspect can leave us drowning ourselves
in pathos. Often the message of the card can come at times
when one is really searching for self-worth but instead we
drop a notch because
of the unkindness of
others. Another
dimension is where
we turn the card over
without acknowledging
the serious place of
judgment.

Intuition
*The Judgment card has
positive and negative
aspects. In the positive
sense we are being
awakened from a long
sleep, a period during
which we lacked clarity,
and now insight is
dawning upon us in
a psychic rebirth and
resurrection. In the
negative sense, we are*

being called to account for past actions, and to justify in the light of truth what we have done in the past. Judgment speaks of a time of reckoning, a time of bringing to light those things which were hidden.

EDWARD AVIZA, *THINKING TAROT*

World Card

Spiritual key
We affirm that the world will be as one. At the heart of this is cosmic harmony.

General meaning
A female figure entwined with a purple sash holds two wands. An unbroken wreath encircles her. Around the borders are four spiritual creatures.

This is the picture of the world as it will be. We have previously encountered the four spiritual creatures found here on the Wheel of Fortune card. On this futuristic card they are drawn from the book of Revelation where they inhabit the divine realm. Here their presence signifies harmony between the spiritual realm and the world. They look down to the earth with favour. Waite indicates that each creature also represents one of the four Hebrew letters making up God's name YHWH (Yahweh). Each creature rests on the cloud, again standing for God's presence. The wreath likewise reinforces the sense of cosmic harmony because it is unbroken. At both the top and bottom of the wreath we see it is fused by the divine sign of eternity.

Who is the woman dancing in the card's centre? She is the feminine sign for wisdom. In ancient times it was common to characterize wisdom as being female in form. For the Greeks she was known as Sophia. Her ultimate mission is that through enlightened understanding there will be harmony in the world. She has relied on the wands – the wands of God's grace: they are in equilibrium, further emphasizing that harmony has finally come into the world. The colour purple in both occult and biblical thought represents the pinnacle of spirituality; how appropriate it is, then, that Sophia should be draped by this purple sash.

The World card brings us to the culmination of our journey through the Tarot. The preceding 20 cards of the Major Arcana all point either to a long-lost world of paradise or to the longings for a renewal of the world. The World card encapsulates the aspirations for the Aquarian age that Paradise Lost may be regained. This restoration is accomplished in the last two chapters of the book of Revelation where the Garden of Eden, as described in Genesis, is reclaimed. The Bible finishes as it begins. Other religions have the same sense that our experience of lostness will one day be overcome as we return to our original blessedness. The serenity of the Lovers card is recaptured.

Positive and negative outcomes

We all identify with personal and global brokenness, chaos and injustice. Although these things overwhelm us this card instils a sense of vision and purpose. This is not the way it needs to be. By drawing on grace, wisdom and true spirituality a new day dawns for all. The depiction biblically is both a now but not-yet changed world. As we positively live our own empowered lives, transformed by the message of the Tarot, let us also be agents of global change. We should not limit our concerns and vision to just ourselves. We are stewards of creation. The prophet Isaiah calls us to envisage the renewed world as including the whole environment – rocks, rivers, plants and animals. The card also depicts this all-encompassing grand cause.

The negative outcome is that it can challenge us with a macro-plan when we are struggling to survive in the micro-world of our personal affairs. Sometimes we are not helped by the call to look at the big picture when we have to deal with personal tragedies and difficulties in our journey. The other side is that the card convicts us of living a life of constant partying while avoiding environmental, social and global concern.

Intuition
We either fear that human culture is falling apart, or we can hold the Vision that we are awakening. Either way, our expectation is a prayer that goes out as a force that tends to bring about the end we envision. Each of us must consciously choose between these two futures.

    JAMES REDFIELD, *THE TENTH INSIGHT*

Fool Card

Spiritual key
There is a person who makes sense of the whole story in the Major Arcana. At the heart of this is the Fool.

General meaning

This is the most powerful card in the entire deck. The Fool strolls towards a precipice unconcerned. The world is alive with his presence and he carries the most powerful spiritual symbols of all.

The bright sunshine accompanies the Fool because his presence dispels all darkness. He walks among the mountain tops – the abode of the creator. Across his shoulder he carries the shepherd's staff, which is also found in the Hermit card, and at the end of the staff is a bag containing a free gift for those who meet him. In his other hand the Fool holds the white rose, which only appears on the Death card. At his feet there is a white dog following

him, different from the evil dog on the Moon card and is a symbol for those who follow their master.

The Fool, who is young in years, is the true spiritual guide. He holds the shepherd's crook, because it is he who brings spiritual direction. The good shepherd knows his sheep by name and they know his voice. Following the shepherd brings eternal life as he holds the white rose taken from the Grim Reaper. The shepherd as our guide is a free gift.

The precipice is a sign that the Fool will lose his life on behalf of others. This connects us to the Hanged Man card where we see one who dies on a living tree.

Who is the Fool? A.E. Waite, the architect of the classic pack, unveils the truth that 'he is a Prince of the other world on his travels through this one' (*The Pictorial Key to the Tarot*, p. 152). The one who uniquely fits what has been foretold is Jesus of Nazareth; he brings eternal gifts, dies for others, and comes from above.

Yet the card requires more. The image of the Fool is of one whose influence passes over the precipice. Joseph Campbell and Richard Roberts observe that the Fool, whom the joker of modern decks reflects, clearly symbolizes the dying and resurrected sun-god (*Tarot Revelations*, p. 253). James Frazer in his monumental study of religion, *The Golden Bough*, identified a universal longing for such a figure in religions and myths. As Jung's archetypes disclose, we all need the champion, the universal hero found in movies and stories who defeats trials and death for himself or herself and also for us. This is the prince who awakens Sleeping Beauty with a kiss from her death-like sleep and leads her into nirvana.

Positive and negative outcomes

The positive factor is that there really is someone who makes sense of the big picture and gives everlasting meaning. The beauty is that the Fool also interacts with our moments of joy and sorrow in the everyday events depicted in the Minor Arcana. More than just a friend, the Fool is our guide, master and hope.

The negative outcome is that if we miss the Fool we will miss the secret of the cards. Come dance with the divine!

Intuition

That is the eternal question, is life all there is of life or do we only know one hemisphere before our death? Speaking for myself I have no idea what the answer is but the sight of the stars always starts me thinking.

VINCENT VAN GOGH, *LETTER TO THEO*

Chapter Five

USING THE MINOR ARCANA

The Minor Arcana is divided into four suits: Wands, Cups, Swords and Pentacles. Each suit consists of 14 cards, the ace, cards numbered two to ten, plus the four court cards: king, queen, knight and page. The Minor Arcana operates at a micro-level and helps us to understand how all the insights of the Major Arcana interact with everyday life.

Personal interpretations of the Minor Arcana

As we reflect on the cards in the Minor Arcana one or two will usually resonate with our current life situation. To experience how this works, you could mark or jot down which cards' descriptions and interpretations relate to you now. You might find one – the six of Wands, say – which is special to your heart and which you want to keep in mind. Name the card.

Now at this juncture it may be helpful to bring out a deck as the cards are explained. If no deck is to hand, this is no great problem because the Minor Arcana symbols are easy to explain. The Major Arcana cards from Waite's deck have been photographically reproduced in this book. These are the focus because of their potency, and they rarely change in the Waite tradition. As we now turn to the Minor Arcana, we are providing a summary description of these secondary cards. From deck to deck variations can be found in the pictures, but the summarized sense described here will always be found. The scenes on each card can be negative or positive. Each court card as well as the ace only depicts one wand or cup, while cards two to ten carry their numerical equivalent of cups, wands, and so on. It is important to note that the number of symbols on each card is not always significant, but attention will be drawn to the number when warranted.

THE SUIT OF WANDS
The wand is a long, thin wooden stick. Consequently, this suit classically represents the element of fire (because wood burns). Fire relates to energy, enthusiasm and a sense of renewal. In the scriptures it is a symbol of the spirit of God that through grace purifies, energizes and renews.

Ace of Wands
Picture simply a cloud, which is a symbol of God's presence. Out of the cloud comes a hand that clasps a flowering wand. In this imagery the ace of Wands is saying to us that energy and renewal begin with dependence on the divine. In our current difficulties: let go, let God.

Two of Wands
Why would a person be standing between two wands looking at a globe of the world? If we are drawn to this card, it could be saying that there are two options before us and we need clarity and inspiration to decide.

Three of Wands
The figure looks out to sea contemplating opportunities to come. It is time for the rush of energy for a creative venture.

Four of Wands

Here is normally a picture of people at work and play. We can allow the spirit to renew us by bringing us a sense of attainment in our daily life.

Five of Wands

This card can portray four people jostling another person using their wands. Here we are confronted by a lack of unity, perhaps finding its source in the Devil card. This is a summons to transform relationships through mediation.

Six of Wands

The six of Wands depicts a person surrounded by others in affirmation. Our confidence in life is affirmed by others. We have the energy to accomplish whatever is before us.

Seven of Wands

Why are we in a defensive posture fending off others? Here we may be enmeshed in a very personal conflict that is destructive to our foundation, as it comes from below. We need energy for the necessary battle.

Eight of Wands

There is a moving landscape with the wands. We are on the move, travelling and pursuing goals. We are to keep the fuel of enthusiasm burning.

Nine of Wands

Surrounded by so many wands, we are weighed down with conflicts. It is time to reassess relationships and circumstances with a renewed outlook.

Ten of Wands

Here is usually portrayed one figure carrying in a bunch of wands. Represented here are the shackles of our work and public commitments, our lives full of 'have to's. Now is the time to reassess priorities and find the energy that comes with a lightened load.

Page of Wands
The page looks at the wand. The page is someone young in our life who is starting a new phase. The young person is out there alone, brimming with creative energy. Encouragement is needed.

Knight of Wands
The knight is on a horse, clutching the wand. He is more mature than the page and is actively in pursuit of goals. The knight's focus needs to be tempered by the wisdom of what is significant spiritually and holistically as portrayed in the Major Arcana cards. Are you the knight?

Queen of Wands
The queen sits on the throne clearly at peace in what she is doing. Her throne is adorned with lions – symbols of fire and strength. If we are in this renewed state we must also beware of the black cat, the Jungian shadow.

King of Wands
The king is seated, usually surrounded by salamanders who swallow their tails (eternity), the lion (strength), and the crown of tongues of fire (motivation and energy). The king in his everyday life has encountered the Fool. In daily life this is a picture of the ideal of strength, vision, motivation and eternity.

THE SUIT OF CUPS

This suit stands for water. Water relates to what we are, while fire symbolizes what empowers. Water portrays right motives, creativity and spiritual awareness. In the scriptures it is a symbol for Jesus, who is the water of life and who offers this awareness to us.

Ace of Cups
The divine hand emerges from the cloud clasping a cup above which a dove is dropping a wafer with a cross on it. We are invited to participate in the cup that has been transformed by the dove – the motif of the

spirit. We need spiritual awareness, which comes by feeding on the sacraments of God (word, prayer, communion and baptism).

Two of Cups

The male and female ideal classically face each other in the presence of a serpent and winged lion. The aspiration for harmony in relationships may unfold in our personal circumstances. The individuals here remind us of the Lovers in the Major Arcana. The signs of both the serpents (in the symbol of the doctors' caduceus of healing) and the winged lion (spiritual strength) point the way forward.

Three of Cups

The card portrays characters in a state of rejoicing and celebration with each other with their cups raised. The card is encouraging us to a commitment to relationships, which always flows when one is spiritually aware.

Four of Cups

A solitary figure is offered a cup emerging from a cloud, while other cups lie before him. Here we are contemplating the material cups of life while being offered the spiritual way.

Five of Cups

Why are we clothed in black with our backs turned and cups scattered? Sorrow and grief are our lot. The Major Arcana indicates this is a reality we all experience. We should not hide from it, but should seek the comfort of the other cards.

Six of Cups

Picture children playing in a perfect village. The card encourages us to enjoy the peace of our spiritual attainment, like the children who are bathing in the security of village life.

Seven of Cups
Traditionally in this card a contemplative figure stands before a cloud of cups that overflow with negative and positive objects. Our inner spiritual life is surprisingly calling us to a new direction. Now is the time to investigate what is good for us.

Eight of Cups
Normally a traveller is portrayed journeying at night by the light of a full moon through a barren land. Barrenness is our spiritual state. It could be useful to recheck the Moon card at this moment. We are destined, however, to walk to higher ground.

Nine of Cups
There is a person confidently seated, smirking. We have fulfilment in our spiritual life but perhaps tinged with some smugness.

Ten of Cups
Here is a rainbow of cups. Underneath is a happy family. The rainbow is a sign of peace that adds to the dimension of the family's well-being. We and those in our care live best when we are together.

Page of Cups
The young man in his pursuit of pleasure finds in his cup a fish. The fish is the early symbol of Christ and Christ-consciousness.

Knight of Cups
The knight wearing a cloak adorned with images of the fish is heading for the water of life. Now is the time for such spiritual succour.

Queen of Cups
A.E. Waite tells us that the queen on this card should be depicted grasping the ark of the covenant, which contained the ten commandments. As she looks, we have also come to the point at which we are to look at the wisdom of God.

King of Cups
The king wears a fish amulet around his neck because he is self-disciplined in the way of the water of life. As the king has attained, so we too have now reached the place where creativity, right motives and spiritual awareness need to be held in calm balance.

THE SUIT OF SWORDS
This suit stands for air because the sword beats through the air. Air relates to having a clear plan for living through mindful decision making. In the scriptures the sword is a symbol for the very words of God we need to live by.

Ace of Swords
Picture again the divine hand emerging from the cloud with a sword upraised. This time we are offered the word of God as it pierces into our lives and world, providing clarity for our thoughts. We need this word to have a clear plan for living and understanding in our world.

Two of Swords
The figure is blindfolded, holding two swords. The recipient of this card is at a crossroads, facing a critical decision about the plan of life to follow. The sword clasped in the left hand and crossing the right shoulder has a crescent moon above it – the pathway found in the Moon card of the Major Arcana. However, the sword clasped in the right hand and crossing the left shoulder points to a better way. Which way will we go?

Three of Swords
Here a red heart is penetrated by three swords, surrounded by grey clouds. The heart is pierced in the storms of life, affecting us in body, mind and spirit. The sadness of life cannot be avoided, but it does not comprise the final word about where we can go.

Four of Swords
This card will normally display a tomb inside a church. Like the stone

figure reposing on top of the casket, we need to reflect on the ultimate purposes of life.

Five of Swords
Unlike the five of Wands, this card reveals that those jostling us are in retreat. We have won an argument and feel self-satisfied that the others involved are dejected. We can get what we want, but we may not want what we get back because of our mindset.

Six of Swords
Why are we and our companions journeying on a barge? In our decision making we and our loved ones must turn our backs on negative thoughts and fruitless plans, and take the disciplined journey towards serenity of mind and purpose.

Seven of Swords
Now a stealthy figure is sneaking away with the swords. We have thought and done things in secret and we are convinced we can get away with them without being found out. Our clever stealth, however, sows the seeds of its own doom. This is a solemn word about being off-track.

Eight of Swords
Here is a pathetic figure, blindfolded and bound, and encaged by many swords. The choices we have made have imprisoned us in a wasteland bereft of clarity and integrity. It is time to face up to self-deceiving thoughts and actions.

Nine of Swords
Normally this is a picture of a person sitting up in bed at night, head in hands. It is our turn to face the dark night of the soul,

but the red roses on the bedspread signify that divine love and hope are just a heartbeat away.

Ten of Swords
A figure lies on the ground pierced by ten swords. Our negative mindset has brought us down so low that we feel stabbed in the back over and over again. The way forward is to embark on a new course of thinking and to be released from the dark situation we find ourselves immersed in.

Page of Swords
The page in gay abandon swings a sword.
The recipient of this card is relating to a youth whose plans are fresh but not tempered with wisdom. This youthful vigour will work best when inspired by clarity gained from the Bible and from experience.

Knight of Swords
The knight wields a sword, moving swiftly, stimulated by fiery thoughts and riding a white horse (a symbol of purity). Our plans for living are clear and purged by the divine spirit. Now we must enter the race of life's challenges, but we need to be wary of burning out or looking for novelty over against substance.

Queen of Swords
The enthroned queen offers a benediction to those who approach her throne as she holds an upright sword. We can receive the blessings of correctly discerning life's priorities, having clarity of thought and knowing the true plan when the divine word is applied to our circumstances.

King of Swords
Waite depicts the king on the throne, holding his sword facing us in judgment. He can signify one who tests all thoughts and plans, but coldly follows the letter of the law. If we are going to take the clear path we must avoid this legalism and let the divine word lead us to the divine spirit.

THE SUIT OF PENTACLES

This suit stands for the earth. The earth relates to practical living in the material world. The pentacle is a five-pointed star. Each point represents one of the four elements (earth, air, fire and water) with the apex pointing to the divine spirit. This symbol reminds us of the harmony that ensues as the creator spirit blows through the natural world.

Ace of Pentacles
Now the divine hand that emerges from the cloud holds the pentacle securely. A practical approach to living operates optimally when we live in harmony and allow the spirit to lead us each day.

Two of Pentacles
Two pentacles are being juggled together in a loop of rope, and the loop is a symbol for eternity. We are juggling two alternatives; and when we choose which one, we need to see our choice from an eternal perspective.

Three of Pentacles
A true depiction of this card will always centre on the three pentacles in an arch that leads to an inner sanctum. They stand for the triune Godhead who is close by in the midst of constructive activity. We need to be aware how God cares for us in the nitty-gritty things of daily work.

Four of Pentacles
Why is this card portraying a person with pentacles underneath each foot, and one held tightly and another as a crown? We have consolidated what we own and become obsessed with sheer material factors. Where is the divine spirit in our lives right now?

Five of Pentacles
Two beggars stagger in a winter's night. The love of material things and money becomes the root of all kinds of evil and makes us beggarly in

spirit. The pentacles placed in the stained glass window suggest we are spiritually empty and need spiritual nourishment.

Six of Pentacles
The two beggars kneel before another who is dispersing coins from the scales of justice. We need to be fair and pursue justice for those less fortunate than ourselves. Are we spiritually rich or concerned only with our material comforts?

Seven of Pentacles
A figure ruefully toils the soil contemplating past agricultural outcomes. We have reaped some reward for our labours and are contemplating what we have stored up for the future. What do we value most here: our material blessings or our spiritual growth?

Eight of Pentacles
A craftsman is making a set of pentacles. In daily life we need actively to hone our skills and acumen and be practical in the way we handle our work, study and play.

Nine of Pentacles
This card traditionally shows a majestically dressed woman strolling in the garden, a bird perched on her hand. We should have contentment as we reflect on our accomplishments, and enjoy them without being distracted by 'wet blankets' who criticize us.

Ten of Pentacles
An aged person warmly gazes on a young couple. As we retire from work we should have joy in our family life and be able to focus on wisdom in our maturing years.

Page of Pentacles
The page balances a pentacle in his hands. He is seriously committed to the disciplines of life and this diligence is something we need to bring into focus now.

Knight of Pentacles
The stationary knight clasps the pentacle. He accepts responsibility and is dedicated to working through the routines of life. We may need to engage in careful thought about our priorities and be firm in our resolve.

Queen of Pentacles
In a peaceful environment the enthroned queen reflects on the pentacle. She meditates quietly on all her accomplishments, which have been balanced and tempered. She has attained a state of serenity in herself and in her world. Does our life reflect the health, well-being and vitality of the queen?

King of Pentacles
We can take encouragement from the king, because he has fulfilled his ambitions and material success. The card points us towards self-confidence and certainty about what we do. How else does one explain a king who on his throne not only holds the pentacle but clearly controls it?

Chapter Six

THE PASSAGE – SPIRITUAL EXERCISES THROUGH THE TAROT

We do exercises with the Tarot on radio and television, at spirituality festivals, and in churches, universities and schools, on the Tarot's spiritual dimension. Here we present the reader with six exercises, which we have found to be most beneficial. There are two methods for approaching them. The first is to select the one exercise that you feel is most essential to your circumstances. Later you may want to explore the other exercises. Of course the 'Personal Transformation' exercise is one we all must undertake at some stage.

The second method is to examine our five signifiers: Lovers, Wheel of Fortune, Hanged Man, Hermit and Star. One of the signifiers may personally resonate with you as you reflect on the five. Begin with that one.

To do the exercises we suggest the following. If you own or have access to a deck of Tarot cards, lay out your cards according to the diagrams and follow the text in the exercise. If you do not own a deck, then you will rely on the diagrams and text. As is the case with other Tarot books, those without a deck will need to flick back to chapters four and five for the appropriate cards. It helps to refresh our memories. In the exercise section read each interpretation of the card carefully, marking or noting those you need to return to for further reflection or direction. If you have a deck you could turn the card over.

We have opened each exercise with simple directions on card layout. If you wish you could read the brief case study that then follows. The case study is given not to divert you from the experience of the moment (we do not want to be distracted by the profiles of others), but rather because a personal story can be helpful in identifying the possible stages of life with which the exercise especially resonates. We conclude each exercise with a meditation with the person from the case study; meditations lose something if they are impersonal.

The sixth exercise is different. It does not have a signifier. It also differs in that we spend more time sharing the story of our client. We have done this as a model for those who may be unaccustomed to our non-predictive use of the cards. We hope you find it helpful.

Exercise One: Personal Transformation

In this exercise the signifier is the Lovers card and there is a 14-card layout as illustrated on page 111. In the text we will see that there are two frames within this layout. The first, as we will see, is a penetrating look at our own spiritual dilemma. The second positively maps out the way forward to grace and peace. This is a powerful enactment of a personal psycho-drama, that is the story of our inner self being drawn out through symbol and action. Psycho-drama normally helps us to reflect on who we are and how we feel, and then sculpts for us where we can be. In this psycho-drama we are guided to identify how we feel spiritually disconnected, and then redirected to discover our true consciousness.

CASE STUDY

Lorraine's background was nominally Christian. She sat at our table in our Community of Hope booth at a Mind–Body–Spirit

Festival. As she started to chat she chose the Lovers card. We asked her why? It triggered a memory. She spoke of her childhood surrounded by religious symbols in religious education classes at school, which included the idealistic story of Adam and Eve. Her experience of life had led her to see that spiritually she felt out of kilter. She shared that by 'spirituality' she meant being in tune with herself, her loved ones, creation and God. That was the heartbeat of the card. Lorraine, like most of us, was still longing for a permanent sense of grace – kindness, acceptance and peace. She could recall different moments when she seemed to be uplifted. Lorraine wanted something more enduring, as pictured on the card.

THE LAYOUT

Frame One

The Lovers card shows a woman and a man in a state of complete harmony with each other, the creation and the creator. They feel good about life and have an aura of peace. It is the state of paradise, which humankind once enjoyed but which we no longer experience in its fullness. We intuitively sense this and we universally ache to return to paradise. The card is a faithful mirror of who we are meant to be in the image of God.

The Tower card affirms that we have lost this sense of harmony. Here we are falling from greatness into personal chaos and cosmic desolation. Further cards we will soon look at reflect why this is so.

The Hermit card represents each of us on a spiritual search trying to make sense of all of this. We have found that those who identify with the Hermit are not going to settle for the Tower's portrait. Notice the Hermit holds the lantern and shepherd's staff to guide us on the journey.

Place the three of Swords on top of the Tower card. It reinforces how we are pierced personally in body, mind and spirit. The sadness of our life cannot be avoided but the card itself does not comprise the final word.

Lovers
card

Tower
card

Devil
card

Hermit
card

Death
card

Judgment
card

three of
Swords

Magician
card

nine of
Swords

Hanged
Man card

Fool
card

World
card

Chariot
card

Strength
card

The Devil card unfolds how the Lovers have fallen into spiritual bondage and everything is shrouded in darkness. They have become chained to the horned creature and taken on his spiritual characteristics as seen in their horns. Yet they still carry aspects of their former greatness and image as we can see by their tails. The tails are fruits from the two trees seen on the Lovers card. We are a mixture of greatness and brokenness.

The Death card reminds us of the consequences of this disharmony. We will all one day meet the Grim Reaper. No one has sufficient status or wealth to overcome his power. His banner reveals the ticket we need to journey to the other side. That ticket is the white rose of true spirituality.

The Judgment card shows us all answering the trumpet blast of the angel at the end of time. When we look at this card we must ask ourselves, 'How am I preparing myself for this spiritual encounter?' The pennant flying on the angel's trumpet points us to a universal symbol of healing and reconciliation: the red cross. The red cross is what we need to find in this life so that we are ready to meet our creator.

Place the nine of Swords on top of the Judgment card because it connects the cosmic judgment to us personally in the here and now. Today is the time for us to look at who we are in this life. The mystics have emphasized that we grow when we confront the dark night of our soul. The red roses on the bedspread signify that divine love and hope are just a heartbeat away.

Frame Two
We are persuaded that transformation in all aspects of life can be found only in God. As Deepak Chopra has put it, 'the aim of spirituality is to learn to co-operate with God. Most of us have been raised to do the opposite' (How to Know God, *p. 298). The second phase seeks to make this connection.*

Kick off with the Magician card. The card shows us the true spiritual master in the spiritual realm. The sign of eternity above the Magician's head shows us that the Magician is the creator. In the Magician's upraised hand is the wand of grace. Grace is an unmerited gift. The Magician offers us this grace. With the other hand the Magician points towards the earth, indicating that grace must come into our world and our lives. The Magician touches all the elements of earth, air, fire and water. If we are going to find this gift, someone must bring it into our realm. This is found in the next card.

The Fool comes into our world and brings the gift to us. Notice the Fool holds the white rose of true spirituality. He holds this because the Grim Reaper is not entitled to it. Over his shoulder is the shepherd's staff, which the Hermit used for spiritual direction in life. He appears to some as 'foolish', but really the Fool is our guide and the pinnacle of all wisdom. As he steps towards the precipice, the Fool will lose his life on behalf of others.

This connects us to the Hanged Man card where we see one who dies on a living tree. The Hanged Man card brings us to the identity of the Fool. The Fool represents Jesus of Nazareth, who came into our world as one of us and gave up his life on a cross. Jesus did this to tackle the darkness that is portrayed on the Judgment and nine of Swords cards. He bore the burden for us. In the Fool card we find we are released from the negative power of our own failure, the Devil and Death cards. Jesus did this on behalf of the whole world.

The World card shows that we are interconnected. The joint process of the Magician and the Fool brings transformation into our world. As hearts are changed so are relationships and the cosmos. The Utopia of the Lovers is restored.

Jesus did not remain dead. The Chariot card signifies that

Jesus arose from the grave triumphantly and shattered the power of the Grim Reaper for ever. This is an empowering card because it also signifies that if we entrust ourselves to Jesus, we are given resurrection power to take the journey. The God-like nature within us is restored.

The Strength card represents the flow of the resurrection power. God's spirit enters our lives and we discover the necessary spiritual strength and transformation we desire. This enables us not only in our own lives but also to live out our relationships with others. The grace we receive not only brings us forgiveness, but also assures us that we are loved by the most significant being in the cosmos who pours his loving energy into our own lives. We no longer walk alone but are transformed into the same spiritual state as the Lovers had.

MEDITATION
At the conclusion of the reading Lorraine expressed her openness to having some prayer that focused on the message of the cards. We thought that there was nothing more appropriate than the classic hymn that is popular in alternative lifestyle festivals as well as the church:

> *Amazing grace! How sweet the sound,*
> *that saved a wretch like me!*
> *I once was lost, but now am found,*
> *was blind but now I see.*

Exercise Two: Healing
The Wheel of Fortune is the signifier card. This exercise is a nine-card spread in the shape of a circle. A healing circle is unbroken.

CASE STUDY
Jack chose the Wheel of Fortune. He shared about his physical ailment and the emotional and spiritual pain that it had brought to him and his family. He had explored Reiki in his desperation for

healing. He was discouraged in that nothing seemed to work. He wondered whether anyone beyond his immediate family really cared about his whole person.

THE LAYOUT

The Wheel of Fortune as a card of the Major Arcana reminds us that on the macro-level life is a roller-coaster ride with its ups and downs. The turning wheel represents the cycle of life. So the card speaks to us that illnesses and pain are certainly a part of this cycle. What the card also reminds us is that we need to navigate our way positively through these spiralling events.

There are three Minor Arcana cards that also pick up this theme of the roller coaster on a micro-level in our daily lives. One or all of these cards will indicate the source(s) of the roller coaster.

The ten of Swords indicates that our ailments encompass our emotional sources. We are so drained that we feel the dark situations of life are constantly stabbing us in the back.

The five of Cups indicates that our ailments are connected to personal grief and sorrow, perhaps because of illness, the loss of a loved one or a job, or friends moving away.

The five of Wands shows that our despair finds its origin in conflict and a lack of unity in the areas of our lives that are most significant.

The Minor Arcana offers insights on the way forward.

The ten of Cups suggests we need to look for hope but not taking this journey on our own. We should share the burden, embrace our families, and receive from others.

The ace of Wands shows that all inspired healing and recovery programmes embrace the fundamental principle of the 'Twelve Steps', and rely on the higher power.

The Major Arcana cements the way forward on the macro-level.

The Strength card points us to strength for living in

Wheel of
Fortune
card

ten of
Swords

Star
card

five of
Cups

Lovers
card

five of
Wands

Strength
card

ten of
Cups

ace of
Wands

our adversity. We can overcome and endure until recovery. Strength is found in the infinite spirit. The female figure points to inner peace and the lion to an outer courage.

The Lovers card unfolds how in our relationships integrity and harmony emerge when we have complete openness to one another in the presence of the divine. If our affliction is relational, the Lovers card calls us to forgiveness and reconciliation where possible.

The Star card takes us beyond an understanding of the causes of our dysfunction and suggests steps for processing the same. It offers us the ultimate cure. The cup that flows onto sea and land indicates that healing is available for our emotional being, and physical well-being. Jesus the divine healer is the water of life.

MEDITATION:
As the cards' message concluded, Jack asked us for a blessing. We laid hands on him, and prayed a prayer of Peter Marshall:

> *I have known you as the saviour of my soul; now I would know you as the saviour of my body. I would find in you this day the Great Physician. I pray simply and humbly, with a deep conviction that you can still heal and you do want to heal me. As I discover your strength in this time of weakness may I never forget your mercy nor cease to give you thanks as health returns.*

Exercise Three: Purpose
The Hanged Man is the signifier for this exercise. This is an eight-card layout in the shape of the letter 'S', signifying a pathway.

CASE STUDY
Suzie had had readings with psychics on her future. Like many young people she was looking for a big picture – who am I, is there a cause or a spirit to belong to? She refused to believe that all of life

was meaningless. She shared with us what Liz Greene wrote in her foreword to A.E. Waite's Key to the Tarot: *'The Tarot cards are fundamentally a description of the human journey from birth to death.' The cards are intended for more than prediction; they are to help us understand our role in the cosmos.*

THE LAYOUT

The Hanged Man card starts us on the journey to an authentic purpose. It is not in self-centredness but in living a life of caring and self-sacrifice. Like the model of Jesus, it requires a healthy self-awareness and self-esteem.

The Emperor card reminds us of the power of one. A warrior spirit that stands for values and integrity.

The Empress card highlights how a purposeful life also involves the feminine potential for nurture. Venus and the heart symbolize a deep love that feels for others and the world. Our commitment must comprise more than attitude and be based on more than hype: it must be heart-felt.

The Temperance card draws us to the need to balance the Emperor and Empress for the purposeful life that influences and makes a difference. We have bi-polar sides: light and dark, male and female, positive and negative, and life–death urges. To make a vibrant contribution we must be harmonized within.

The Moon card serves as a warning to us about the evils and temptations that would lead us astray. It isn't always easy knowing what those diversions can be.

The Magician card has the sign of infinity. The Magician connects us with the eternal power and wisdom of the divine. When we are grounded in the divine we have clear direction. The infinite reflects on all elements and aspects of life.

The Justice card shows that the pathway to an authentic purpose requires a heart committed to fair-mindedness and fair play, in a person of virtue. It internalizes the message of the Emperor card.

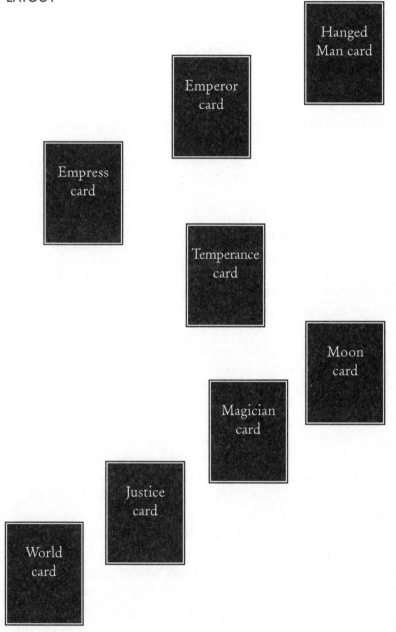

The World card focuses our vision both here and now, and for ever. It is a picture of harmony and restoration with all creatures and the whole creation at peace. Here is a vision we have to own both by taking a firm stand and by seasoning it with love. Apart from our own efforts the wands remind us that we achieve this in partnership with divine grace.

MEDITATION
Suzie sought a prayer that would encapsulate this message and encourage her for what lies ahead. We thought Francis of Assisi said it best:

> *Lord, make me an instrument of your peace.*
> *Where there is hatred, let me sow love.*
> *Where there is injury, pardon.*
> *Where there is doubt, faith.*
> *Where there is despair, hope.*
> *Where there is darkness, light.*
> *Where there is sadness, joy.*
>
> *O Divine Master,*
> *Grant that I may not so much seek to be consoled as to console,*
> *Not so much to be understood as to understand,*
> *Not so much to be loved, as to love;*
> *For it is in giving that we receive,*
> *It is in pardoning that we are pardoned,*
> *It is in dying, that we awake to eternal life.*

Exercise Four: Guidance
The signifier is the Hermit card. You will notice that the cards are to be placed on a tray. The tray symbolizes there are boundaries to what we are prepared to allow to direct our lives. On one side of the tray are the cards from the Minor Arcana that represent the micro-dimension of decision making, the everyday choices we must

make. A sash divides the tray's centre. On the other side is the Major Arcana, its cards drawing us into the macro-dimension of guidance.

CASE STUDY
Sandy came brandishing her aura photo. We were familiar with auras, having had our own taken. We affirmed there is good evidence for the aura, but questioned how useful a tool it is for guidance. Sandy shared her frustration with not knowing how to find guidance. She was a young executive who was used to decision making and mission–vision strategies, but who was struggling to find the same direction for her own life.

THE LAYOUT
One or more of the three cards on the left-hand side might apply to our situation. We can always refer back to the chapter on the Minor Arcana for other cards that might apply to us.

The two of Pentacles means you are juggling two alternatives and like most important decisions in life they have eternal ramifications, for instance in your career path or marriage, or whatever is impacted beyond the moment.

The three of Wands suggests you are contemplating creative new ventures that at this stage lie beyond anything that you can see or imagine.

The eight of Wands indicates you are already on the move, travelling and pursuing your goals. Perhaps it is time to reflect.

These are the Major Arcana cards that draw us into the macro-dimension of guidance:

The Hermit card is the signifier of this exercise. It shows us the universal archetype for all who seek meaning and direction in life. The initial key is to find a place for solitude for meditation. The implements that the Hermit clasps are pivotal in finding guidance: the staff of wisdom and the divine lantern. The staff is the one who can guide,

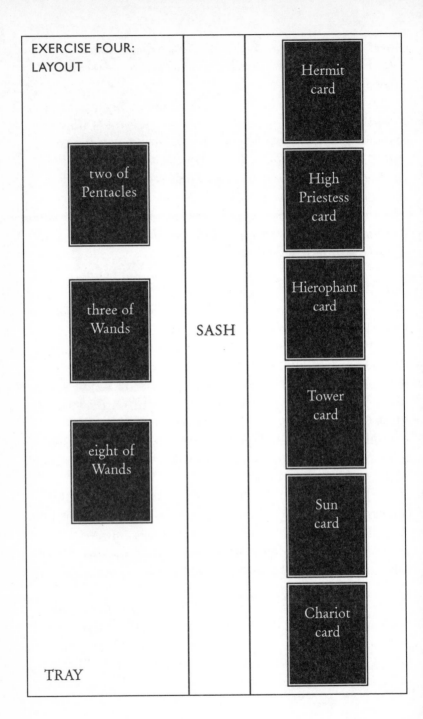

EXERCISE FOUR:
LAYOUT

two of
Pentacles

three of
Wands

eight of
Wands

SASH

Hermit
card

High
Priestess
card

Hierophant
card

Tower
card

Sun
card

Chariot
card

TRAY

and the lantern is the word of God. As we meditate and reflect in the presence of the divine one, our understanding begins to unfold.

The High Priestess card unfolds how we must focus ourselves on the divinely inspired scroll. It is the Torah – or the Jewish scriptures – that she is reading, and continues on with the story and message of Jesus. The practical teachings of the scriptures give us priorities and principles for decision making.

The Hierophant card points unswervingly to the crucial role that a spiritual mentor can play in our growth, development and search for answers.

The Tower card highlights the wisdom of being cautious and avoiding reckless, spur-of-the-moment decisions. Self-aggrandizement might lead to the actual loss of our crown of success.

The Sun card reminds us that most decisions require the simplicity of a little child. You do not have to have all the answers in order to move forward like a child.

The Chariot card invites us to place our trust in the one who drives the chariot. He is the victorious, triumphant figure who has conquered in all realms. As we follow the steps above we hear his whisper to us as we face the challenges of life.

MEDITATION

Sandy was intrigued by the deeper sense of the cards. She responded to our suggestion of spiritual insight into her decision making. We shared the following stanza popular in Celtic circles:

> *Christ with me sleeping,*
> *Christ with me waking,*
> *Christ with me watching,*
> *Every day and night*

Every day and night;
God with me protecting,
The Lord with me directing,
The Spirit with me strengthening,
For ever and for ever more. Amen.

FROM *CARMINA GADELICA* COMPILED BY
ALEXANDER CARMICHAEL

Exercise Five: Eternal Hope

The Star card is the signifier in this seven-card layout made in the shape of the numeral seven. It represents numeric perfection.

CASE STUDY

Thomas and Mary were graduates in religious studies. They questioned the origins and purpose of the Tarot. They understood it was not primarily from Egyptian sources nor was its aim prediction. They had read works such as Tarot and the Millennium *by the authority Timothy Betts, who proposes that the Tarot images can be traced back to pre-Renaissance times, and that the probable inspiration for them is to be found in church art and the illustrated manuscripts of the book of Revelation. This book unveils the signs and message of the second coming of Christ and the reign he will bring. Prophetic signs are very much in vogue right now. We shared with Thomas and Mary how the Tarot does express the message of a coming kingdom – a universal aspiration in movements such as the New Age, or in human philosophies such as Marxism.*

THE LAYOUT

The following interpretation follows on from the pre-Renaissance sources.

The Star card shows seven small stars, one large star and an angel pouring out water on the earth. In this pre-Renaissance context, the seven small stars stand for the seven angels of the seven churches mentioned in the

EXERCISE FIVE: LAYOUT

opening chapters of Revelation. The earliest Renaissance decks disclose a shocking apocalypse, though in recent decks it is more hidden. The large star is actually Wormwood, the great evil star that falls to the earth (Revelation 8:10–11). The angel pouring out water portrays the third vial judgment of Revelation 8 – the judgment on the seas and rivers. The card is a classic apocalyptic sign of environmental disasters summoning the churches and people of faith to be ready and spiritually centred.

The Moon and Sun cards reflect the prophecy that, before the return of Christ and the kingdom, the moon and sun will become smitten and one-third of their respective light-giving potential will be darkened (Revelation 8).

The Tower card depicts the hail that strikes the earth, with the symbolic city, Babylon, falling into ruin before Christ returns (Revelation 8:7; 11:19; 16:21; 18).

The Chariot card dramatically depicts the triumph of Christ over the powers of evil – the agent of eternal, personal and global transformation.

The Judgment card sparks hope because it represents the resurrection of humankind, at the end of time, to a transformed world (Revelation 21).

The World card offers us a current of unending hope in a world that seems to be consumed with drama and disaster. It predicts a revitalized cosmos which is ushered in by Christ and which embraces those who love him and follow his way. It challenges us to live in that eternal vision here and now.

MEDITATION
Thomas and Mary shared with us a reflection of spiritual visionary Marilyn Ferguson, in her book The Aquarian Conspiracy:

> *Over the centuries those who envisioned a transformed society knew that relatively few shared their vision. Like*

Moses, they felt the breezes from a homeland they could see
in the distance but not inhabit. Yet they urged others on to
the possible future. Their dreams are our rich, unrealized
history, the legacy that has always existed alongside our
wars and folly (p. 458).

Exercise Six: The Sixth Sense – Stages of Life

CASE STUDY

Teresa was attracted to our booth when she spotted our sign about
spiritual exercises through the Tarot. Before we began the exercise,
Teresa initiated a conversation about herself. She began by saying
she was at a crossroads in her life. What was uppermost in her
mind was what she should do with the rest of her life. She was
single, about to turn thirty, and was disenchanted with her life,
career and relationships. Teresa was in one of those stages we all
pass through, such as the transition to adulthood, being an 'empty-
nester', mid-life and retirement. Her immediate concern was to find
some clarity and direction.

As the conversation unfolded Teresa spoke about her
struggle to have an identity. The surface indicator of this
sprang out of her name. Although her given name at birth
was Teresa, her parents had nicknamed her Tessa. The
problem with being known as Tessa was that this made
her feel a bit of a puppet under her parents' control. She
was feeling constricted in most areas of her life and she
attributed this to her relationship with her parents. Was
she Tessa or Teresa? Now she was striving to assert her own
identity as an adult woman by reclaiming her given name
of Teresa.

This exercise – stages of life – does not have to begin
with any particular signifier card. It can spring from any
of the five signifiers used in the previous exercises or it
can arise simply from the descriptions of the cards set
out in chapter four. Look at the cards and if something is

triggered about your identity – adjusting to life's phases, crossing thresholds – then let it flow.

With Teresa we had a nine-card configuration in the shape of an X.

THE LAYOUT

The Lovers card is the first one Teresa chose. It gave her the sense that harmony in her relationships, especially with her parents, was a most desirable thing. However, she acknowledged that the harmony depicted on the card had not been reflected in her journey. She felt impaired inside her spirit and did not sense the presence of the divine in her life. When she saw the Lovers card she intuited that there must be a divine imprint within, which she desired to have awakened in her life. We agreed that recovering the divine image inside was crucial to any growth and spiritual understanding. We placed this card in the middle to signify how this harmony and yearning was central to her life's journey.

The three of Swords was the next card and we placed it at the top left-hand side. Teresa saw herself in this card: pierced in every area of life and thought. This spoke to her of how difficult it had been playing the part of Tessa, when within she had been crying out for recognition of who she really is. We also explored how the creator, though seemingly absent here, could indeed meet her in the middle of these trials and pain.

The Judgment card turned up next and it was laid diagonally between the three of Swords and the Lovers. Teresa reacted with a pained expression. All of her life she had felt judged as unworthy by her parents. She said she had failed time and again to meet their expectations. We looked at the red cross on the angel's pennant. The red cross is a symbol of reconciliation. We considered together how there was a profound need for reconciliation in her life with her parents. We also reflected on how the card also spoke to her spiritually. She affirmed that instant

EXERCISE SIX: LAYOUT

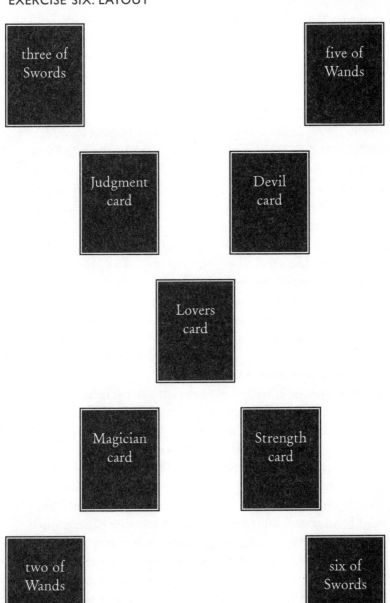

answers were not for her, and that she now needed to undergo a time of preparation spiritually if she wanted to experience wholeness within.

The five of Wands was the fourth card selected and we placed it at the top right-hand side. Teresa immediately said that this depicted exactly what she felt: people and circumstances were opposing her on all sides. The card simply reiterated how she was confronted by a lack of unity, perhaps finding its source in the Devil card. Even though this card spoke to her about frustration, we paused to see how she might reframe the way she looked at life. Perhaps the card was a summons to transform relationships through mediation.

The Devil card was the fifth card to be selected. It was placed diagonally between the five of Wands and the Lovers. Teresa identified a lack of freedom in her spirit and her life. We looked at how this sense of bondage in her personal relationships tied in with the bigger universal picture of spiritual oppression that we all experience. The contrasts between the Devil and Lovers cards were most poignant and apparent to her.

The two of Wands was the sixth card selected by Teresa. It shows a person clasping a wand in one hand and holding a globe of the world in the other. The person is looking towards the sea. With two options open a choice must be made. We placed this at the bottom left-hand side. Unlike the negative sequence of cards that had unfolded so far, this one seemed to offer Teresa some hope. She could put things into a more positive frame of reference. She could have a fresh perspective on life and the world around her. The big issue was: would she be willing to take a risk and confront those negative experiences and individuals in her life? Did she discern here something of the presence of the creator at work in her?

The six of Swords was the next card she selected and

we placed it at the bottom right-hand side. Teresa saw the message spring out at her. She had to turn her back on negative thoughts and fruitless plans, and take the disciplined journey towards serenity of mind and purpose. The one steering the raft evoked in her a sense now of the close proximity of the creator. She could embark on a new course in life and cross those risky thresholds with God in her life to guide and comfort.

The Strength card was the eighth card and it was placed on the right-hand side between the six of Swords and the Lovers. Teresa nodded as she could see the new picture of her life come into focus. She could perceive how spiritual strength and nurture could be best sought in God's spirit. The golden light of God's spirit shining on her was unconditional. She could see here that her self-worth did not depend on how her parents saw her, but rather what mattered most was how God loves and accepts her. She was open to dying to her past and to opening herself up to the empowerment of the Holy Spirit.

The Magician card was the final one selected in the exercise, and it was placed on the left-hand side between the two of Wands and the Lovers. Here Teresa could clearly see her need for grace and how the yearning of the divine image inside her could find fruitful and purposeful expression through the Magician card. Just as Teresa yearned for that awakening and transforming experience, we all need to come to grips with the Magician card. The biggest and riskiest threshold of all to cross is the one where we allow the Magician through the Fool to heal our soul-sorrow and give us the incomparable joy of spiritual rebirth.

MEDITATION

Teresa's first step to spiritual renewal came when we prayed together and read these words about God's love:

Love is patient and kind; love is not jealous or boastful; it is not arrogant or rude. Love does not insist on its own way; it is not irritable or resentful; it does not rejoice at wrong, but rejoices in the right. Love bears all things, believes all things, hopes all things, endures all things. Love never ends.

1 CORINTHIANS 13:4–8

EPILOGUE

In our opening chapter we raised some universal questions such as: How can I be the best person I can possibly be? How can I find my place in the world? Who am I, and who might I become? Does any of it make sense? And even if it does, who cares anyway? These are reflected in the universal archetypes, dreams, myths, stories and symbols of the world. Sometimes trite answers can be given to these meaningful questions. After our sojourn through the Tarot we see elegant simplicity coupled with depth of spirituality in facing these ultimate questions of life.

The message of the cards ultimately leads us to the Fool. The Fool has always been with us, calling us from death to new life, empowering us on the roller coaster of life. He is our universal hero, 'the wind beneath our wings'. He invites us to be his dancing partner. As we begin to move our feet in the divine dance, the choreography progressively leads us to abandon all the negative energies properly depicted in the Tarot cards. As we are swept into the Fool's positive embrace, we intuitively know who we want to explore life with.

The Tarot beyond prediction is a call to broaden our horizons beyond our consciousness and to reconnect our souls with the divine source of all life. Let's dance.

READING LIST

Edward A. Aviza, *Thinking Tarot*, New York: Simon & Schuster, 1997.

Alessandro Bellenghi, *Cartomancy*, London: Ebury, 1988.

Timothy Betts, *Tarot and the Millennium*, Rancho Palos Verdes: New Perspective Media, 1998.

Joseph Campbell with Bill Moyers, *The Power of Myth*, New York: Doubleday, 1988.

Joseph Campbell and Richard Roberts, *Tarot Revelations*, San Anselmo CA: Vernal Equinox Press, 1987.

Ross Clifford and Philip Johnson, *Jesus and the Gods of the New Age: Communicating Christ in Today's Spiritual Supermarket*, Oxford: Lion, 2001.

Ross Clifford and Philip Johnson, *Riding the Rollercoaster*, Sydney: Strand, 1998.

Ronald Decker, Thierry Depaulis and Michael Dummet, *A Wicked Pack of Cards: The Origins of the Occult Taro*, New York: St Martin's Press, 1996.

Terry Donaldson, *The Lord of the Rings Tarot*, Stamford CT: US Games Systems, 1997.

Alfred Douglas, *The Tarot*, Harmondsworth: Penguin, 1972.

John Drane, *The Bible Phenomenon*, Oxford: Lion, 1999.

T.S. Eliot, *Selected Poems*, London: Faber & Faber, 1954.

Paul Fenton-Smith, *The Tarot Revealed*, Sydney: Simon & Schuster, 1995.

Michael Frost, *Seeing God in the Ordinary*, Peabody MA: Hendrickson, 2000.

Cynthia Giles, *The Tarot: History, Mystery and Lore*, New York: Fireside, 1994.

Corinne Heline, *The Bible and the*

Tarot, Marina del Rey CA: DeVorss, 1969.

Stuart Kaplan, *Encyclopedia of the Tarot*, Vol. 2, Stamford CT: US Games Systems, 1994.

Sheldon Kopp, *The Hanged Man: Psychotherapy and the Forces of Darkness*, Palo Alto CA: Science & Behavior Books, 1974.

Martin Kriele, *Meditations on the Tarot: A Journey into Christian Hermeticism*, Warwick NY: Amity House, 1985.

A.T. Mann, *The Elements of the Tarot*, Dorset: Element, 1993.

George Miller, 'The Apocalypse and the Pig: or The Hazards of Storytelling', *The Sydney Papers*, 8/4, 1996, pp. 38–49.

John Warwick Montgomery, *Principalities and Powers*, Minneapolis: Bethany, 1973.

John Warwick Montgomery, ed., *Myth, Allegory and Gospel*, Minneapolis: Bethany, 1974.

Sallie Nichols, *Jung and Tarot: An Archetypal Journey*, York Beach ME: Samuel Weiser, 1980.

Robert V. O'Neill, *Tarot Symbolism*, Lima: Fairway, 1986.

P.D. Ouspensky, *The Symbolism of the Tarot*, London: Universal Books, 1989.

Naomi Ozaniec, *The Illustrated Guide to the Tarot*, New York: Godsfield Press, 1999.

Rachel Pollack, *Seventy Eight Degrees of Wisdom*, revised edition, London: Thorsons, 1997.

James Redfield, *The Secret of Shambhala*, New York and London: Bantam, 1999.

Janina Renee, *Tarot Spells*, St Paul: Llewellyn, 1997.

Mouni Sadhu, *The Tarot*, Hollywood CA: Wilshire, 1968.

Carl Sargent, *Personality, Divination, and the Tarot*, Rochester NY: Destiny, 1988.

J.R.R. Tolkien, 'On Fairy Stories', in C.S. Lewis, ed., *Essays Presented to Charles Williams*, Grand Rapids: Eerdmans, 1981.

A.E. Waite, *The Pictorial Key to the Tarot*, Stamford: US Games Systems, 1990.

A.E. Waite, *The Key to the Tarot*, revised by Liz Greene, London: Random House, 1993.

Brian Williams, *A Renaissance Tarot: A Guide to the Renaissance Tarot*, Stamford CT: US Games Systems, 1994.

Charles Williams, *The Greater Trumps*, Grand Rapids: Eerdmans, 1979.

C000178257

OXBI
ENTRANCE

THE REAL RULES

Elfi Pallis

Tell Books
London

TELL BOOKS
PO Box 55671
London W9 2WA
www.tellbooks.com

This edition published by Tell Books 2009

First published by
Tell Books 2003

ISBN 978-0-9545944-42

Designed by www.anu-design.ie
Typeset by Academic + Technical, Bristol www.acadtech.co.uk
Printed and bound by MPG Biddles Ltd www.biddles.co.uk

Contents

Acknowledgements

This book would not have been possible without generous help from a large number of people. First credit belongs to the dozens of students, past and present, who mapped out their varied routes towards Oxford or Cambridge for me. They also shared what were often deeply moving tales and offered valuable insights. Similar credit must go to the many state school teachers who found the time to proffer technical advice, success stories and educational frustrations. It is a measure of the awe in which the two universities are still held that most people in either group did not want to be named. This necessitated the use of pseudonyms, though the stories told are unchanged.

Further thanks go to the members of ArRum, a London club for young Muslim professionals seeking to reflect the cultural diversity of Islam. Despite busy lives and responsible positions, these graduates managed to convey to me an ethnic minority experience of the Oxbridge entrance process.

For academic guidance I am indebted to Deborah Eyre, Joan Freeman, Ruth Heilbronn and Diane Montgomery. A number of current and former Oxbridge dons kindly talked me through their subject's general entry requirements. Among those were Peter Carey, Gabriel Dover, Françoise Friedman, Steve Hunt, Catherine Hood, William James, Avi Shlaim, Claudio Scazzoccio and Richard Stone.

Iain Chalmers, Elizabeth Laird, David McDowall, Anne Rodford, Karl Sabbagh, David Wolton and Roger van Zwanenberg added further advice.

Special appreciation must go to my editor, Liz Friend-Smith, whose tactful suggestions and love of precision were crucial in shaping this book. Lastly, Robert Smith provided moral support, literary help and the professional dramatist's sense of how to tell a story.

Naturally, none of the above is in any way responsible for the contents of this book.

The author and publisher are grateful to the following:

1. HarperCollins Publishers Ltd. for permission to reproduce an extract from *From the Land of Green Ghosts* by Pascal Khoo Thwe (HarperCollins, 2003)
2. Oxford University Press for permission to reproduce an extract from *A Jerseyman at Oxford* by Robert Randolph Marett (OUP, 1941)
3. Johnson & Alcock Ltd. for permission to reproduce an extract from *All Souls in My Time* by A.L. Rowse (Duckworth, 1993).

About the author

Elfi Pallis is a sociologist by training, but has worked as a print journalist, researcher and TV producer. She also produced a number of radio programmes on educational issues. Saturday workshops she used to run for exceptionally talented pupils led to her editing the London quarterly of the National Association for Gifted Children. When she discovered that workshop children from state schools failed to progress to Oxford or Cambridge, she set out to write this book.

The author now mentors academically able sixth formers at a variety of inner city schools. Many of those she has worked with have gone on to Oxbridge.

1

Is there a road into Oxbridge?

There is no such place as Oxbridge, but it features in many families' dreams. The word, a blend of two town names, is a crucial part of its mystique. So are the turreted buildings, black-gowned students and bewilderingly complex entrance procedures.

There is, of course, far more to Britain's oldest universities. Your teachers may have mentioned their academic record, the great discoveries made and the Nobel Prizes won. If you are raising a bright, high-achieving teenager, Oxford and Cambridge can sound like a wonderful place for her, but also unreal or unwelcoming. And with so many richer, privately schooled pupils going there, how can you tell whether your state school educated daughter stands any chance at all?

The answer, on first sight, seems both positive and obvious. In recent years, Oxford and Cambridge have gone to great lengths to publicise that they invite applications from all sorts of talented young people. A Government-supported campaign run under a variety of names, but mainly known as Access, has resulted in every state school being contacted by at least one of the two universities. Millions of pounds, much of it taxpayer's money, have gone into promoting Oxbridge to a wider public. As a result, you might already be considering this slightly awesome university choice. Or perhaps you have been told by your son's teacher that the promising lad ought to apply.

In order to ease the initial decision-making process, this book explains what sets the two universities apart and why it is worth studying there. Their most attractive features, I believe, are far too little known.

Deciding to apply, though, is not at all the same as getting in. To guide your teenager towards this aim, the book carefully lays out the long, fiddly and not all that straightforward Oxbridge entrance process. Giving you the information absent from the official

1

literature, this book shows you how to do things right from the very start, well before you fill in the application form.

Rather than just sending off the girl and hoping for the best, this enables you to maximise her chances of acceptance. To that end, the book unpacks the kitbag of qualifications and qualities that candidates must bring with them to succeed. There are chapters about A-level choice and grades, colleges, academic activities, personal statements and Access initiatives. Readers are taken through the key interview skills and the rigid entry rules of the Oxbridge medical schools. Minor mysteries too, like what to wear to your Oxbridge interview, are resolved.

Before embarking on this road, though, it is best to know more about Oxford and Cambridge, two universities some 80 miles apart yet so similar and so coordinated in their approach that they are usually referred to as one. It is also crucial to address all those fears and myths that surround them.

Chances are, you will have heard discouraging stories. Some will be about the old-fashioned subjects studied there, which can worry a parent keen to ensure their offspring a good career. Others are about the strange way in which these subjects are taught.

Then there is the cost of sending a teenager to such a famous place. Isn't Oxbridge awfully expensive? Would another, less famous, university near home not do the same job of teaching you Maths, History or Economics?

Most discouraging can be the doubts about whether Oxbridge really wants candidates like your son or daughter at all. You may have read about Oxford's Millenium rejection of Laura Spence, a Whitley Bay schoolgirl with five top A-levels and a strong working class accent. So, is all that publicity bumph a genuine invitation or just a professor's equivalent of "you really must come to dinner sometime?"

It is only when these questions are resolved in your mind that you and your teenager can hope to successfully negotiate Oxbridge Entrance.

WHAT MAKES OXBRIDGE SPECIAL?

Oxford and Cambridge are intellectual powerhouses, but what makes them that is a quite intangible factor. The two universities do not contain "all the best academics," as many of their graduates like to claim. Mental ability, a gift for teaching and the research skills which can lead an academic towards exciting new discoveries are also found elsewhere. At lots of British universities brilliant young academics inspiringly pass on cutting-edge knowledge to their students; professors, whose research has won them international acclaim, share their wisdom in seminars, lectures and laboratories.

What Oxbridge dons (as its academics are called) have, though, is time. Thanks to Government funding, which tops up the two universities' own inherited wealth and that of individual colleges, their student-teacher ratio is far lower than anywhere else. This allows their dons to employ a leisurely, personalised teaching system, the tutorial. It was affectionately described by Robert Ranulph Marett, a Jersey lad who went up to Oxford in the autumn of 1894 and later became its Professor of the new science he had invented, Anthropology:

> Oxford bases her method strictly on the Socratic use of the dialectic, that is conversation, as a means whereby an older man engages with a younger man in a friendly interchange of views, with truth as their common object... a companion of maturer experience can greatly help him to think critically... though he must do so, not by laying down the law, but by showing the inquirer how to put to himself the right questions ©.
> *74w from p. 121 from A Jerseyman by Marett, Robert Ranulph (1941) By permission of Oxford University Press*

Little has changed in this method since, although both conversation partners might be female these days and the subject under discussion Computer Science.   TUTORIALS

The tutorial is not, strictly speaking, unique to Oxford and Cambridge. Although most other universities allocate their students a tutor, their system is far less intensive. Half a dozen students might share one tutor, or a personal tutor might see the student only once a term. Most learning outside Oxbridge takes place though large hall lectures and smaller groups called seminars.

Oxbridge tutorials do more than guide the student "towards the truth". They make it possible for her to critically absorb a huge amount of information. Staff may also show great flexibility. Even a first year can satisfy her curiosity about a course-related subject by raiding the college library, writing an essay on what she found and discussing it with her tutor. If the student's tutor has not read a specific book mentioned by her, he may well do so for the purpose of discussion. He is not burdened by the needs of hundreds of other students, long teaching hours or piles of paperwork, as are even the most brilliant, committed academics elsewhere.

Although Oxbridge students have a huge range of lecture options, this group-based learning is not their main form of study. Much of their progress is expected to come from the conversations held with and work done for their individual tutor. It is a privileged learning system, but also one that puts great responsibility on the student. If she is keen, she will plough through mountains of written material, write long weekly essays and debate aspects of her course with her tutor and other students.

A student expecting to be jollied along is in for a shock. His tutor may not admonish him if he fails to pull his weight and although there are intermediate exams the lad must pass, they don't really count towards his degree; this is based on how he performs at his final exams, not on continuous assessment. Being told that "we are not here to teach you, you are here to learn" can be a liberating experience for a fast, inquisitive teenager.

The method works best for students who are quite independent-minded and willing to work hard. A student seeking firm guidance towards narrowly defined goals, on the other hand, might find it scary or confusing. It means mixing with adults and being treated like an adult while still allowing you to sleep until lunch – at least if you are an arts student.

The staff meanwhile still have time left to attend to their own research. Thanks to this, and to fabulously equipped research facilities in all fields, even the youngest don can expect to quickly make his mark in a competitive academic world. And his fame, in turn, will reflect back on Oxbridge.

THE NETWORK

Oxford and Cambridge, though, are not just two high intensity learning and research centres. They also play another, equally important role in British life as discreet power brokers. When making his first speech as Chancellor of Oxford in June 2003, former Conservative Minister Chris Patten expressed this by asking rhetorically: "What should Oxford University aim to be and to do? As yesterday so tomorrow, our task is to shape and create the future. It is as simple and audacious as that."

This is not an empty boast. Britain has 109 universities, yet almost all its modern Prime Ministers studied at just two of them. So did most of those who determine what we see on TV or read in the newspapers. Mark Thompson, the director-general of the BBC, is an Oxford graduate, as is Rupert Murdoch, the owner of a media empire that includes Sky TV, The Sun and Times Newspapers. The BBC's chief interrogator, Jeremy Paxman, and the editor of *The Guardian*, Alan Rusbridger, who snap at the establishment's heels from the centre left, gained their degrees at Cambridge. So did the editor of the rightwing Daily Telegraph, Will Lewis.

Oxbridge mass-produces judges, senior civil servants, politicians and most of the committee chairs appointed to pick the next great young artist or city boss. It also supplies much of the top level staff of other universities. Oxbridge dons pride themselves on their easy access to successful ex-students and the corridors of power.

As a result, the universities are, to many of their traditional students (not all!) a place for networking, for making useful, prestigious links that will last them a lifetime. "You might not remember me, but we were at Jesus in '99" is a meaningful phrase to any of its graduates. It is also a good way of asking for a job.

Meanwhile, successful ex-students drop in for college dinner and everybody who is anybody turns up as a speaker. An undergraduate who has impressed his tutor may meet famous scientists and authors, ennobled industrialists and enraged public campaigners. And because an Oxbridge qualification counts everywhere, a high proportion of graduates quickly emigrate to higher wage economies, which probably makes their expensive education a net loss for the taxpayer.

But it is an ever-renewing circle. Junior politicians are launched onto an unsuspecting public from medieval quads and eventually return, in old age, as college wardens or university chancellors. History students become famous British novelists and teenagers studying lower life forms turn into property tycoons thanks to contacts made over a college drink. Most Oxbridge graduates eventually become parents who regard a place at Oxbridge as their kids' birthright and go ballistic when anybody suggests letting more outsiders in.

FUN CITY

The best reason for going to Oxbridge remains its lively academic atmosphere. This does not mean everybody is terribly academic, or even above-average bright. A handful of students, most of them male, will have been admitted to keep up the glorious reputation their college has enjoyed for a few hundred years in rugby or rowing and might leave with a poor degree but muscles that would be the envy of the Incredible Hulk.

The rest of the student body, though, can be pretty brainy. At Oxbridge it is OK to show off just how clever you are, to pepper

5

your conversation with long, fancy words; to have frantic all-night arguments about crazy, complex ideas; and to develop the most obscure artistic tastes. Alternatively, it is fine to walk around with your nose permanently buried in a physics book.

Thanks to the superb leisure facilities, Oxbridge students need not even sacrifice other interests for the sake of nurturing their brains. Instead, they are encouraged to pursue them, often to a semiprofessional level. Generous funding for student society means that an undergraduate is able to combine the most diverse activities: History with directing a musical, Geography with ballroom dancing, or Physics with water polo. To a smart all-rounder who used to be very careful "not to show off" in a mixed ability set, this can feel like paradise.

It can also, so potential candidates should be warned, feel like hell. The workload, if you want to get at least a middling degree, is quite shocking. Students learn to prioritise or collapse in a heap after too many sleepless, deadline-cursed nights. Courses can be too abstract for some tastes, tutor and tutee don't always hit it off and a student from an ethnic minority or working class background may pass several uncertain months before she considers herself at home. Still, the tears shed at graduation parties are real enough, and not just due to the champagne donated by parents whose money pit is about to become self-supporting.

CAN YOU AFFORD IT?

Having glimpsed those immaculate lawns and high maintenance ancient buildings on TV behind Inspector Morse, you may well assume that sending your daughter to Oxbridge is far too expensive for someone like you. Unlike with most things in life, such pessimism is unjustified – for the moment at least. Many parents, alas, remain unaware of this.

When asked why there are not more students from ordinary families applying to Oxbridge, nearly all the dons I spoke to attributed this to shyness or, as they put it, low self esteem. Parents, on the other hand, often mentioned quite a different factor: money. They could not possibly afford, they said, to educate their child at a famous university like that. In fact, many regarded the mere idea of sending a son away to study when he could do so right in their own home town as wasteful.

However, this can be short term thinking. Generally, living out is likely to broaden your son's outlook. He may hear about careers he never considered before, talk to and visit students whose parents do interesting, unfamiliar things. If your own family and friends all work in similar fields, and so do the parents of his classmates, university can catapult him into a world of more varied options.

Also, the more desirable jobs are often obtained through personal contacts. Graduates tip off one another and academics make recommendations, but this only works for those who have established close links in the university years. Students who live at home and go to college simply to attend lectures tend to keep their old friends, rather than make new ones. They don't hang around after a lecture to chat. As a result, the young man who is still out of work months after graduating will probably be the one his financially careful parents kept at home.

What is yet more useful to know is that Oxford and Cambridge currently charge the same tuition fees as nearly all other UK universities, namely £3,225 a year. Even better, up-front fees were abolished in 2005. This means parents no longer need to dip into their pockets at all. Instead, young people who have completed their degree, found work and are earning more than £15,000 a year are expected to pay back the fees like a bank loan. They can currently do so in small amounts and over several decades.

But what about the future? While a sharp fee hike has been recommended by some politicians to cover rising education costs, this has proved a highly controversial suggestion. Moreover, it cannot be brought in until 2012 at the very earliest on legal grounds. Even then, the new fees would only be applicable to students about to start their course.

LIVING IT UP

As most potential university students come to realise, tuition fees are not the only item of expenditure you need to budget for. So, what about rental costs at Oxbridge?

Well, college rooms generally cost around £90 a week, depending on the facilities. Oxbridge rents tend to be lower than those charged by other top universities. Thanks to generous university subsidies, most students live in during their entire course and pay no more weekly rent for a room in an historic building with a view "to kill for" than they would for a bedsit in some concrete maze. Their college covers the cost of internet connection and other maintenance bills. Also, since Oxbridge terms are much shorter than those at other educational institutions, there is less rent.

Food too need not cost you an arm and leg at Oxbridge. Each college tries to ensure that a student eating in its dining room or cafeteria will pay no more for this than he would at most other universities. A good meal can be had for the cost of a ready supermarket dish. Outside the college gates, popular student haunts like Pizza Hut and McDonalds charge the same wherever you go.

Unlike in other university towns, students incur no travel costs, and there is a built-in night life. Every college has a bar, as well as a club room, the Junior Common Room (JCR), and most have their own theatre or a cinema society that shows recent films on a big, proper screen. Pints can cost very slightly more than in most redbricks, but university club nights, called Bops or Entz, cost less. Being smallish towns, neither Oxford nor Cambridge can sustain any really flash clubs, so there is no need for dressing up (although your daughter might disagree). Students are also entitled to cheap tickets for gigs or shows in town.

Even those annual newspaper shots of students attending the college May Ball in full evening dress can be misleading. Dinner jackets and ball gowns are often hired or bought at the excellent local Oxfam shop, which circulates them among the student generations. And while May Ball tickets may cost a hefty £90, they include dinner and all you can drink. There are also several ways of not paying: anyone willing to promote the event, clean up afterwards or do a couple of hours waiting at tables gets in for free. This is a popular option, since by that stage of the university year funds are often tight, and all the students I spoke to insisted that there was no stigma attached. Members of the May Ball organising committee, a post open to all comers, also get in free the subsequent year.

One female Cambridge don has run a protracted campaign to get the May Ball abolished, as she feels it gives outsiders quite the wrong impression of College life, but she is annually defeated by the student body. "We girls really like it, because it's a bit like being a princess for the day, and the men quite like what they see," Jess, who is the daughter of a train driver and the president of her college May Ball committee, told me with a giggle.

BARE ESSENTIALS

Text books, an essential of student life, cost the same at Oxbridge as anywhere else. However, only here can a student get by without ever buying a single one. Reading lists may be terrifyingly long, but no student has to make do without. The main university libraries of

Oxford and Cambridge contain copies of every book ever published in the UK. Books are also available from other sources, so that any work mentioned in any course is normally available to all. An English student at Oxford, for instance, can find anything on his reading list or just mentioned by staff either at his college library or at the library of the university's English faculty or, if it is fairly obscure, at the university's reference library, the Bodleian. And, by the way, most of these lovely libraries are open 24 hours a day.

Of course, some people prefer owning books to borrowing, and there is no shortage of wealthy Oxbridge students who buy. Some do it because they to want underline, scribble in the margins and generally vandalise the printed page; but others just like to own everything mentioned in class. This has a very useful side effect. On the first day of each new year, these students sell off their books (or at least the ones still in tolerable condition) for a fraction of the original price to people in the year below.

The expensive photocopying of key chapters, which is so common in other universities with a limited book supply, is almost unknown at Oxbridge.

What about the peculiar black outfits that you always see students wear on TV? Well, most students at Oxbridge, like elsewhere, live in sweatshirts and jeans. Formal occasions, such as exams or special dinners (which are a bit like wedding meals, including the long speeches), call for a dark suit or two-piece, plus a cap and gown, bought from a local shop, a graduate or, again, Oxfam. Only very few colleges nowadays insist that students must wear formal dress for ordinary dinners, so gowns tend to last forever. The only unavoidable expense is the £13.99 white tie which male students have to wear with the suit. Apparently, whenever you try to borrow one, it always has tomato ketchup on it.

For those seeking to recover from the wine flowing at these events, there is a choice of sports facilities which are truly amazing and totally free. In fact, there are few experiences for which you actually need to pay; one is membership of your university debating society, the Oxford or Cambridge Union. Joining these historic launch pads of government ministers and government critics for life costs £198 at Oxford, but only £120 at Cambridge. Alternatively, a student can pay £5 a night to attend a debate on an issue of the day. Only the Drinking Societies charge higher fees.

But what about student social life? Well, "Brideshead" it ain't, not any more. A student can go out every night of the week (though they'd better not, if they want to pass) without paying for anything at all. This is not say there is no high spending Hooray Henry set, dressed head to sun-bronzed toe in designer labels. If your son wants to keep up with them, he'll have to get a part-time job. There are quite a few of those in local shops or at the college bar. The universities, although not keen on such distractions, also offer students work in the library, which is reassuring for non-drinkers.

OXBRIDGE GRANTS

The most important fact is the one I have left to the end: Oxbridge offers a substantial grant (not loan) to poorer students. At Cambridge, students from low income households will qualify for a maximum grant of £3,250 a year from 2009, while Oxford will pay £3,225. Students whose parents earn up to £49,999 a year will still qualify for part of this. None of the grant, referred to a bursary, ever needs to be paid back and it comes in addition to the new government grant covering most of students' tuition fees. Few other universities can afford to be that generous.

On top of this, Oxbridge is rich enough to have very substantial hardship funds. A student who has genuinely fallen on tough times will be directed towards the right application forms, especially in the crucial third year. Once in, no student has to leave Oxbridge because of genuine poverty.

In addition, are quite a few minor bursaries, each worth around £100. Designed to reward achievement, these are open to anyone. Some are bestowed for an outstanding bit of course work, while others require the student to complete a specially defined task. Information about all bursaries can be found on the university or college website.

Still unsure how you will pay for your designer cycling shorts? There is one further source of money you can access. Student Finance England (SFE), a government-regulated scheme, will lend you several thousand pounds a year (how much depends on your individual circumstances) at a fairly low rate. Its loans are meant to help with living costs, whether you are at Oxbridge or elsewhere.

The important thing to realize is that once a student has been accepted, most of his basic financial worries can be resolved. Oxford and Cambridge today are pretty flexible societies. Students have similar, but not identical living standards. If your son is on a tight budget, he will not be shunned. There are always other students whose parents cannot pay them to keep up with the Chelsea set.

Should your son wonder how he'll manage, I pass on some advice from a recent graduate: if you want your term money to last, don't smoke and drink only at weekends.

THINKING AHEAD

So, while an Oxbridge education is no longer as freely available as it was until the introduction of tuition fees in 2005, it is unlikely to be out of your reach. Disadvantaged families will, in fact, benefit from the new fee structure and the new, very generous Oxbridge grants.

On the other hand, the vast majority of couples with a child set on Oxbridge probably earn just a little too much to qualify for proper financial help. Given that the current Labour Government is dominated by Oxbridge graduates, pulling up the ladder by making young people pay for higher education was a pretty rotten thing to do.

Having said this, it's worth repeating that an Oxbridge education constitutes a great investment in a career. Employers, many of them products of the system themselves, love an Oxbridge degree, and many don't care which subject the applicant took. A degree in Classics was for some two hundred years seen as the ideal qualification for the post of Prime Minister. We have moved on only a little since: Margaret Thatcher's Oxford degree was in Chemistry; Tony Blair's, in Law.

Which is not to say that all Oxbridge graduates go into "sensible" careers. A few always drop out, or embark on wildly eccentric and quite unprofitable schemes, something perceived as a legitimate choice. This is, however, far less common than most people think. Anyway, should that solitary desert traveller ever feel like touching base and introducing his tribal friends to someone in Britain, his tutor will probably be delighted to oblige. He'll almost certainly know a chap who understands the visitors' dialect, has done research into their culture or might wish to discuss their national aspirations with them.

And should the traveller want to return to society or his studies in some way, the door is always open. Oxbridge graduates retain their opportunities whatever they do (even, it seems, if they commit treason). There is no excuse for any of them to say that he could not develop a career.

MIX AND MATCH

If it is the other students you are worried about, don't be. Oxbridge undergraduates these days come from a wide range of backgrounds. Not that the mixing process always goes smoothly, especially at the

11

start. Discovering that someone with a Scouse accent may have read more of James Joyce comes as a shock to many a public school boy. Nor do enough teachers tell their pupils that it is possible to have a deep love of British medieval history and yet not be white. Luckily, the brainier Oxbridge students tend to cotton on to these facts reasonably fast.

By the end of the first year, certainly, friendships have usually been formed that will cut across income, class or colour lines. Many of these will last a lifetime. Oxbridge graduates keep in touch and tend to employ, gossip about, and marry one another.

Telling your daughter this may still not be enough to remove her doubts about Oxbridge, especially if she attends a school that does not usually sends students there. Rather than give up, you might find it helpful to remember that at seventeen all adult suggestions sound bad. So does university in general. The girl is being asked to consider a long-term project, for a start, and at a moment at which the question whether she will have somewhere to go next Saturday night is far more urgent.

A more forward-thinking student may have her own ideas. Even if you're a bright, well-read young woman determined to become a TV chef, though, it is wise to research career paths. Did you know that Nigella Lawson did modern languages at Oxford?

Parents may also need to address the most immutable of teenage emotions: fear of loneliness. Having looked though the prospectus and admitted that the course and facilities look pretty good, your teenager will turn to you and say firmly: "I can't possibly. None of my friends are going. It'll be horrible. All the other students will be from somewhere else. I'll be totally on my own."

Don't laugh. And don't bother pointing out that, as an adult, you know that one's best friends are quite rarely the people one has smoked one's first fag behind the bike sheds with. Or that it is possible, maybe even exciting, to make friends with people different from yourself.

Instead, just deal with the basics. Firmly agree that your son's current friends are great, and may well remain his friends for life. After all, he will see them in the extra-long Oxbridge holidays. Then remind him that he actually wanted to go out into the world and meet some new people. If you are bright, interested in ideas and/or academic subjects, Oxbridge is a great place to do just that.

And, of course, there will be ways he can hang out and meet people he is not already attending seminars or lectures with: at the student common room or the bar, on the college sports field or the university drama society. Moreover, Oxford and Cambridge are small towns and he will be bumping into fellow students at Foot Locker, at the local Boots and in Tesco Metro.

BUT WILL I BE SNUBBED?

This is the real fear, the subtext behind many teenage hesitations. Your son may well be flattered by the idea of being thought academically bright enough to apply for Oxbridge, but worried that, once there, other students will make him feel he does not belong.

You shouldn't sneer at such fears because they reflect an historic reality. When Roger Dataller, a South Yorkshire collier, went up to Oxford on a miners' scholarship in 1928, after years of preparation at night school, he encountered a world of petty snobbishness chronicled in his book *A Pitman looks at Oxford*. In this world, students from private schools treated all others with total contempt. Even sport did nothing to bridge the gap. "In my first term at Oxford I played soccer," a fellow working class student confided in Dataller soon after he arrived at the university. "Everything went swimmingly the first game. I played back. The other back was Lord – son of –, He wasn't bad at first. He'd chat a little when play went up the field. Then he discovered who I was. Never spoke to me again. Never tried . . ."

Until well into the 1970s, Oxbridge churned out embittered young men (and occasionally women) whose much longed-for Oxbridge education was won at the price of social agony and isolation. Their degree, they knew, would impress others enough to land them good jobs, but they would forever feel that they themselves had failed to impress. Oxbridge was a public school club, dominated by richer, more confident young people who all seemed to know one another and whose vocabulary, accent and manners made everybody else feel a clod.

But this was generations ago. Now Oxbridge is eager to emphasize its varied student body. At Oxford, I was encouraged to meet Gail, a current student from the same region and social background as Roger Dataller. A quick, bubbly girl with a distinct Yorkshire drawl, she is writing a history of her local football club, Barnsley, as part of her course and describes going to Oxbridge as "the best thing I ever did."

Which is not to say that Oxbridge is a totally modern, homogeneous place. It still has quite a few male, upper middle class customs, made more obscure by their incomprehensible Latin names, but they are not designed to trip up ordinary students. The university guides sent to all those accepted explain what students are expected to wear and do. Also, every newcomer is contacted in advance by a "college parent", a student from the year above. Not only will this student try to answer any worrying questions, but she will be at hand in the first week to guide the newcomer.

So, tell your daughter not be scared by popular misconceptions. Despite what you may have seen on TV (*Brideshead Revisited, The Glittering Prizes, Inspector Morse* and all those dramas about the Cambridge spies all have a lot to answer for), Oxbridge is no longer the homeland of the toff who specialises in put-downs. Not everyone is poor, but whenever I was there everyone was watching Big Brother.

THE NUMBERS GAME

Oxbridge admissions staff have not come quite as far as their students in terms of adapting to a changing world. If your son is now thinking of applying, it may reassure him to know that the two universities, between them, admit over 3,000 state school students a year. This equals around 56 per cent of their British student intake. It can be less reassuring to know that these are mostly middle class kids and that students from private schools, who teach eight per cent of British children, constitute most of the other 44 per cent. This makes Oxbridge a possible destination for a bright student from a state school, but not exactly a certain one.

Given these facts, and given that the Chancellor, Gordon Brown, described the rejection of Laura Spence in January 2001 as "an absolute scandal", you might like to know what the Government, keen on improving opportunities for all, is doing about this. Well, in January 2003 it announced plans to appoint, in three years' time, a so-called Access Regulator, who would tie a university's Government funding to its success in admitting more students from disadvantaged backgrounds.

Much of this was aimed at the country's oldest universities, and when Education Minister Margaret Hodge visited Cambridge in February 2003 she explained the need for such a regulator by spelling out the current situation: "Let's not pretend that Cambridge is wonderful by letting people in on low incomes," declared Hodge.

"Cambridge does not. Only 9 per cent come from the three lowest socio-economic groups."

That remark went down like a lead balloon, and senior Oxbridge academics rushed to lobby the Minister's Oxbridge-educated superiors. Within days, Prime Minister Tony Blair told the Commons that pupils ought to gain places "based on merit, not on their class background." By April 2003, the new Education Secretary, Charles Clarke, had promised that the regulator would not set external targets or quotas for university intakes.

In October 2004, Sir Martin Harris, like Charles Clarke a graduate of Cambridge, was finally appointed as Britain's first Access Regulator, or rather as Director of Fair Access. The change from the original job title proved to be significant. When journalists enquired what his organisation would do about the latest Oxbridge admissions figures, they were put right. Admissions, so staff at the Office of Fair Access (OFFA) explained, were altogether outside its remit. It only concerned itself with increasing applications.

It was to take another four years before it dawned on the government that OFFA could perhaps do a little more. In April 2008, John Denham, the Secretary of State for Universities, announced that it would be given powers to scrutinise the admissions procedures of every university to check it was fair. The declared aim was "transparency", but the question of sanctions against offending institutions has yet to be resolved.

SO, CAN PEOPLE LIKE US REALLY GET IN?

The answer is yes, absolutely, but you would be unwise to rely on Oxbridge automatically recognising your daughter's ability, or on an effective Government intervention in favour of state school pupils. Those candidates who do get in tend to be not just bright, but also very clear about just how the Oxbridge entrance process works.

On the other hand, a lack of focused preparation harms many promising applicants. Even pupils formally identified as "gifted or talented" by their state schools and offered academic enrichment activities every year fail to gain an interview, never mind a place, at Oxbridge.

As a result, state school pupils remain underrepresented and underappreciated at both universities. Still, this is not to say that you cannot improve the odds considerably for your bright son. All you need to do is follow the advice in this book.

The best way to start is by treating an Oxbridge education not as a dream, but as a perfectly reasonable aspiration, no matter what you are earning and where your teenager goes to school. This does not mean it automatically goes to those who would most benefit from it. Oxbridge entrance is not actually an ability test, as the universities like to think, but nor is it a lottery. It is a snakes and ladders game based on a set of unwritten rules, known to all the parents who went there and to all public school teachers.

This book, based on dozens of interviews with Oxbridge academics, sixth form teachers, Oxbridge students and Oxbridge rejects, as well as on a study of the available literature, spells out those rules. Taking you through them step by step, it reveals the true road to the only two British towns known as one, Oxford and Cambridge. Most importantly, though, the book does not stop there: having taken you right up to the Oxbridge gates, it identifies the hidden forces which keep them as narrow as they are and suggests opening strategies.

MEASURING OXBRIDGE

Universities differ in lots of ways, some of which are particularly important when deciding where to apply. The quality of a university's teaching and research, the learning facilities available, the degrees obtained and the level of employment after graduation are generally regarded as key factors. Most broadsheets, notably *The Times* and *The Guardian*, therefore publish annual university league tables based on them. The Higher Education Funding Council of England (HEFCE) also publishes comparative records of university performance.

On all these tables, both Oxford and Cambridge tend to occupy positions at or near the top.

There is another way of grading a university, which is by the company it keeps. Most universities are affiliated to one of three groups, *The 1994 Group, Million+* and *The Russell Group*. Of these, the Russell Group of twenty long established universities is the most eminent one. Its members employ staff with top qualifications, seek to maintain the highest academic standards and are internationally renowned for their work. Oxford and Cambridge form part of this group, but also hold a special position due to their great age, reputation and financial resources.

Having said this, it is important to realise that it is crucial to look out for variations by subject when it comes to university choice. Even an excellent university may not be at the top in, for example, physics, or may not specialise in a subject area which a student might be interested in, for example nuclear physics.

Moreover, the excellence of individual academics may not show up in a university's general rating. Outstanding researchers, university teachers, theoreticians and writers can be found in a great variety of places. While Oxbridge offers a great education, it should therefore never be regarded as a bright student's only suitable choice.

2

The brightest and best

Having decided that Oxbridge might appeal to your teenager, the next stage is to work out whether the girl or boy might appeal to one of the two most picky universities in Britain. You cannot apply for both places, but their tastes are so similar that you do not, at this stage, need to make a choice.

So, what kind of students does Oxbridge want? The simple answer is in all their publicity bumph: they want "the brightest and the best." This is excellent news for today's generation, because things were rather different in the past. In his autobiography, *All Souls in My Time*, the historian A.L. Rowse recalls that when he applied for his first lecturing job at Christ Church College, Oxford, in the 1920s, the question put to him by the appointment panel was: "Would you be more interested in teaching the more intelligent pupils, or the less intelligent?" Rowse replied "the more intelligent" – and was promptly rejected©.

When an Oxbridge working party in the late 1950s proposed to restrict entry to academic students in response to Government pressure, the master of Pembroke College, Cambridge, R.B. McCallum, implored his fellow dons to maintain "a rational suspicion of over-intellectualisation... there are young men and woman who by their heredity and upbringing in more leisured and cultivated homes have some special contribution to make."

Even a 1965 Commission of Inquiry could not persuade all Oxbridge dons to select by brightness alone. The eminent Classics don Sir Maurice Bowra warned that "young men (and perhaps young women) who are chosen for not strictly academic reasons may not feel entirely at home in a society of which the members are for the most part chosen for their academic promise, and this may be bad for their self-respect."

This was a tragic prospect indeed, but it too could not stop the onwards march of brightness, driven by an influx of new, often state-educated dons, as well as by Government threats to cut university subsidies. In 1996, Professor John Stein, admissions tutor at

Magdalen College, Oxford, declared that "all our students are admitted on their individual academic achievements alone." Stein would briefly come to national prominence four years later, when justifying the university's rejection of Laura Spence, but the principle stood. Laura's place, said Stein, had gone to "another talented candidate from a similarly modest background."

QUALITY STREET

When reminded of the old ways, today's Oxbridge dons respond with the embarrassment which a young man visiting home with his first girlfriend might feel as his mother affectionately brings out a framed picture of him sitting on his potty. Oxbridge, like the young man, has long outgrown that childish stage. One Oxford admissions tutor I met proudly told me that he had just rejected the son of a university professor.

"The brightest and best" is an extremely vague term. It does not tell you what qualities or personal record Oxbridge candidates need if they are going to stand a chance in the highly intensive selection process. There is no measuring rod that is marked with the words "Brightest and Best" at the top and, presumably, "Daftest and Worst" at the bottom. So, how can you possibly know whether the hunched figure gripping his mobile with one hand, a tattered copy of Beowulf in the other and a bag of crisps with his teeth fits the Oxbridge bill?

An IQ test is certainly not the answer. Oxbridge does not administer the standard test and is not interested in the results if it was taken elsewhere. The SATs tests used by American universities are seen as too easy for potential Oxbridge students.

There has been some cautious experimenting with universities' own "aptitude tests", which trawl for sound background knowledge and a quick, sharp mind. Cambridge was the first of the two universities to devise such a test for all applicants to its science courses. This was initially hailed a great success but, several years after its introduction, some dons worry that private school students are now being intensively coached for it, thereby distorting the outcome.

Oxford has taken a more optimistic view and the number of universal subject tests set by the university has steadily grown. Despite state school complaints that over-academic wording can favour middle class applicants, such tests now regulate entry to a dozen of its most popular subjects. Oxford also uses an externally devised Law test, the LNAT and both universities make medical applicants sit an external exam called the BMAT.

It is not entirely clear for how much these tests count: in recent years, even a top score did not win some candidates an offer. Most Oxbridge places, anyway, still go to students who have not sat any professionally designed entrance exam.

So, what does count? In search of some details about "the brightest and best" whose application Oxbridge awaits, I interviewed numerous dons involved in the admissions process and others who had spent some of their working life at Oxbridge before moving on to other top universities. Although my interviewees taught in widely different fields, from History to Physics and from Mathematics to Medicine, the lists they produced were almost identical.

There was a kitbag of very specific qualities which, all of them felt sure, marked out the potential Oxbridge student. At the top was intellectual curiosity, meaning a desire to learn more about a familiar subject and find new subjects to learn about. The right candidate was interested in exploring problems, not just in rattling off solutions. A highly motivated young person, she had a flexible mind and, ideally, a creative bent. The dons also invariably mentioned more general qualities like independence, resourcefulness and determination.

These are very impressive qualities indeed, and if your teenager does not have them all, don't panic. Almost nobody else's does either, certainly not at the tender age of seventeen. Any expert on teenage development will tell you that pupils gearing up for university entrance are only at the start of their intellectual growth curve. They have not yet developed definite character traits, a permanent learning style or a clear sense of their own abilities. They will acquire these later, as a result of time, experience, trial and error.

BRIGHT SPARKS

This is not to say that brightness never manifests itself early on. The boy who gets obsessed with a different grown-up subject each month, which can be anything from architecture to zoology, and then reads every scrap of paper he can find about it, could well be Oxbridge material. So could the girl who is almost exclusively interested in IT, but does not merely use it to play: instead, she is forever trying to create new games and will also use the computer for Maths or Physics related problem solving.

Talent in the humanities (or arts, as Oxbridge calls them) can take longer to show up. A future English student writes well, ploughs through the library shelves and may wonder how his favourite tales are constructed years before he starts shaving. Future philosophers and theologians, on the other hand, are more difficult to spot. Although avid readers, they can be dreamy, unfocused and helpless, rather than independent, determined or resourceful. And that little pest who keeps asking difficult questions when she should be finishing her homework may just be the candidate Oxbridge is looking for. Brightness, as experts will tell you, can show up in a variety of guises and in combination with all sorts of character traits.

So, the dons' list merely describes a pretty unattainable ideal. Like the teenage girl who dreams of a relationship with Leonardo di Caprio but ends up dating the gawky lad next door, Oxbridge has to make do with the talent available in the real world. Still, it would be nice if at least two items on its wish list, intellectual curiosity and a real interest in exploring problems, were there, even in embryonic form.

Cynics may argue (and more than one cynical state school teacher has done) that it is the job of a university to inculcate these very qualities in their students. Many universities indeed do so every day of the week. In fact, Oxford and Cambridge can be brilliant at turning a bright and dreamy teenager into a deep and focused young thinker, but both seem strangely unconfident about this.

All this means that your teenager's Oxbridge ambitions may well be realistic and therefore worth pursuing. As long as the girl or boy is blessed with some of the above traits and perceived by most teachers as intelligent or academic – two terms which suggest a university-oriented type of brightness – the road is open.

HOW TO BE ACADEMIC

To be on the road is not the same as having reached one's destination, of course. Given that most Oxbridge applicants have at least some academically desirable traits, this leaves a student with the question of how to develop his own enough to stand out. Is there anything you can feed that teenage brain with, apart from smelly capsules of fish oil?

Fortunately, you can find suitable, brain-enhancing activities in many places, often independently of any school. A bit of online or library research, along the lines suggested below, will unearth a huge range of options. Most are publicly funded too, which means that they will be free or at least cheap, and all are good at creating the academically "interesting young people" admissions tutors like.

So don't worry if your son's comprehensive has no science society, or if he is nervous about joining it, in case he is persecuted as a swot.

But how should you choose? The answer, if you are a parent, is that you can only suggest. The rest is up to your son. You want him to feel that he is an explorer, not burdened with more pesky chores. So, merely explain that the best activities expand academic learning, but also show that a student is capable of initiative and hard work. They may even send strong, positive messages about him to teachers and universities.

Identifying activities which will perform this multiple task may take a bit of thought and forward planning by the lad, but this quickly pays off. School subjects become more comprehensible and university choices increase. The right activities may also provide a student with interests or hobbies he will enjoy throughout life.

STARTING THEM YOUNG

Where you start on this quest depends largely on your son's age. If the boy is still young and you live in a larger town, just take him along to the odd children's event at your nearest library, museum, NAGC Explorers' Club or cultural centre. It does not matter if it is a talk, a workshop or an exhibition. If he shows any interest, check whether the notice board offers relevant leaflets or further events. Or is there, perhaps, a junior science club?

And once you've both gone to the event and it has not been a disaster (most events are amazing, but occasionally a lecture can be dull, workshops under-staffed or geared to the wrong age) let your son take charge. Ask whether he might like a book that will explain more. Accept that interests will change and suggest that understanding can be enriched by looking at quite unrelated issues. The subject of light, for instance, can be explored through the disciplines of physics or art.

An older pre-teen can probably be persuaded to attend a workshop only by explaining that it will help her with a particular school project, but it is worth suggesting. Once there, your daughter will not only pick up educational tips but meet other young people interested in a field which may have marked her out as peculiar at school. She will also get used to different styles of adult academic language, to different accents and vocabularies.

Such a visit gives the girl a chance to experience what could, if encountered for the first time, be intimidating physical environments. The premises of the Royal Geographical Society or of

Somerset House in London, where many junior academic events are held, are not a bad preparation for the imposing architectural splendour of Oxbridge. (Don't point out the old building's features in awe, just move comfortably amongst them.)

Of course, outings like this will only work if your daughter cares to find out more. There has to be some flexibility on your part, too. If the girl is into art, but only wants to see contemporary installations, don't try to make her pour over Russian icons. Do encourage her to explore all aspects of her field via exhibitions, books and internet sites. Ideally, not all her pursuit of the subject should be via the net; while it can help explore things at great depth, there is no real substitute for personal contact with adult experts and other young fans when it comes to sustaining an interest. If you can get a word in edgeways, try to get across (ideally by questions, not by statements) that every subject has its rules, history and protagonists.

IN AT THE DEEP END

While starting academic life young is a good thing, the reality is that Oxbridge appears on many family horizons only once a pupil reaches her teens. This is also the stage when being among one's peers matters most, so keep an eye out for group events and workshops.

Some of the best are now run with government funding by the CfBT Education Trust and the umbrella of its Young, Gifted and Talented scheme. Pupils living anywhere in England can join its free Learner Academy, which offers both online and local events designed to show that intellectual pursuits can be fun stuff. The organisation's summer schools offer sixth formers who are on their school's gifted & talented list a chance to explore new academic fields with the help of enthusiastic university staff. Lots of leisure activities are included and students entitled to free school meals are not charged anything at all. Others may qualify for reduced rates.

A student who already has a clear focus of interest has further options, especially in the scientific field. Most scientific societies in England, Scotland and Wales run their own junior branches. Designed to encourage interest and spread expert knowledge, they are either free or charge as little as £8 per annum. For this money you usually get a magazine, invitations to scientific outings or field trips and a chance to meet other members.

How though do you become a society figure? The best route is via the internet. Reptile lovers, for instance, will find that they can join a junior herpetologists club (www.thebhs.org), which offers local talks, wildlife walks and involvement in conservation projects. To find a society to your taste, go to the BBC website (www.bbc.co.uk) and type in, say, "Astronomy Society". Alternatively, there is the Royal Society's virtual science club (www.royalsoc.ac.uk), which runs online debates on big issues like the use of GM and gives you entry to its lectures.

And if your son knows what he'd like to study at Oxbridge, but is worried he has joined the wrong science society or club, tell him not to worry. Science has general principles and rules, so an interest in reptiles can prove helpful, even if you later decide to study physics.

Maths lovers can aim for the British Mathematical Olympiad (www.bmoc.maths.org). If you sign up with BMO, its staff will provide you with a steady supply of interesting problems. If you're really good, they will send you on one of its summer camps at Oxford or Cambridge for a week of Maths lectures, problem-solving sessions, competitions and social events. For those who get into the finals, the next stage is a free trip to the International Mathematical Olympiad. Coming up is Kazakhstan, to be followed by the Netherlands in 2011 and Argentina in 2012.

English candidates can keep their noses in a book longer, but a regular burst of creativity develops literary skills. Writing for (a however modest) publication also teaches you not to miss deadlines and double-check every word. If your daughter's school won't publish her stories, reports or poems, of if there is no school magazine at all, she could always try to get them into one of an infinity of online magazines. Some of these offer prizes for the best work.

Those even vaguely considering a university course involving history may have to start out on their own. Once your son is clear what he wants to know more about, which can be a place or a period, even a family holiday with his cousins in Ireland can, with a bit of forethought, become an opportunity for research. Suggest the lad makes contact with one of the many local history societies, again via the BBC's website (www.bbc.co.uk).

READ ALL AROUND IT

A sixth former who already has a specific Oxbridge course in mind needs to focus more sharply. The rather vague advice you are often given at this point is to "read all around it". Just in case you are wondering, this does not mean that you are expected to slowly girdle the nearest tree while holding open a copy of *Plant Pathology*.

Instead, what to do depends on the subject you have picked. An aspiring biologist simply needs to add to his stack of knowledge. A specialist magazine such as *New Scientist* or *Scientific American*, found in any public library, will tell him about new discoveries in the field and the problems raised by older ones.

A good science book, aimed at adult readers, will help him see the point behind his own experiments. Instead of just getting the powder in his lab dish to turn green, as predicted in his school text book, an A-level chemistry student will learn to perceive what the scientist Richard Feynman has called "the beauty of the inner structure". He'll discover how scientists think and how they arrive at their understanding of the natural world.

For a pupil hoping to study something not taught at school, "read all around it" means grasping her way towards a quite mysterious subject. A budding architecture student, for instance, may dream about the cool new buildings she will design, but first she needs to look at (and perhaps sketch) some existing ones. This might be followed by a book on architectural history or styles. Next, she'll want to explore the physics of engineering, which prevent that brick ceiling above from falling on your head. Specialist magazines, although they exist, may not make sense until the university stage.

Equally, "reading around" a subject can mean exploring it through various other media. INTUTE (http://www.intute.ac.uk) gives you free access to articles written by researchers and academics on a huge range of subjects. JSTOR (www.jstor.org) contains outstanding features on most areas of academic interest, though it can only be accessed from public libraries. The BBC offers interested students great radio programmes on science (most of which are broadcast on Radio 4) and great TV ones on art, history and archi-tecture. Many of the more intellectual BBC series are now archived or available as a Podcast, so you can explore them whenever and wherever you like. The BBC's site also contains lively, detailed fact sheets on lots of subjects.

To a potential literature student, on the other hand, "Reading around it" means keeping your eyes firmly on the printed page. As a sixth form mentor, I did not know whether to laugh or cry after hearing from one bright boy planning to read English Lit. I had recom-mended a favourite novel to him and when he did not contact me after the summer holidays, I sent a slightly worried email. The answer was clearly meant to reassure me: "Haven't had a chance to look at *Brighton Rock*, but I've done some internet research on it."

That student, sadly, had lost the plot altogether. No amount of research would make any sense unless he read the novel itself first. Only then was it time to explore what the net, or rather a few, carefully selected sites, had to offer him. In his case, this probably meant going to Converse (http://aspirations. english. cam. ac. uk/ converse/ home.acds), a site run by Cambridge.

CAUGHT IN THE WEB

Quite a few other websites can be a boon to the aspiring Oxbridge student. What matters, though, is finding a reliable source. Those run by universities, academic societies, specialist magazines and quality newspapers offer full-length, expert-written features on almost anything you might like to research.

Just reading what comes up first on Google, as a staggering number of sixth formers still do, can mean that you end up being not just under-informed but wrong. Anyone can set up a website and, if carefully linked to others, it might come up on page one. Corporations are highly skilled at promoting their goods online under the guise of offering information.

Even much respected sites are not always problem-free. Wikipedia recently had to admit that a 24 year old Kansas student, pretending to be a professor, had altered over 20,000 of its entries as a joke. If you need a reliable digital reference work, use the Encyclopaedia Britannica.

For a junior researcher, the BBC's excellent, compact fact pages are almost too tempting. Skimming a couple of reports, summaries or extracts, which are easily found there, can make you feel smart within minutes. Unfortunately, this may be an illusion. If you plan to impress a major university, you need to draw at least some extra knowledge from a primary source, which usually means a book. Only this will provide you with sufficient details.

There is only one exception to this rule: even the most ambitious Maths A-level student can probably get by without ever moving from the screen. Thanks to sites like http://www.nrich.maths.org/ public/index.php or http://plus.maths.org/index.html it is the net, rather than the library, which can offer her the endless supply of problems, debates and explanations on which born mathematicians thrive.

OXBRIDGE CANDIDATES

Having a sound knowledge base is the basis of Oxbridge success, but many pupils who have worked hard to build it still won't apply because they feel unsure what kind of person the two universities seek. To help you decide, here are short profiles of four imaginary Oxbridge candidates, based on the dozens of young people I interviewed for this book.

Kate goes to a comprehensive which used to be a grammar school in a small Midlands town. She is extremely hard-working and when she gained eleven top GCSE's the headmaster suggested she should try for Oxbridge. Although the idea had not occurred to anyone in her family, they were delighted. Her father is a van driver and her mother looks after three younger children. The family is evangelical and Kate is active in Church work: she helps to run a youth club for girls, plays netball and sings in the choir. An avid follower of events in Africa, she is also the head girl of her school.

Sam moved to an urban sixth form college after attending an inner city comprehensive. He has been interested in science all his life and had read his way through several Oxbridge texts already in his AS year. His father is a welder and his mother works as a part-time machinist. When he gained what were exceptional GCSE results for his poorly rated comprehensive, they were unsure what this meant. It was Sam's physics teacher who put him on the college's "gifted and talented" list, so he could be offered academic enrichment work. He also encouraged Sam to apply to Oxbridge. Sam spends his free evenings either with his girlfriend, playing online chess or listening to Hip Hop in his room. He also has a Saturday job as a warehouse porter.

Jill attends a selective state grammar school in an affluent southern suburb. The smallish school regularly sends around four pupils a year to Oxbridge and when Jill proved to be an excellent language student, she was put into its Oxbridge group, even though her GCSE's were good, rather than brilliant. Jill's parents run a thriving specialist shop and encouraged her to follow a range of interests. She cycles, plays the viola to concert level, won a prize for her sculpting and is active in the School Assembly, which led to her being sent as its delegate to a national schools conference. During her language exchange, she ran a musical movement class.

John goes to a small rural public school near his father's farm, which takes pupils of all abilities and sends about eight students a year to Oxbridge. John gained twelve, mainly good GCSEs, taken over two years. He is not a great reader, but is the chairman of the school's physics society and the treasurer of a recycling scheme it runs for the local village. He also plays squash and is on the school's rowing team. John commands his school's cadet force, has completed the Duke of Edinburgh award scheme and plays the tuba in his spare time.

Well, who got in? If you instantly blurt out "only John!" you are still living in the 1960s. If you think everyone of these remarkable people did, you are an incurable optimist. The real answer is everybody but Sam.

But why is that? To the careful reader, it will be obvious that every student except Sam could point not just to academic ability but also to a wide range of interest and activities. These created the kind of personal profile which, according to experienced headmasters, Oxbridge dons liked. Brains mattered most, but there had to be evidence of independent use, usually provided by an academic interest beyond the school syllabus. In addition, "good candidates" had often done a spot of voluntary work, practiced some sport or were involved with music. Many had also held a leadership position, however minor. Students who fitted the bill were most likely to get in.

Most of the candidates admitted certainly were busy young people. As one Physics student put it to me, "You want to come across as quite driven." The Cambridge educated author Philip Hensher, writing in *The Independent* of 15th April 2002 under the title "Sorry, but Oxbridge graduates are the best", took this point rather further by claiming, "The sort of people who at 18 have the drive to get into these universities are the sort of people who are going to rise to eminence in later life."

Although he has what psychologists might regard as the clearest indicators of academic ability, Sam did not fit that bill. This is not his fault. While he reads avidly, he has few opportunities to discuss his interests. His comprehensive long ago sold off its playing fields and laid off its music teacher. He lives in an area with little public transport and his parents do not have a car. Nor do they have the money to supplement the activities his sixth form college offers. Also, Oxbridge does not accept a school's definition of a pupil as "gifted and talented".

This way of picking pupils has traditionally worked against state school and especially poorer applicants. They could seem dull and unmotivated in comparison with young people from private schools. There, teachers run regular school competitions whose prizes can add distinction to a pupil's record. Many provide their teenagers with carefully manufactured adult CVs: cultural, scientific and sporting activities are laid on and can even be mandatory. Besides, pupils are often boarders and cannot go to the movies instead.

As a result, teenagers leading sheltered and tightly structured lives would sometimes come across as more determined, resourceful and academically curious than bright young people who were handling the complexities of inner city life. Proving that you have "the drive", which Philip Hensher identified as a key feature of the best, can be harder if you are poor.

CHANGING TIMES

Perhaps not being poor yourself, you may wonder why you should care. The answer is because of one last and vitally important thing about Sam: he is a thoroughly modern teenager and so is most likely to resemble your son. Listening to CDs or playing computer games (or going to gigs, or shopping) are favourite leisure pursuits among the brightest of today's teenagers. With every generation physically maturing a little earlier, today's Oxbridge candidates often have an active sex life, or at least actively seek to acquire one by clubbing, etc.

Fortunately a new generation of dons blessed with CD racks, store cards and torrid love lives of their own feel that modern life-styles are compatible with academic thought. They have no trouble grasping the abilities of non-traditional Oxbridge candidates or doubts about admitting them. More than one told me with feeling that he never wanted to hear about the Duke of Edinburgh Award again. Unfortunately, it was not safe until recently for candidates to generalize from this.

In his review of this book's first edition (2003), Geoff Parks, the Cambridge director of admissions, described it as "doing an excellent job of identifying and describing what is good and distinctive about the two universities and why it is worth going to them", before dismissing the importance of extra-curricular activities. "Selection", he pointed out, "is based overwhelmingly on academic potential". This is undoubtedly true, but given the presence of so many students with a wide range of cultural achievements, it was hard to believe that extra-curricular activities were, as he claimed, "entirely incidental."

Nevertheless, a couple of Oxbridge dons promptly went on student websites to indignantly declare that they, personally, had never asked candidates about such a thing as sport or music. Consequently, academic ability was all that counted at their university. Students, they said, would be wise to disregard any references to extra-curricular activities.

This was not always good advice, as other dons, sometimes working from the college rooms next door, merrily went on grilling students at length about these same incidental activities at the Oxbridge interview. Questions like "What could you contribute to college life?" or "If you could only pursue three extra-curricular activities here, which ones would you pick?" remained fairly common. More importantly, applicants who could handle them were more successful than others, sometimes at the same school, who could not.

So, has there been any change? Colin Hall, head of Holland Park School, one of London's inner city comprehensives, does not think so. In an interview with the Financial Times published on April 19th 2008, he claimed that his students were culturally discriminated against when applying to Oxbridge. "I imagine it must be very difficult to chose between someone who's outstanding at Maths and someone who's outstanding at Maths and can also quote TS Eliot and play the violin," he said ironically.

This leaves us with two questions: are extra-curricular activities still important or not, and what was their original point? After all, doing very well in your school subjects is a pretty good indication of academic interest and ability. Why should future historians hit the race track or concert hall? Which benefit, exactly, do future scientists gain from rattling a collection box? And what is the point of an post that a teenager can hold?

No general answer was ever forthcoming, but it is clear that entrance criteria often just reflected individual preference. A friend teaching at a private school during the late 1990s recalls the guidance offered to him by a visiting Oxbridge don, who was also one of the school's governors (a not uncommon situation). "Not much point sending us a linguist this year," proclaimed the distinguished figure. "Too many good ones coming up already. But let's think: there's a new college fellow. What he might go for is an interest in microscopic sea urchins and a taste for Chopin."

Other dons' explanations were far from revealing. During my book research, one leftish, public-school educated admissions tutor described extra-curricular activities as merely something you could dip into in order to break the ice at the interview. A very conservative one, educated at a state grammar school, suggested they proved that the candidate was good at time management. A young female don from a top comprehensive argued that such activities "show that you've got a bit of a life."

When it came to sport, there was more of a consensus. The ancient Greek belief that there is "a healthy mind in a healthy body", today associated with totalitarian rulers who like to see their name spelt out by the bodies of massed gymnasts, featured in several replies.

VICTORIAN VALUES

In fairness, the emphasis on music and sport has its roots in something slightly more spiritual, the ideal of Muscular Christianity embraced by the Victorians. Originally coined by the author E. Cobham Brewer to describe the qualities of the perfect Christian knight, the concept was developed by Charles Kingsley, a professor of Modern History at Cambridge and in later life the author of *The Water Babies*. In the 1860s Kingsley, who supported universal voting rights, put forward the argument that physical prowess could and should co-exist with moral and mental activity. This meant that there was nobility also in the working man.

The idea of a Christian manliness that combined quite aggressive action with mental pursuits was next taken up by Matthew Arnold, a professor of Poetry at Oxford. Arnold, though, had a different agenda. To him, the male student's sporting values could prevent the same working man from taking over. Strength and piety were the qualities needed by a Victorian gentleman, in addition to learning. They were also handy for defending British civilisation in its Imperial outposts. Arnold advised educators to strive for "harmonious perfection, only to be won by unreservedly cultivating many sides in us."

It is this salad of somewhat contradictory Greco-Victorian values that for generations helped to determine who would be a successful Oxbridge applicant. Academic ability was a must, but when it came to choosing between different candidates, "the best" were often those who spent their leisure time like a Muscular Christian. While girls of a similar background were sometimes willing to play along, even the brightest, most ambitious modern working class boy was likely to reject the Victorian ideal with horror. This worked in favour of wealthier pupils from traditional schools.

A mix of generation shift, government concerns and Oxbridge soul searching has gradually altered the picture. Also, the changes have become explicit and thus binding on all dons. For a start, they can no longer grill students about their sporting prowess. Such questions, Geoff Parks told the public in 2006, "are now in the past". By 2007, Oxford was stating that there were no credits for extra-curricular activities and Cambridge that "all admissions decisions are based on academic criteria, and excellence in an extra-curricular activity will never 'compensate' for lower academic potential".

Oxbridge, this suggests, does now accept that widening participation is incompatible with vague, old-fashioned entrance criteria, a fact first pointed out by this book in 2003. Students, teachers and parents should rejoice at the news.

SHOULD YOU SHAKE A LEG ANYWAY?

If you are a potential Oxbridge candidate happily hunched in front of your screen, the announcement that you don't need to ever think about Scottish country dancing or cricket may go down rather well. This does not necessarily mean that you should load up the next computer game.

Why? Primarily because reading, writing and researching beyond curriculum requirements do not come under extra-curricular activities but under academic interests. Also, many of the qualities and skills Oxbridge does seek are most easily acquired in this way.

Drama is a case in point. While directly relevant only to an English Literature or Modern Languages course, learning how to hold the stage can benefit students targeting other subjects. An Oxbridge interviewee who thinks before she speaks and nicely articulates her words may be judged more intelligent than one mumbling rush answers. Students who have been involved in dance often come across as thoughtful and calm.

Or take politics, as leadership is now known. Campaigning for change teaches you to argue your points clearly and convincingly, as well as to counter other people's. By becoming a member or chair of an organisation, however small, you'll develop self-discipline and teamwork skills. Don't worry that strong views might alienate Oxbridge. Dons tends to look equally benignly upon a candidate writing for the Conservative Party's Heartland magazine and for Socialist Worker, upon a canvasser for the Green Party and a contributor to Young Labour eZine. What matters is that a student can rationally defend her views, but also grasps that these are not immutable facts. The two universities have been in the business of producing leaders, as well as thinkers, for hundreds of years and are not easily shocked.

An applicant keen to hone his arguing skills without going out into the world might want to join a debating society. Once common, such societies are now quite rare in state schools, but there is little to stop you from starting up your own. There is almost invariably one teacher keen on verbal battles who will help you find topics, time-table space and unbroken chairs.

While the concept of a debating society may be too far removed from some pupils' lives, concerns about human rights are not. Groups like Amnesty International, which has branches in many schools, offer members a chance to talk. So do school conferences, set up to discuss burning issues from the European Union to Militant Islam. Students will research and prepare the event, organise and publicise it and often invite outside speakers. It's a great way of learning how to clarify your ideas, phone up total strangers and cope with last minute disasters.

Volunteering for a local charity has benefits too. Unlike those charity sponsorship projects which charge you a fortune to do unskilled work in a far-away, sunny country full of poor people who'd love to be paid, local ones really help local people. Placements can be hard to find because the under-18s legally now need to be chaperoned, but keep looking. One project, *Inspired* (www.vinspired. com/), set up by the Department for Education and Skills, offers 16 to 24 year olds a chance to pass on their own skills, from sports coaching to creating websites.

Do especially consider volunteering, at least for a brief period, if you are planning to take a year off. Oxbridge Maths tutors especially are not wild about gap years because students forget so much. Teachers, though, often encourage the idea. It may seem especially harsh to suggest disadvantaged young people should play Lady Bountiful, but charities claim that volunteering benefits both sides: it fosters maturity, increases confidence, develops skills and helps you to meet fascinating people at both ends of the social spectrum.

Activities like those, or the fact that you've been appointed your school's head girl or break-time librarian, also tell others something positive about you. The Oxford head of admissions, Mike Nicholson, has praised candidates for "exhibiting significant responsibility in roles that they have within their school, colleges and/or local community."

Playing an instrument has a variety of potential spin-offs, apart from conceivably getting you into one of the prestigious Oxbridge Music courses. Being in an orchestra or a band teaches you about group dynamics; playing on your own encourages you to concentrate or, if it is a leisure activity, to relax. Singing can even benefit you financially. Colleges at both Oxford and Cambridge offer choral scholarships worth several hundred pounds a year.

But what about sport? If you love it, the answer is obvious. Even if you remember those ghastly, sweat-soaked gym shorts with dread, try to admit that physical exercise can come in handy. A bit of running or aerobics will stop you from getting fat while you comfort-eat before exams. Winning a kick-boxing match will make you feel great and just kicking a ball at the dog can unstress you after a bad day's revision.

It's even worth checking what will be on offer at the Oxbridge college you are aiming for and limbering up for it. Sport has come a long way since an Oxbridge candidate was asked to make clear whether he was "a dry bod or a wet bod", which meant whether he played the "dry" university sports of cricket or rugby, or preferred "wet" rowing. Now badminton, mountain biking, water polo, netball, snooker and table tennis all have their fans. Football, played by both sexes, is today more popular than rugby at both universities. It's also great for meeting new people.

Other activities can improve personal confidence. Writing poetry, setting it to music and producing your own CD helps you see yourself as literate, creative and organised. Teaching drawing skills to disadvantaged kids can make you feel worthy, grown-up and responsible.

Such activities can even give you something to talk about in the first, awkward seconds of the interview, although the response will depend on your degree subject. The fact that you directed your school's drama society production of "Blasted" will impress an English don far more than an Engineering one. Your membership in a junior mountaineering club could thrill a Geography don, but not a Philosophy one. Be prepared to say what specialist knowledge you have gained and what uses it might have.

And don't automatically assume that, however useful, such an involvement will take much of your precious time. We are only talking about a couple of hours per week at the most, and not always spent away from home. The road from first year A-level work to Oxbridge interview is quite a long one.

In the meantime, don't be overawed by the potentially scary words "brightest and best". Just like in a washing power ad, this is a promotional term, rather than a straightforward description of the product at hand. Oxbridge has a high proportion of very smart young people, but when your son goes on his taster visit, he is sure to discover that most are pretty normal, nevertheless. There are not enough genuinely driven, charitable, opera-singing, cricket-playing, leadership-oriented, microscope-fixated geniuses in this world to fill a university, never mind two.

3
GCSEs, AS and A-levels

Beyond brightness, interests and certain character traits, applicants also need some official bits of paper such as exam results. Taking note of school exams is not, contrary to popular belief, an ancient Oxbridge tradition. Until 1939, Oxford and Cambridge admitted students without any formal entrance qualifications. Any young gentleman with enough schooling to read a few Greek and Latin texts was welcome – assuming he could pay.

Until the middle of the 19th century, most students didn't sit any finals either. They simply claimed their degree upon an attendance certificate from their college. If you could afford Oxbridge you were entitled to all the blessings it could bestow.

Less well off young men with a grammar school education could apply, once an academic had recommended them, but acceptance often depended on them also gaining a small grant from a church, charity or Oxbridge itself. Most grants went to prospective clergymen. Competitive tests were only for the handful of very poor candidates admitted each year. A.L. Rowse, the son of a clay miner, started his career as a historian by winning the sole Oxford scholarship place available for the whole of Cornwall.

The result was that Oxbridge fell behind continental universities like Paris and Marburg once those had started to prefer qualified students. A steady flow of reforms, fiercely resisted by public school heads and many university dons, was gradually pushed through so it could regain its intellectual lead. From 1940, grammar school pupils willing to stay an extra term could get in by passing the new Oxbridge entrance exam. Well off candidates, however, were still accepted on the nod of a college head.

The Oxbridge entrance exam was resented by many applicants, mainly because it was conditional on them staying on at an often fee-charging grammar school, and because it did not apply to everyone. In 1987, a new system was introduced, covering all applicants, although colleges retained some discretion to offer places to exceptional applicants.

Since then the academic school exams, GCSEs, AS and A-levels have become the standard qualification required by UK students applying to Oxford or Cambridge. This seemingly puts Oxbridge on a par with all other British universities, which have been using these qualifications since they were introduced. Still, great differences in what is acceptable remain and pupils need to be clued up about them very early on. So, below is a guide to Oxbridge thinking on exams, based not just on official publications but also on dozens of private conversations with college dons.

A-LEVELS: HOW MANY AND HOW GOOD?

Today's UK pupils take an infinity of exams, but what formally counts at Oxbridge are only GCSEs, AS and A-levels. Scottish Highers have long been accepted and are evaluated in line with those. So is the Welsh, European and International Baccalaureate. Candidates studying for the new Cambridge Pre-U Diploma are now welcome too. Oxbridge is less keen on the new Advanced Diplomas introduced by the government in 2008 and currently accepts only the Engineering one, at least if the right ASL options are taken.

What exam record, though, does your son or daughter need to stand a real chance of success? And how much allowance is there for the different types of schooling?

The answer, in terms of GCSEs, is simple enough. Oxbridge candidates are expected to have the normal number of GCSEs taken by students at their educational establishment. In practice, this can mean eight at a comprehensive or 12 plus at a public school.

When it comes to GCSE grades, allowances are again made for the type of school: at least half of a state school candidate's grades should be As or A*s, the rest Bs, with perhaps the odd C in a practical subject. Those sitting the exam in the private sector need to aim for at least As. Oxbridge is willing to concede that, at the GCSE stage at least, someone in a class of thirty-five pupils cannot be judged exactly like someone in a class of fifteen. As we reach A-levels, though, this awareness disappears. The rules become more complex and are shrouded in mist.

One of the worst bits of misinformation I encountered came from the education department of my local council. I had phoned them on behalf of a new neighbour. The woman, who speaks little English, had wanted to know whether there were any extra classes her teenage son, listed by his comprehensive as "gifted and talented", could take in preparation for Oxbridge. A female voice of authority replied crossly: "There are other universities, you know. All the applicants there have five A-levels at A or A*. They are all gifted."

Almost everything in the council dragon's statement, except for the first sentence, is factually wrong. To start at the end: the National Association for Gifted Children (NAGC) estimates that 2 per cent of the population are of exceptional ability, which means "gifted." The total number of "gifted" entrants among the 300,000 new students accepted by British universities each year is likely to be 6,000. Not all of these, by any means, wish to go anywhere near Oxbridge. Even if all of them did, there would still be places left over for other, fairly bright kids. Oxford and Cambridge, between them, absorb around 7,000 new undergraduates every year.

Now let's deal with A-levels. On these, too, myths abound. The official requirement for Oxbridge entry are three A-levels, as for most other universities, and half of all successful candidates have sat no more.

However, candidates from the private sector, where an entire Year 12 may apply for Oxbridge after a decade of being taught in small, single ability groups, are usually advised by their teachers to sit four A-levels. So are many students at the remaining state grammar schools. Five A-levels are pretty rare and are never demanded anywhere.

MAKING THE GRADE

But what about grades? The answer is, for the moment, pretty straight-forward. To get an Oxford interview, a student's predicted A-level grades should, ideally, be AAA. Students are not expected to have any of the new A* grades introduced in 2009. Still, if a teacher foresees BBB or less, instant rejection is likely. A student with predictions of AAB will usually be asked up, one expected to score ABB probably not.

Cambridge, on the other hand, now seeks candidates with grade predictions of A*AA, though it does not usually specify a subject for the A*. To gain the new grade, students will have to not so much display factual knowledge as the ability to solve problems and think independently.

It is an approach which, so Cambridge believes, will help to make the admissions process fairer. According to the university's head of admissions, Geoff Parks, "more independent school offer-holders would have been screened out by A*AA offers than students from any other group."

If a student with lower grade predictions gets to sit an aptitude test, this offers her an additional chance, but she'll have to gain pretty high scores. In any case, Cambridge will continue to make lower offers to some disadvantaged applicants.

What is also good to know is that the story does not end there. While grade predictions need to be very high, hesitant teachers and parents should be aware that a place offer made after an applicant's successful interview can be slightly lower. Individual Oxbridge colleges (a subject we shall get to) have always been entitled to admit the odd candidate with modest grades, if they so wish. How else would Prince Charles have spent his undergraduate years at Cambridge?

This discretion now tends to be used at the opposite end. Truly disadvantaged candidates from comprehensives may be offered a place based on AAB. A famous college that has been pilloried in the press for having few "ordinary" students will suddenly make its sole working class applicant an offer of ABB. Cambridge publicity material mentions even BBB offers, though none of the many schools I contacted had heard of such a case. In practice, 97 per cent of current Oxbridge students got in with three As.

AS levels, once dismissed by Oxbridge dons as too easy, now play a growing role because their results are available by application time. Admissions tutors do not just look at AS grades but often at each individual module mark to find the most able pupils. GCSE grades matter hugely too, as they have been shown to more accurately predict academic success than A-level results. Students who get top GCSE marks often do best in their university finals.

So, it remains true that no amount of talent will get a student into Oxbridge unless their school can provide them with decent exam results. This is a rule that sets it apart from other Russell Group universities. One inner city teacher I interviewed proudly told me that one of his brightest but poorest students had just received an offer of CCC to read medicine at Queen Mary College, London. Such unconditional offers, made to express a university's trust in an applicant's outstanding potential, don't really exist at Oxbridge.

HOW TO GET AN A*

The simple answer is: by knowing more than just facts. Academics have long complained that too many university applicants can only parrot the information fed to them at school. So, in 2009 government educationalists responded by redesigning many of the key A2 questions. What these now seek and reward through a new marking scheme are problem-solving skills and a broader understanding. Students will be faced with unfamiliar contexts, encouraged to think for themselves and expected to give longer, more detailed answers than in the past. These should draw on the concepts, theories or techniques relevant to their subject.

In a biology exam, for instance, you may not just be asked to name the cardiac blood vessels shown in a drawing of the human heart, but also be told to describe *and explain* the events that occur during a ventricular systole in the cardiac cycle". Confronted with an unfamiliar graph, a student must certainly be able to tell the examiner what it means in numerical terms, but may also be expected also say whether it does or does not support a specific hypothesis.

While this assumes that good answers will simply arise from students' brain cells being working extra hard on the day, the "holistic understanding" sought can, in fact, be developed well in advance. Teachers highly ambitious for their class tend to encourage classroom debates on problems and their causes. If you're trying to teach yourself, help is available in the section of this book called "Read all around it".

No less important than reading is writing practice, best gained by undertaking an extended project during your A2 course. Lastly, students who are able to express themselves well and at length generally have strong grammatical skills. You can acquire those painlessly from a book called *My Grammar and I (or should that be 'Me')* by Caroline Taggart and J.A. Wines.

MORE GRADE RULES AND A FEW MATHS SECRETS

Oxbridge will be specific about the subject in which it will accept a B. If your daughter expects to read History and is taking A-levels in History, English and Biology, for instance, then any B-grade offer made will be in the unrelated subject, Biology.

It is also worth knowing the obstacles encountered by some students aiming for the Oxford or Cambridge Maths course. While the ability to think mathematically is innate, it needs lots of nurturing to reach Oxbridge entrance standards. These are quite a long way from the requirements of the Maths A-level syllabus and it takes Further Maths to bring you closer. Unfortunately, many comprehensives do not offer this A-level course. Their students can, at best, take an AS level in the subject. While this qualification is, in principle, accepted by most colleges, it does not really prepare you for the Maths entrance tests set by Oxbridge.

As a result, state school candidates struggle to get in: in 2007/8, their success rate when applying for the Cambridge Math course was a mere 17 per cent. So, try to book yourself into a Further Maths A-level course if at all possible, even if it is held outside your school.

Information and test papers can be found online, but students who succeed often do not rely on them alone. Instead, they also tackle challenging problems found on a good Maths website such as NRICH (http://nrich.maths.org/public/index.php) on a regular basis, and look out for Plus magazine (http://pass.maths.org.uk/). Both these sites have been produced by Cambridge mathematicians.

Cambridge candidates also need to prepare for the STEP Maths exam. Concerned by the poor success rates of comprehensive school pupils, the university will from 2009 offer them an intensive study course in preparation for this. While Oxford does not offer such a course, it admits a slightly higher proportion of state school students after its own entrance test. Those who found it hard but still got in are then supplied with extra material to work through in the pre-university summer months.

Students who prepare for the entry process by themselves are not necessarily disadvantaged. What they need to know is that successful candidates tend to have a strong, active interest and a firm but not always very broad knowledge base. One Oxford admissions tutor stated that pupils who did well in his Maths interview had a grasp of calculus, a method of writing a good proof, and a more abstract notion of what "a function" was.

The Mechanics option in the Math A-level course can also help, so dons say, as will A-level Physics. Unfortunately, since 30 per cent of those teaching Physics in state secondary schools do not have a degree in the subject, it may not help much. This takes us further along the admissions route, into A-level subjects.

PICKING THE RIGHT SUBJECTS

Once upon a time, this was a simple matter. Candidates needed only Latin and Classical Greek. By sheer coincidence, these languages were the sum of every young gentleman's education. They were not studied by anyone else. By keeping them compulsory, Oxbridge excluded both women and working men for 700 years.

Almost all of today's candidates have studied other and more practical subjects. A-level choice, though, can be a horribly confusing business for those without Oxbridge links. After all, comprehensives and sixth form colleges offer up to forty A-level subjects. How can your stressed daughter, faced with all those exciting options in her school's fat, brightly illustrated course brochure, possibly decide which ones to take?

Well, the choice is far smaller than both of you might think. What you need to know is that both Oxford and Cambridge prefer applicants to take three A-levels in academically demanding "hard" subjects like English, Maths, Chemistry or History, which they have studied at school in considerable depth and over many years. This is why even the most expensive public school will offer no more than twenty A-level subjects, including a range of languages.

This rule applies even if the "soft" A-level subject is also the one your daughter is planning to do at university. For instance, a student dreaming of a future as a psychologist might think that A-levels in Psychology, Sociology and, perhaps, Drama would be the ideal qualification. She would be wrong. What Oxbridge would expect is at least one "hard" science subject such as Chemistry or Maths (because Psychology involves scientific work) plus one "hard" humanities subject, such as English. A third "hard" A-level further improves a candidate's chances. A-level Psychology is fine but not essential, so don't worry if the girl's school does not offer it.

The same applies to Law. A-level Law is rated as not intellectually demanding enough at Oxbridge, so applicants for any Law degree course offered there should go for more traditional subjects. English is almost a must, plus perhaps History and some "hard" science subject. Oxbridge Medicine too (on which there is a whole chapter later on) will normally consider only candidates with three "hard" A-levels, whatever their background.

Oxford's degree in Politics, Philosophy and Economics (PPE), which churns out a steady flow of MPs and is the only media studies course as far as broadsheet editors are concerned, cares less about A-level subjects. It is keen on History and likes Maths (which helps with the statistics), but will consider any "hard" A-level or even a "soft" but smart and relevant third. The Cambridge course in Politics, Psychology and Sociology (PPS), its own version of PPE, again likes the first two A-levels, but will let applicants combine them with "soft" but relevant subjects.

Cambridge can be more particular than Oxford here and actually lists those A-levels it will accept on its website. While this is very useful to know, the list may come as a shock to some teachers. Even a subject like Critical Thinking, which is brilliant at developing students' reasoning skills, won't count ("because it lacks academic contents") – except maybe for Philosophy.

None of these are iron rules. Faced with a child genius who has taught himself nuclear physics while caring for his dying grand-mother on a condemned housing estate, a college may choose to accept him, whatever his A-levels or grades. A politician's son from a distant British interest zone much in the news could find himself invited in with any odd qualifications.

However, if your son or daughter does not fit this bill, but is just the clever child of non-university parents, they will need to play it safe. They can certainly not take their cue from any student profiled in Oxbridge promotion material: some of these, with their clutch of mainly "soft" A-levels, are very untypical.

ARTISTS AND SCIENTISTS

Oxbridge sciences, as already said, include Psychology; Oxbridge arts are everything from languages to History and Philosophy. While the arts/science divide continues to exist, it is not as rigid as it once was. Successful science applicants very occasionally have a mix of A-levels, but most admissions tutors at both Oxford and Cambridge far prefer three science ones. Having less may be read as a lack of scientific commitment. If your daughter has built her own mini computer lab, but is also interested in baroque paintings, Fine Art might therefore have to be A-level number four.

The arts are more flexible. A set of A-levels consisting of History, English and something clever like Maths is now a highly acceptable qualification for almost any non-science course. Very rarely, a student sitting History, Maths and Physics might be considered for a History course, but she would need to convince the interviewer that her interests really have shifted.

Students wishing to study Archaeology and Anthropology or Geography have perhaps the widest range of options when it comes to A-levels. Here, one "soft" A-level alongside two "hard" ones is usually acceptable, and very occasionally even two.

When it comes to languages, the rules are different yet again. Those wishing to do a modern language course, such as German, need a top grade A-level in the subject. However, candidates wishing to do an Oriental language, such as Chinese or Thai, do not need to have studied it at all. Their four-year course will include intensive language training and a year abroad.

Latin and Classical Greek are today essential for only one subject: Classics (know at Oxford as "Greats"). Both Oxford and Cambridge, however, have turned this into a four year BA course, which allows applicants from comprehensives to pick up those dead languages as they study for their degree.

HARD CHOICES

So, what should you advise your wavering son? The admissions tutors I interviewed had no doubt: go for almost any "hard" A-level mix in, ideally, either science or arts. Once an applicant has proved that he can think via his A-level subjects and grades, Oxford especially can be flexible about precise course requirements. Tutors in the arts (but less so in the sciences) often perceive A-levels largely as proof of an applicant's capacity to learn. They do not expect fully fledged experts. Only students planning to take a degree in one of their A-level subjects need to show detailed prior knowledge.

Certain combinations, though, maximise a student's options. Science fans with A-levels in Maths, Physics and Chemistry can apply to a huge range of courses from Engineering to Medicine. A-level English, History and Maths (or a foreign language) are a sound basis for most arts courses, in the way Latin and Greek were once.

Remember too that three top A-level grades are easier to obtain than four and will make a state school candidate attractive to all colleges, including the most famous ones.

What if your daughter has independently made up her mind? Going through the school's large range of A-level subjects on offer, the smart and curious girl has picked the ones that seem most exciting and fit her wide interests. Unfortunately, all three are "soft" A-levels, chosen not because they are easier but because she has done enough English, Maths or Biology, she feels, and does not plan to do these subjects at university.

This, of course, is her choice. She is almost an adult now, as she will no doubt remind you. There is no point in trying to impose your will. Getting any A-levels is a long, hard slog, and I was warned by several sixth form heads that unless a student selects their A-levels on the basis of at least some real interest, they could well drop out. Many top universities acknowledge this fact.

If your daughter really wants to go to Oxbridge, she will have to compromise. Don't browbeat her into changing her A-levels, just get her to accept that candidates who get in with three "soft" A-levels are as common as hen's teeth.

Then look at which of her "soft" subjects might still be worth doing. Media Studies and Textiles are definitely out. Oxbridge defines them as non-academic. An A-level in General Studies doesn't count either, but it greatly broadens pupils' understanding of the world and so helps with some entrance tests. Other subjects, especially Politics, Economics, Sociology, Religious Studies, Computing and Drama, are fine in the context of a relevant degree.

Now do the figures. If your daughter's state school has links with a certain college, she can reasonably expect to get into several of its degree courses with one "soft" A-level. A well-disposed admissions tutor might even, on a whim, consider her for one of its less prestigious courses with two. However, in a competitive environment these are not really very good odds. Colleges have been known to suddenly drop "their" comprehensive in favour of some other worthy cause. Candidates need to be acceptable to more than one place, in case their chosen one has more talented applicants that year than it can take.

Your daughter might also have a horizon so broad that three "hard" A-levels cannot possibly satisfy her. If the girl really wants to write English well, learn about sociology in some depth, live in Spain and be a historian, then she does need to do four A-levels.

There is one other good reason for taking four A-levels. This is if your hard-working son is willing to give up midweek nights out (though not, of course, football practice) for good grades, but is unsure if the degree course he has picked will suit him. Oxbridge is fairly easy-going about students changing subjects in their first weeks, but if he wants to make a bigger switch than, let's say, from Ancient History to Modern History, he will still need relevant A-levels. A set of four A-levels broadens his choice, at least among arts subjects.

However, do keep the grade issue in mind. It is no good ending up with the results AABB if your teenager could narrow his aim and gain AAA, the magic level required. And be aware that while Oxford will only insist on three specific grades, however many A-levels you take, Cambridge has been known to specify the grades it wants in all four.

FOUR LEGS GOOD

Let's say your ambitious daughter has come round to the idea of four A-levels (as long as one of them is Spanish). Unfortunately, her problems are far from over. Many comprehensives cannot deliver them. This is not because they don't want to, but because of under-funding. A shortage of qualified teachers and pressure from other duties result in many students finding that the A-level options that they had chosen are only offered in one particular time slot. This may not be when the student is actually free. Those wanting to combine science with arts subjects such as languages frequently discover that their timetables clash. This is one more reason why the vast majority of applicants doing four A-levels come from private schools.

Now the truth is that missing out on a language A-level is far from fatal for adult life: students who have a grounding in French will have no difficulty becoming fluent in the language later on by means of evening classes or videos. Others acquire fluent Portuguese by working in Brazil or fluent Urdu by marrying someone whose family speaks nothing else. Brains do not actually suffer total melt-down at the average graduation age of twenty-two.

When it comes to other subjects, though, being unable to take a fourth A-level can close your options. This is because the Oxbridge attitude remains highly ambiguous.

One the one hand, all the dons I spoke to insisted that it is not necessary to have four A-levels, never mind five, in order to follow even the most demanding course. After all, almost everyone managed fine with three until about a decade ago. On the other hand, many of the same dons declared themselves impressed that nearly half of recent candidates "were bright and hard-working enough" to get four A-levels. This does imply that four A-levels count as a major achievement.

THE A-LEVEL MARKET

A-levels are not simply the reflection of a teenager's talent and hard work. They are also consumer goods. It is more difficult to buy a top grade vintage car in this country than a top grade A-level. Some education experts fear that even the new A^* grade, designed to reward innate intelligence and now sought by Cambridge, can be won by costly methods.

The market supplies what the consumer wants and can pay for: so, if Oxbridge wants its applicants to have mainly As, whether they studied for them in a rural crammer with five pupils to a class or in a comprehensive in which the Maths teacher has a Geography degree, half the pupils have English as a second language and the crumbling science lab predates Apollo 11, then those parents who can afford it will reach for their cheque book.

Almost any public school nowadays, especially if it has boarding facilities, will steer your reasonably bright child towards a clutch of good A-levels. It has the language and science labs, the qualified teachers, the single ability groups and the one-to-one tuition that will do the job. There will be lots of support and few distractions. A-levels will be carefully matched to a pupil's perceived ability, to ensure top grades. Young people's own interests often count for rather less, but the end result is in the bag – if you are willing to pay £10,000 upwards per child per year, that is. Got two children? Tough luck. Advantage, as far as Oxbridge is concerned, is a term used in tennis.

But is there any other way of looking at A-levels? Steve Allen (not his real name) the head of science at a sixth form college whose pupils come from poverty line homes and include many refugees, has no doubt. "Oxbridge," he argues, "is not contextualising our pupils' achievement. To them an A is all that counts, and four A-levels are better than three. They don't understand that the young people we send have made enormous gains. We have students who live in a bedsit with their whole family, yet get very good grades, despite their insecure existence and family problems."

Would students with less than three top A-levels be able to keep up? Steve suggests that his do even better than that. "Once accepted into a good university, our students often become top of their year and the university is pleased it took them. They are hard-working and resilient. Oxbridge should take more of a chance on kids like ours, they over-shoot once they are accepted." As an example, Steve cites one of his students, the son of a packer, who went from a C at A-level Physics to a First in his finals at King's College, London. A-levels, Steve argues, tell you about a disadvantaged applicant's past, not their future.

Every year, Steve and his fellow teachers at the school encourage a dozen of their most promising students to apply for Oxbridge; they are determined to maximise their potential. And their students do get Oxbridge offers, at least some years, but these are nearly always based on AAA or, at best, AAB. Such offers, the staff feel, are so unrealistic they might as well be rejections. Oxford is not comparing like with like, the teachers complain.

It is a view echoed by many colleagues elsewhere, invariably off the record. Teachers who have no qualms about shouting at their school's $6'0\ 6''$ Karate champion for running on the stairs will drop their voices to a whisper and glance nervously over their shoulder when criticising Oxbridge. They are desperate not to offend the universities that can do most for their pupils. Each of them, though, knows of a gifted mathematician or other scientist interviewed at Oxbridge who then failed to get the required AAB. Maths, Chemistry and Physics require intensive, daily, small group teaching for top A-level results. Research methods have to be explained, findings interpreted. These are not teach-yourself subjects.

In public schools, it is almost unknown for a student not to get the required grades. This is not because state school pupils are lazier. Those who do get in tend to have educated parents who can help. They also often attend selective grammar schools or successful comprehensives in comfortable neighbourhoods.

Some of those working with exceptionally able children are also unhappy with A-levels being given so much weight. One of these is Deborah Eyre, who founded the National Academy for Gifted and Talented Youth (NAGTY) at the University of Warwick. Professor Eyre shares the view that A-levels are an unreliable predictor of university success. The current trend towards grade inflation, she believes, is working against many talented pupils. A scheme adopted some years ago at Warwick led to the acceptance of students from the most poorly equipped and funded institutions, further education colleges, on lower grades. The result confounded its critics: the FE group actually got more Firsts in their final degree exams than the best A-level students.

A study by the Government's Higher Education Funding Council (HEFC), released in July 2003, lends further weight to such views. Having tracked the progress of all 18 year old A-level students who entered degree courses in 1998 and graduated in 2001–2, its researchers found that, on average, a state school pupil performed as well as a private school one who had up to four A-level points fewer, the equivalent of comparing AAA with ABB.

The fact that A-level success must be seen in a socio-economic context is gradually dawning on some Russell Group universities and has already led to more realistic offers, even from departments academically rated just as highly as Oxbridge. Some actively seek out new types of candidates. At a seminar about medical school entrance organised by London universities, which was attended by the careers teacher of a "tough" London comprehensive, an admissions tutor recited the usual mantra about medical schools wishing to attract the very best students.

"Just tell us what you want, we'll send you candidates with six A-levels, if that's what it takes!" was the instant response of a private school head.

"It is not your students we're interested in here at this point," replied the tutor with obvious irritation, "we're trying to achieve a more representative intake, doctors who can empathise with more of their patients."

The careers teacher left in good spirits, but also aware that no such views have yet been expressed by Oxbridge.

Even worse, when another university with a high public school intake, Bristol, announced in 2003 that it would make slight A-level level allowances for disadvantaged pupils, there were howls of protest in the media. Frantic voices warned that letting in some state school students on lower grades was not only discrimination but a form of "pernicious social engineering" or "inclusion by the back door" and, as Simon Heffer put it in the Daily Mail of March 5th 2003, "an assault on the most hard-working people in Britain". In London's Evening Standard, Stephen Pollard from the Centre for the New Europe suggested that "in America such thinking has come close to destroying the very basis of academic standards".

One education expert wheeled out by the Headmasters' and Headmistresses' Conference, which represents the heads of private schools, actually claimed that "to go for such crude rebalancing at this level will create more unfairness than already exists".

Beneath the hysterics, you could just detect the gloom of a father who had been paying thousands (frequently £100,000 over a school career) to ensure that his son got into one of Britain's top universities, only to find that "his" place had gone to another kid.

ADVANCED EXTENSION AWARDS

But how do you prove that you're really the smarter applicant? A student keen to show that he has more to offer than just (!) top A-levels and wide interests can now take yet more exams. Advanced Extension Awards, known as AEAs, are designed to academically challenge gifted applicants and deepen their subject grasp. These written tests, replacing the old S-levels, are currently available in nineteen different subjects. Passing one or two course-related AEAs with a distinction will raise your profile in the eyes of some Oxbridge dons, especially if you can talk intelligently about it.

WHAT DOES IT ALL ADD UP TO?

The answer, despite all these grim tales, is that success is possible for state-educated students from even the poorest backgrounds, and today more than ever. One reason for optimism is that both Oxford and Cambridge are officially committed to widening the range of their candidate's backgrounds, undoubtedly out of idealism but also because future Government grants to Oxbridge may depend on it. Even more importantly, every year nearly four thousand state school students, including several hundred from working class backgrounds, already enter these universities.

Almost all of these students have managed to get top grades, so it is worth helping your child to do the same – perhaps in between lobbying Government for a regulatory body that will actually ensure a more representative intake.

But how is it done? Your teenager can find the answer in every basic study guide. To get top A-levels, a sixth form student should pick A-levels for which he has at least some aptitude, pay attention in class, establish a home study routine and plan out his work carefully, so all of it will be completed. He should also seek help from teachers, textbooks, websites (such as www.bbc.co.uk/schools/sosteacher) or any knowledgeable adult, rather than hope that what is still unclear to him will not come up.

There are also things that mothers and fathers need to know. Below is the best A-level advice from the parents of highly successful students and education professionals. What will be relevant depends on your circumstances and on the time left.

WHAT NOT TO DO (AND HOW NOT TO PANIC)

Don't go on at your son about how he really must get top grades for his A-levels. Grading is what other people, namely the examiners, will do. He does not really have the power to determine their decision, which will depend not just on the quality of his work, but also on the standard set by other students. Instead, calmly encourage him to cover all the ground – a realistic and far less scary target. It simply means working through the books, chapters, problems, hand-outs, sample papers and/or revision notes he has been given.

Don't be swept along by his inevitable moments of despair. If he is about to chuck all his books into the fire, don't just agree with him that perhaps Oxbridge is really not for the likes of you. Instead, suggest a break and gently remind him that young people from his background do get through this frustratingly heavy work load every year. If he's still stressed, take him out for some fun, to buy a small gift for someone you both know, or perhaps for a sporting event. Then, find a moment to ask whether you can help. Are there any books he needs? Would he like you to video a relevant programme for him?

Keep reminding the lad that there is help in class too. Seeing himself as an independent young adult may have prevented him from requesting it. If a teacher's explanation still leaves him confused, it may help to consult shop-bought revision guides or websites like www.mathsnet.net and mpn.meikleriggs.org.uk.

Real exam panic calls for more active steps. An A-level student who has not uttered a word for days or bursts into tears as soon as he takes out his course-work will not simply snap out of this. So, don't keep this problem in the family: ask his teacher whether she knows what state he is in. Can she think of any specific reason? Are there any short-term tasks she can set him to move him on? Sometimes one seemingly impossible task paralyses an able but insecure student.

If the panic does not subside, you might want to address it more directly. Suggest that the lad takes a day off for an intensive dose of football or swimming. Physical exercise helps to reprogramme the mind towards a more focused state.

Then, if necessary, get professional help. A session with the school counsellor may reassure your son that his goals are realistic. Alternatively, he could try listening to a relaxation tape, or watch one of those "achieve your aims" type self-help DVDs which use mild hypnosis. These can be remarkably effective. Drawing on psychological aids does not mean that your son is going mad.

While trying to help, make sure you're not impersonating a bulldozer but the AA, a service for emergency break-downs. Move the lad along, then let go. Accept that some mornings he will spend an hour staring at the wall, or kicking a ball into it. It's all part of the study process.

A-LEVEL TIPS

1. It helps to understand the real A-level time scale. While pupils will be preparing for their A-levels two years in advance, the last year is the most crucial. So, try not to schedule a big family trip abroad, the renovation of your home or your messy divorce for this period. Also avoid moving home halfway through the sixth form years, if that involves a change of schools. Adjusting to new class mates, a different syllabus and exams set by different boards can be very tough.

2. Studying is work and saps your energy: that teenager stretched out on a book-covered floor with his eyes half closed and listening to what cannot possibly be music is (hopefully) memorising the church structure of Old England in between worrying about whether his girlfriend will like his radical new haircut. He might well be too exhausted to look for food, so coach him gently towards it. He'll protest that he is not a kid anymore, but probably appreciates the effort.

3. Make sure that your daughter doesn't use up too much of her precious energy in this period on paid work. If she currently has an after-school and weekend job to fund her clothing habit, this will probably have to go. Otherwise, she will be far too tired to concentrate properly, either at school or at home. She might be able to earn a little money: a Saturday morning at the supermarket till or a Saturday night sitting an exceptionally calm baby are fine, but anything more is likely to affect her results. The poor girl will probably be distraught at the idea that her new spring wardrobe might have to wait until after June, but you should stand your ground. People are not actually being evicted from clubs for wearing a six months old crop top. Could you perhaps offer a new bag or a Hennes voucher in the meantime? If nothing else, this will prove to her that studying can pay off.

4. If your son is working not for extras but in order to keep your family afloat, the answer is not quite so simple. First make sure all of you receive the benefits you are entitled to. The government's Education and Maintenance

Allowance (EMA) offers pupils £30 a week to stay at school if their annual household income is no more than £20,817. Child benefit, which is paid to parents, normally stops at sixteen, but you can claim it until your son leaves school.

There is also Child Tax Credit, which will be paid directly into your bank account if you are responsible for the children. You don't need to be employed to qualify for this. If you work at least 30 hours a week but are on a low income, you may, in addition, be entitled to the new Working Tax Credit. To find out how to apply, phone the tax credits helpline on 0845 300 3900 or go to www.inlandrevenue.gov.uk/taxcredits. You can also visit or call your nearest Inland Revenue office.

You must also discuss your financial situation openly with your son. Make it clear that you thoroughly approve of his university plans and that you don't resent the cost of keeping him: you'd be surprised how many kids think that their parents do. Try to also get across that the drop in his own after-school income is only a temporary blip. Good grades will get him into a good university, which in turn should lead to a good job and an income which, if you are hard-up at the moment, may be almost beyond his imagination.

Make sure, though, that the lad does not try to bridge the gap with credit. Some card issuers will happily sign up 18 year old non-earning pupils The result can be urgent, massive debts, a bad start for his university life.

However, if your family finances really will collapse without your son's contribution, don't give up on the idea of Oxbridge. Just make sure that his school is fully aware of your circumstances and mentions them in its Open Reference. Alternatively, he himself might want to talk about his paid work and why he needs to do it in his Personal Statement. Family poverty is not a character flaw he needs to be ashamed of. Allowances are made for seriously disadvantaged students and an admissions tutor genuinely committed to "widening access" (there are quite a few) might be impressed with the lad's persistence.

Lastly, don't encourage your son to see his A-level work as a competition with his class mates. True, some kids thrive on rivalry, but for many exams are the time when they need peer support most. His sixth form will be going through this mix of slave labour and adrenalin rush together and, rather than worry whether his best friend is getting on any better, he might want to team up with him. The two might waste some time discussing chart hits rather than studying Chemistry charts, but having company takes the panic out of revision. This often enables a student to arrive at previously missed solutions himself.

4
Getting the exam experts in

Having said all this, I must point out that none of the above steps will get your son into Oxbridge if the school's teaching is poor. If his school's results are consistently below the national average because its teachers do not have degrees in their A-level subjects or because of severe discipline problems then no amount of hard work by your talented lad can tip the balance by itself. He'll need external help.

What help you'll be able to get depends largely on the time your teenager has left. Nobody will have any magic solution to offer if you find out a fortnight before the crucial exam that large chunks of the syllabus have remained utterly incomprehensible to him. As the drunk, sitting in a puddle, told the lady who had asked him the way to the local savings bank: "Madam, you don't want to start from here."

On the other hand, if school reports or test grades indicate earlier in that year that the boy, who might even have been defined as "gifted or talented" by his teachers, is achieving well below his potential, then a revision course can be one way forward. It is best not to wait for the results of his springtime mocks; by then most courses will be booked up.

REVISION COURSES

Easter revision courses are run by some state schools, local education authorities and private institutions. None of these courses are a substitute for a student's own hard work. Nor can they provide a student with a full understanding of his or her subject. Some subject mysteries, though, will be resolved and study priorities established. Mainly, revision courses teach students to provide what the examiners really want. Teachers explain to them what they need to write, then make them practice writing under exam conditions. At the end of what is usually a week's intensive work, participants should have picked up enough study skills and exam techniques to show themselves in the best light.

What lies behind this is the assumption that exams are not just about knowing your subject, but also about preparing and packaging what you know in order to do well in exams. Some pupils can do this unaided, but most need to learn. This results in better and, in case of able, hard-working students, in excellent grades.

SCHOOL-RUN COURSES

An increasing number of state schools now run their own revision courses, sometimes financed by the Government's Standards Fund. These are free, voluntary and aimed at encouraging students who the staff feel might benefit most. Teachers seek to ensure that students have worked through the relevant course material, rather than blindly thrashing their way through everything they were ever taught. There may also be another mock exam at the end. Often, however, there is only limited emphasis on exam technique.

Still, your teenager should at least be given a copy of the examiners' mark scheme, which tells her what exactly the crucial extra marks that will take a student up to an A-grade are awarded for; in English, for instance, this will include putting a literary work into its historical context; in History, examiners reward students, amongst other things, for providing a "web of causation", rather than just a sequence of historical events. (The mark scheme can also be downloaded from the website of the relevant examination board.)

How much time there is to resolve individual student's queries depends on the revision course structure. Some individual concerns can certainly now be addressed, since classes will, at least, be smaller than in the school's term time A-level group. The classes might, though, still be fairly mixed ability and run by the students' regular teachers.

A few state sixth form colleges also run such vacation courses and some of those are open to outside students. If your daughter has been unhappy about the quality of some of her teaching, then a highly rated sixth form college (its Ofsted report will be on the college website) could be a better bet, assuming that its pupils are studying for the same board.

PRIVATE COURSES

Private revision courses, once the preserve of the rich and dim, are a growth industry. Some are run on a Saturday basis all year long, but most are holiday ones. Such courses, advertised in the press around three months in advance, offer intense revision work in very small groups, albeit at pretty large fees – anything between £200 and £700 for a week. The cost depends partly on the number of subjects to be revised and partly on whether it includes accommodation. Day school courses are just as good as boarding ones, though you may not have a choice if you live far away. Courses are often run on the premises of private schools and might employ some of their teachers. Students here will usually be guided towards a deeper understanding of their subject. They will also be reminded of fundamental principles and teachers will try to sharpen key skills, for instance grammar in the case of languages. Nevertheless, in most short courses the emphasis will be on what one revision college principal described as "technique, technique and more technique." Some revision courses are actually held inside colleges in Oxford and Cambridge. These are based on boarding and explicitly aim to make your son or daughter at ease there, as part of their preparation for the Oxbridge entrance process.

Before you part with such serious money, though, ask a few questions and don't be swayed by the freshly painted buildings and lush green lawns. It will take more than a generous application of Growmore to turn your teenager into an A-grade student. As a start, you need to know the qualifications of the course teachers. Reputable revision colleges will list those on the publicity material: John Smith, B.Sc. Biology (Cantab.) tells you that Mr. Smith has a Bachelor of Science degree in Biology from Cambridge. If it was a degree from Oxford in an arts subject, such as English, the qualification would be BA English (Oxon.). The letters M.Sc. or MA after a name indicate a higher qualification in most cases, but former students of Oxford and Cambridge can claim this title automatically a year after graduation. Some revision courses are taught by university lecturers or teachers who also moonlight as examiners.

You also need to know whether you are booking your son into a new or established revision college. New tends to be bad until proven otherwise. How big are their classes? Will they prepare your daughter for her specific subject exam and examining board? Do they specialise in helping their students to pass or to get As? And how many hours a day does the teaching actually take? The answers, you will discover, can vary extremely widely.

What you would, ideally, want to hear is that they teach a single subject in groups of no more than six, for at least two hours a day, with extra time set aside for exam practice, feed-back and advice on further revision work the student can do at home. It would also be nice if the revision college took lots of bright students aiming to get into Russell Group universities and, perhaps, Oxbridge. Generally, smaller groups are far better value than longer hours. By this stage, your son needs personal attention. In this spirit, a good revision college will want to hear about the GCSE and A2 exams your son has already taken, plus his current grade predictions. These details enable them to fit him into the right course. If the principal is trying to make you sign a cheque without showing any interest in the boy's record – don't. You are probably being sold a pup.

I am less sure about the apparently rather well taught A-level courses at Oxford and Cambridge. Tempting as these may sound if your daughter clams up when confronted with quaint old university towns and the clipped vowels of their teaching staff, such a course does imply that Oxbridge is her sole possible destination. If she then fails to get in despite her very best efforts, the disappointment can be harder to bear.

HOME TUTORS

Getting one-to-one attention, even for a fairly short period, can dramatically raise a pupil's achievement. A good tutor will explain previously incomprehensible bits of the syllabus, focus on those aspects of a subject which are likely to come up in tests and, in an ideal world, suggest wider reading. He can also make even the driest subject sound exciting, thereby coaching your son towards doing more work.

To get the best results you must spell out the basics. Is the tutor there to help improve your kid's general grasp of a school subject or just to prepare her for an imminent exam? If exam performance is all you are after, the tutor will have to be familiar with the type of questions likely to come up. If he is not currently a teacher, this means that he needs to be given copies of previous years' papers, available from your son's school. The tutor may or may not cover exam skills such as timing, ordering material and clarity of expression. Unless you make clear what you want, no tutor can provide it.

(A word of warning: tutors can make a difference, but cannot magically transform a middling pupil into a top student. If that is what you hope, I'd drop the idea of Oxbridge. For the sake of family peace and your teenager's self-esteem, it would be better to focus on another university. Having two fairly strong subjects is the minimum requirement not just for getting into Oxford or Cambridge, but also for surviving there.)

So, where do you find a tutor? Well, Prime Minister Tony Blair found his sons' tutor at the nearest public day school, and there is no reason why you should not copy him. It is quite OK to ring up yours, picked from the Good Schools Guide, and tell the school secretary that you are looking for someone to do a few weeks' private tutoring. If their own staff are too grand to take the extra job (in the era of huge mortgages, few are) they might well have a friend or a former pupil just down from Oxbridge who is keen.

Don't be put off by a potential tutor's youth. When it comes to exam coaching, someone who left school only a few years earlier and so may have worked through the same syllabus as your son towards very similar exams could well come up trumps. And don't be ashamed to ask the young postgraduate student earning his rent in your sitting room what grades he got and how he got into Oxbridge himself. Is he keeping in touch with staff there? It's a good sign if he is. He might have picked up gossip about new priorities and admissions policy or might even be able to put in a good word.

Alternatively, A-level tutors seeking work advertise in many local papers. They are often retired teachers and some have worked in both the public and the private sector. Ask how long they have been retired (because A-levels have changed much in the last decade) and if they give the school as a reference, follow it up by phone. You never know whether you'll hear songs of praise or some tense, embarrassed waffle. The latter can mean he left under a bit of a cloud – drink or perhaps a taste for under-age boys. Schools rarely prosecute.

There are also lots of tutorial agencies offering their services in the papers. Told what kind of help your teenager needs, they'll try to come up with someone suitable. It's best to insist that this means a tutor who has graduated in the subject he will teach. The kind of person registered with the agency is often an Oxbridge graduate still looking for the perfect city job or for enough bookings as a comedian. A few are young academics trying to pay their mortgage. Some agencies check tutors' references, others are just groups of university friends sharing out the work.

As for the practical side, this is pretty straight forward. Expect to pay between £20 and £25 per lesson, and settle for between one and two lessons a week, depending on the amount of time left. A good tutor can massively improve a willing student's understanding of a subject and his exam skills in two or three months. The emphasis is on "willing": if you have scheduled the tutorials in place of your son's weekly football practice the tutor will be as popular as Bayern Munich.

Before finally striking the deal, clarify with the tutor how long a lesson will be and if you have to pay his fare on top of the fee. Then, fix a time and place and don't allow circumstances to alter them. The time should be after one of your daughter's easier school days or a quiet weekend afternoon. The place, ideally, around your bare kitchen table or your daughter's tidied up room. Being able to spread out reams of paper work is what matters here. This is not the moment to show off your new, extra-soft three piece leather suite.

In some cases, the tutor may suggest to hold lessons on the school premises or elsewhere. This may be tempting, especially if you feel embarrassed about your home, but it is worth keeping in mind that the tutor himself was probably not raised at Buckingham Palace. I'd certainly agree to this only if you can be sure that other, trustworthy people will be present. If the person who will be spending private time with your son was not vetted by anyone, you might even want to remain at home (but not in the same room, of course) during lessons. I'd also make clear to the girl that the tutor, however nice, is technically a stranger, which means not a trusted family friend whose invitations she can accept.

Lastly, it may be wise to review progress after two or three lessons. Ask your daughter how she feels about the tutor. Is he good at explaining a problem? Approachable? Responds to questions? Does she feel that she is learning anything or is she just watching a dopey stranger scoffing the chocolate biscuits you thoughtfully put out?

If things go wrong, don't be shy about starting again. Tell the tutor you are moving away (or whatever), then quickly look for another one by the same route. Tutors are just human beings and vary tremendously. The next one might be a teaching genius.

MOVING SCHOOLS

If you conclude that your son's school is not good enough already at the GCSE stage, you have different options. He might agree – or even badly want – to move to another, more successful comprehensive school for his sixth form studies. What you need to work out, though, is when and where.

The answer to the first question is simple: no later than the start of year 11. The best comprehensives want all applications in by January or February of the previous school year, which means eight to nine months ahead of entry. As for where to move your teenager, the choice is, on first sight, considerable. Legally, you no longer need to live near a school to apply for a place there, and your son is now old enough to travel considerable distances.

Picking a good school seems simple enough. Obviously, both you and your son will want to attend the school's open day for sixth formers, which will be in November of the year before or in January thereafter. This is the time to check out the basics. Does it have the facilities and/or labs he might need? Are you struck by the positive attitude of the pupils who are showing you around? Do the teachers impress you as qualified, likeable and ambitious for their pupils? Does the school send pupils on Government-funded schemes such as Inspire or Access to broaden their horizons? Does it prepare its students for the Oxbridge entrance process and do any of them get in? A good school will send you home with a pile of bumph that will tell you the rest, notably what subjects it offers at AS and A2 level and where they might lead. It should also show the previous year's exam results and which universities, if any, their students have been accepted by. There will be some mention of class size, which in the A-level group should be 20 or less.

A well-structured school brochure will also contain extracts from the school's Ofsted report, although I'd treat those with caution. For instance, it is nice to know that its community links have been rated "excellent", but if your daughter is planning to do English, you really need to know the rating given to the school's teaching in that subject.

Also, "good" sounds fine in an Ofsted report, but actually isn't. The Ofsted range goes from "very poor", "poor", "satisfactory", "good" and "very good" to "excellent". So, "good" is actually pretty middling and you'd want it to be better than that. If the school won't tell you these things, you can go directly to Ofsted. Either phone for the report or go to their website, www.gov.uk and search for the name of the school.

Then, if you're happy, go ahead and fill in the application form, remembering to emphasize your teenager's academic abilities. You have done what you could and must now hope for the best.

Unfortunately, such steps have a really good chance of success only outside the big cities. In London, certainly, top quality

61

comprehensives are hopelessly oversubscribed. When it comes to the sixth form, most take in only a small proportion of outside pupils. While it is worth trying hard, which includes making sure that the school is aware of all your son's strengths and potential contribution to the school's academic glory, he may have to consider other options. The most obvious one is a sixth form college.

SIXTH FORM COLLEGES

State run colleges of this kind have a poor reputation, mainly because they often cater for a very mixed intake of young people. Some may come from failing schools, others from disadvantaged homes. This means that their overall exam results cannot equal those of a school in some executive suburb. However, the college might still be great at developing a pupil's individual potential. And don't be automatically put off by the presence of refugees: some of their parents may well have been teachers or civil servants before they had to escape and will encourage their children to study hard.

Most importantly, a huge amount of Government money has gone into this sector in recent years, which has been translated into state-of-the art facilities from language labs to IT equipment. The funding has also attracted more and more highly qualified teachers. As a result, your local sixth form college could be far more geared towards sending your son to Oxbridge than the struggling comprehensive down the road.

Having said that, the above rules still apply: attend the open day, go through their bumph with a fine-toothed comb and check whether the staff are actively involved in preparing pupils for Oxbridge entrance. I would, perhaps, add one reservation, which is no reflection on the professionalism or the dedication of their teaching staff. Although some students from sixth form colleges get into Oxford and Cambridge every year, the two universities rarely accept them for Medicine and Law. Partly, this may be due to the rigid A-level requirements for these courses (three "hard" subjects at grade A) and partly, perhaps, just a case of Oxbridge being toffee-nosed.

IF YOU CAN'T BEAT THEM...

You may, in fact, dream of being toffee-nosed yourself, of sending your son to one of those schools which, in exchange for annual school fees well above the national minimum wage, smooth their pupils' path to Oxbridge. If you could afford to do so, you would presumably not be reading this, but don't give up quite yet; some private sixth form education is available at little or no cost, at least if your child is really talented and you play your cards right.

What you need to know is that almost all private schools have scholarship schemes. Most of these cover a proportion of a child's fee, usually 50 per cent. The traditional function of this is to enable those of their old boys who have fallen on hard times to send their kids there. Quite a few schools, though, also have 100 per cent scholarship schemes. These have quite a different purpose. They enable a private establishment with a mixed ability intake, which is what most public schools except for a tiny group of highly selective ones really are, to strengthen its academic base. The top A-levels won by its hand-picked scholars will ensure that the school retains its place near the top of the annual league table. Once this has been achieved, it can hike up its fees as much as it likes. In other words, scholarships are not a form of charity and you need not be embarrassed about accepting one.

There is only one problem. While these schemes might even get your son into some of the grandest boys' schools, including Eton and Harrow, full scholarships to girls' schools are like gold dust. The trick here is to think outside the box, at least with an older teen-ager. You need to know that many top boys' school now have mixed sixth forms. Ambitious headmasters at such schools are forever in search of bright girls.

While most existing schemes are aimed at pupils entering at 13, big schools generally set aside about half a dozen full scholarships per year for sixth form entry. Created after the abolition of the Government's assisted places scheme in the 1990s, these scholarships are usually means-tested. In other words, they are aimed at those parents of a gifted child who are on the dole or earning little more than £12,000. If you are slightly better off, the school might drop part of the fees.

The scholarships usually cover all costs, including tuition and, if applicable, boarding. If asked, most schools will also find a way to fund the scholar's absurdly overpriced uniform and other kit. And when your son has lost his flannel blazer and cap for the third exasperating time, a kindly teacher will reveal to you that the annual school fete always includes a "good as new" second-hand uniform stall. Then watch the most genteel of middle class mothers get into a scrum so the money saved can go to Harvey Nichols.

When do you throw your child's name into this particular hat? The answer is very early. While state sixth forms do not usually decide on admissions until February of the year in which the sixth form course is to start, private schools think fourteen months ahead. This means you probably should first contact their admissions officer in July or August of the year before your teenager will be starting her sixth form. Below is a sample letter I suggest you send in order to set the process in motion, but you may want to tailor it slightly to fit an individual school. As you will discover by looking at a school's brochure or website, expectations from scholars can vary; some schools like to find the perfect all-rounder, the boy who performs equally well in all subjects without obvious preferences; others look for exceptional ability in one academic field. Most schools like a pupil who can offer extras like sporting ability or an outstanding musical gift.

LETTER TO A SCHOOL (SAMPLE)

Dear . . . (phone to find out the name of the head),

I am the parent of a child currently attending Year 10 of his comprehensive school. My son has been assessed as gifted by his school (or an educational psychologist, or some other expert), especially as far as the sciences are concerned. He works hard and has consistently good exam results. He is also a keen athlete and plays basketball for his school.

His gifts, I feel, would be best developed in a school such as yours. I would therefore be grateful if you could advise me about your admissions procedures. Unfortunately, I am a low earner and unable to afford current school fees. Perhaps you could let me know whether there are any scholarships or bursaries available for boys in my son's position.

Yours sincerely,

If the school is interested, an application form will be in the post. The school might also ask for documentation such as school reports or teachers' comments. All being well, the boy will then be invited to an interview and exam session lasting anything from a few hours to two whole days the following November. This is a promising outcome, but don't count your chickens yet: a large private school may be offering up to 20 of their sixth form places to non-pupils, but will interview between twice and four times that number. If possible, your son should therefore sit exams for more than one school.

The exam itself usually consists of several parts. A chat with the applicant, perhaps combined with some sort of brief IQ test, will seek to establish innate ability. A set of longer, written tests will determine how much the lad knows about the subjects he has been taught. Some schools favour giving the applicants a kind of lecture, then quiz them about the contents; others ask them to write an essay on a non-school subject, often involving a story in the news. If you meet any current pupils, don't be put off by the unfamiliar way they speak. Obviously, your son's accent will be different, but accents change fast at that age and six months into the school year, he may well shock you by sounding like them.

The school may or may not wish to talk to a parent, but if they do, don't be nervous about this either. They are not looking for airs and graces, but for a commitment to your son's academic goals. This means that you will encourage him to work hard at home if an exam is looming, that you will not disappear abroad just before he is due to go home at half term or that you won't keep him away on holiday long after term started. They get quite enough of this behaviour from the fee-paying parents, thank you.

They will also expect you to back the strict school rules. You'll have to make your son understand that there will be little tolerance of misbehaviour. Private schools maintain discipline and try to prevent breaches of the law, such as drug-taking, by mercilessly expelling culprits. Parents of rebellious pupils, however bright, have reasons to fear the headmaster's dreaded phrase: "He would be happier elsewhere."

Can you prepare for this entrance exam? The honest answer is, most applicants do. You can start by asking the school for more details. Many will offer some information on exam contents, or even previous papers. Obviously, your son should be having another look at his GCSE notes in those subjects he intends to continue with. It may also be a good idea for him to do some newspaper reading. After a few weekends of immersion in The Observer, The Sunday Times, The Sunday Telegraph or the Independent on Sunday, he should be able to express a personal opinion on a few issues of the day: strikes, global warming or plastic surgery are just some examples. Remember, there are no "correct" views on such things, only arguments backed by a few facts.

Although few schools conduct proper verbal interviews, your son will probably be asked to talk a little about his interests. These might have to include cultural or sporting ones, depending on the school. Make sure he can rattle down a short list!

When it comes to the written work, it is obviously important not to overlook any of the mandatory questions by mistake. Most crucially perhaps, an applicant needs to be able to complete an essay within a set time, usually 45 minutes. This means acquiring the skills of timing, structuring and summarising. Check he's got a working watch!

If you're uncertain whether your son is properly prepared, consult ISIS, who might be able to tell you which sample papers your son might want to look at before sitting for a particular school.

WILL HE BE HAPPY THERE?

The answer is, it depends. I've rarely heard of a day school pupil on a scholarship regretting the choice they made. Sleeping in a different world can be more stressful. An outgoing teenager who likes group activities and understands that he is contributing to the school's fortunes will probably settle in fast. Large boarding schools tend to have separate scholars' houses and your bright son might really enjoy living with lots of other fast learners.

On the other hand, most private schools are single sex, and living an hour's train ride from the nearest place selling hair gel does not suit everyone. Having less freedom than at a comprehensive can be a pain, although boarding schools are no longer the prisons which earlier inmates remember them as. Physical punishment and fagging, the public school version of bullying, were abolished nearly a generation ago. There is some privacy and a universal youth culture has reduced the once enormous gap in pupils' lives. One Eton teacher, quoted in the Daily Telegraph, insisted that it can now be hard to tell who comes from where: "By the time you've opened a few doors, you see that everyone has the same rickety CD system and the same posters."

The range of well-resourced leisure activities can thrill a newcomer. Still, a very shy teenager may be thrown by the unfamiliar environment and not everyone fancies the wide open spaces, which may include dormitories, as well as playing fields. There can be other problems: a small school's intake may be too white to make an ethnic minority child feel at ease, or too intellectually average to stretch a fast learner. A few schools get so obsessed with

A-levels that they (metaphorically) stamp on the more original pupil who is doing work outside the curriculum. To invent a game, design a machine or write a poem in school time can be seen as betraying the struggle for top marks.

In short, private education, even if you can get it, does not meet every gifted child's needs. There has to be a fairly precise match between abilities and facilities. Anecdotal evidence suggests that mixed boarding schools work best for working class pupils (think Atlantic College or Bedales) but a current A-level student should not get too excited about these options. While Winchester has launched a £70m. bursary appeal to fund sixty-seven boys by 2018 and St. Paul's seeks to raise £250m. so that it can go "needs-blind" within twenty-five years, the number of free six form places currently available is very small. There are only about three hundred a year, which does not quite make them a superhighway to Oxbridge.

5

What degree course?

Picking an Oxbridge degree course is something many pupils do in the first, exciting weeks of their A2 year, almost as an afterthought. The forms arrive in September, and finishing a class essay in time can, at this point, seem far more important to your son. So might finding out whether leggy Jessie from Maths has really broken up with her naff boyfriend in the holidays. Other pupils are probably not even discussing courses yet. After all, entrance applications to most universities need to be submitted over two months later. So, why worry? If you fuss now, you might well get your head bitten off. "Filling in the form just means applying for a course in what you're best at, right?" Wrong, actually.

Course choice is fairly crucial for enjoying university life, as well as for getting in. The problem is that by the time they fill in their Oxbridge application form, most pupils are perfectly clear about theirs. They want to study the subject in which they got the highest marks at school. Teachers may strengthen this idea by telling the proud dad on parents' day that "she is a natural mathematician" or assure a mother that "he has a real gift for English."

For the pupil with at least a trace of doubt, the school's careers adviser may be the next port of call. Some are wonderful at making even a timid but clever science pupil see herself as a future Professor of Medicine. Others, though, are overwhelmed by the requirements of so many new pupils, universities and courses. In a school which does not normally sends students to Oxbridge their focus might well be on making disadvantaged pupils consider any university at all. So, while all careers advisers have a shelf full of dog-eared books and booklets to lend, only a few will explain to an Oxbridge applicant while she, especially, should take time over them.

Nor is there much emphasis on the link between careers and courses. While it is pretty obvious what you can become with a degree in Law, the same is not true of, for instance, Linguistics. Its name alone sounds like a sexual practice. To a pupil nervous about striking out into the alien adult world in general and Oxbridge in particular, sticking with a familiar school subject also provides some reassurance. So, Maths or English (or History or French) goes on the application form.

WHAT'S ON OFFER

This is a great pity, as a start because your son will never know what he could be missing without a leisurely study of the Oxford or Cambridge undergraduate prospectus, available over six months in advance. Not only has this once dreary document at last caught up with the lively and colourful booklets issued by the former polytechnics, it also no longer assumes that every reader knows what Economics is or what jobs it can lead to. Every year too it contains more non-school subject courses, a few of them entirely new, others newly combined or newly opened to candidates without Latin.

Admittedly, the number of courses offered by Oxford and Cambridge is not huge. After all, for most of the two universities' long history, only three subjects, Classics, Divinity and Law, were taught there. Even the introduction of English Literature was fiercely resisted for decades but, once its academic supporters had won the day, the subject was, in true Oxbridge style, elevated to a national mission. Speaking after his election as Oxford English Professor, George Stuart Gordon announced in his 1922 inaugural lecture: "England is sick, and ... English Literature must save it. The Churches (as I understand) having failed, and social remedies being slow, English Literature now has a triple function: still I suppose, to delight and instruct us, but also, and above all, to save our souls and heal the State."

Academics elsewhere tend to see their role in slightly more modest terms and so managed to create a wider choice earlier on. The new universities, in particular, try to cover every possible student taste, with some offering up to a hundred degree options, from Accounting to Culinary Arts (Pastry), both taught at Thames Valley University. Cambridge, in comparison, tends to list only around thirty degree courses in its prospectus. Oxford lists just over fifty.

Oxford and Cambridge have also taken seemingly different paths. While Oxford has gradually added a small but interesting set of combined courses, such as Mathematics and Philosophy, Modern History and Economics and Classical Archaeology and Ancient History, Cambridge has not, or so a quick skim though its prospectus suggest. Here the early 20th century range of academic disciplines, topped up by one newcomer, Computer Science, survives almost intact.

This impression is misleading. Once a Cambridge student has done her initial year, working hard to absorb a single subject at great depth, she has an amazing range of study options. Thanks to the many experts and expert libraries on tap, a History undergraduate interested in, for example, North African History, will be able to explore even its most obscure angle with a world-renowned expert. And if she wants to combine this with another discipline, say Cultural Studies, this is not just fine but actually encouraged.

In other words, although History and Culture is not a Cambridge degree course, you can actually do it, and probably to a higher level than elsewhere. This so-called "Tripos" course structure means then a student is sometimes even able to move from his official course subject to a fairly unrelated one. If your son has started off in Oriental Studies, but wants to broaden his outlook (or is struggling with Hittite grammar) by year two, he might be able to move to Social Anthropology, Law or Management Studies and continue with this into year three. This means he will end up, in practice, with a combined course.

In science too progress options are huge, though usually only when you have completed the first year of what in Cambridge is called Natural Sciences, but in Oxford comes under either Biological Sciences, Earth Sciences, Chemistry, Biochemistry, Materials Science or Physics. Other science courses, tend to offer the student either a wide module choice or at least some subject combinations. Teaching methods can vary too and you need to remember that, unlike in many other universities, the science approach here will be theoretical rather than applied. If Robert Stephenson had gone to Oxbridge, he might have been encouraged to explore the scientific principles making a steam engine possible, before building one.

It is also worth knowing that some subjects are absent only in name: "The word sociology, being a Latin–Greek hybrid, was not used in polite academic society," recalled Cambridge don Thomas Howarth. So, must you go elsewhere for this popular hybrid? Actually, no. Nowadays all Oxbridge Anthropology courses, as well as the Cambridge PPS course and Oxford PPE (see below) put their students through the Sociology reading list, albeit in between lots of other books.

No subject is today out of bounds to state school pupils. As mentioned before, this includes Classics, which now accommodates the study, from scratch, of Latin or Greek, or both. The Oxford Classics course, a tour de force through Greek and Roman literature, history, languages, thought, art and culture, is not even terribly hard to get into. The only problem is that applicants from comprehensives need to do more independent reading than others to prove their interest. Private and grammar school pupils plough through loads of Classics-related stuff at school.

THINK BEFORE YOU JUMP

As a result of there being so much on offer, working out your course options from the prospectus alone can be hideously confusing. Don't even think of signing on the dotted line before you have read the clearer but also much more detailed information on the course website. Keep in mind too that two courses of the same name may be quite different at Oxford and Cambridge. Oriental Studies at Oxford, for instance, is largely language-oriented. At Cambridge, the same course (renamed Asian and Middle Eastern Studies in 2009) has a substantial history and culture element.

All admissions tutors I spoke to emphasized that it is absolutely fine for students to contact staff with further questions, either by email or (good practice for the interview) by phone. All the telephone numbers, email addresses and websites you might need to contact a faculty or college are listed in the university prospectus. The best person to ask for is the undergraduate studies secretary, a goldmine of information on exciting but unfamiliar courses.

On the other hand, simply sticking to the school subject he knows may well disappoint your son intellectually. For instance, doing school Maths eight hours a week is not at all the same thing as doing the more abstract Oxbridge version for thirty hours a week. Reading fiction for pleasure and writing essays about the narrative of your book is very different from concentrating on literary theory, as you would with Oxford English Lit., or on literary structure, as you would at Cambridge. Of course, some bright students absolutely thrive on this approach and will spend endless blissful university hours discussing iambic pentameters in English or Fermat's Last Theorem in Maths. Others, though, will love the inspiration found very much further afield.

So, encourage your son or daughter to take their time. It's best to think of course choice not as the automatic continuation of a student's school career, but as a new and carefully considered beginning.

PICKING TO GET IN

Course choice at Oxbridge also matters greatly (and far more than at many other universities) in terms of acceptance chances. What does this mean in practice? Well, let's say that your daughter has returned from an Access trip to Oxford or Cambridge determined to live for three years under the ramparts of a medieval nunnery, but also to study her favourite school subject. Unless she is a really outstanding pupil, this can be a problem. Each year, there are vastly more Oxbridge candidates than places for English, Maths, History and courses involving French. Poor teaching too often handicaps candidates for school subjects more than others.

If your daughter is determined to go to Oxbridge, but also to do French, the only foreign language taught in all English schools, she might have to choose between these two perfectly reasonable ambitions. Suggesting this to her could trigger a tantrum bigger than the one she threw, aged three, when she couldn't take home the deep hole she had dug in the playground sand pit. And, if she has read her way through the French novels shelf in your local library or is beginning to take an interest in Parisian existentialism she is quite right to ignore you.

Clinging to French just because it comes easy to her and she is curious about the world, though, might be the wrong decision. Oxbridge offers lots of alternatives – and we are talking mind stretchers, not cheap substitutes here. A pupil who fearlessly walked the horrifying tightrope of French grammar may actually find it more rewarding to tackle a non-European language with a whole alphabet of its own. Future explorers can, at the same time, learn about the history or culture of a new, unfamiliar country through courses like Oriental Studies or Anthropology. Or, if the girl has a more theoretical bent, she might want to explore the science of languages, Linguistics, together with a new modern language of her choice.

All these are stimulating, often extremely well taught courses and they have another very attractive feature: they admit around a third of all those who apply. State school candidates are especially good at getting into the Cambridge Archaeology & Anthropology course: in 2008, 55 per cent of them were successful. Graduates of Arch & Ant, as it is known, also do well in life: the Governor of the Bank of England, Mervyn King, is one of them.

Many such courses not even require prior knowledge of another language, certainly not a non-European one. Others have admissions tutors who will be delighted to hear that your daughter speaks Polish to her grandmother or learnt Arabic in the mosque. She will still have to prove her interest in the course by reading around it, but her background can give her that slight edge.

And if the girl does get in, she might get a very good degree. Many a language student finds herself alongside some of the classic Oxbridge "coasters", rich but less academic students who have picked their mother tongue as a course subject and coast along on the strength of that. But to do well takes more than basic language skills, and if she works hard on all aspects of the course, your bright daughter might well overtake the coasters and get a First. On the other hand, if the girl insists on clinging to her school subject, she might not even get into Oxbridge.

TARGET PRACTICE

One of the open secrets of Oxbridge entrance has always been that you can get in by targeting a course which has a high rate of successful applicants. Rates vary greatly: courses such as Economics and Law accept less than one in six candidates, while History, English, French, Experimental Psychology and Medicine accept about one in five. The success rate of Chemistry, Materials Science and Classics applicants, on the other hand, hovers around 43 per cent. Nearly half of those who apply are likely to get in.

For unusual language combinations, success rates can be even higher: only Oxford and Cambridge can afford to run courses which, during certain periods of history at least, hardly anyone wants to attend. Some of these courses are relics of the British Empire, which exported thousands of young men with a grounding in the various "native languages" to the Colonies. Elderly Oxbridge dons still recall the frantic War Office search in 1941 for graduates in Serbo–Croat who could be dropped behind enemy lines in German-occupied Yugoslavia. Younger dons will talk of a similar search in 1999, when the British Government prepared to enter Kosovo.

Until recently, few people would have thought that Sumerian, the ancient language of what was Mesopotamia and is now Iraq, had any public use. However, the looting of Iraq's museums in 2003 deprived the world of valuable ancient documents and made the study of the remaining ones crucial.

As a result, courses which combine language training with historic or cultural studies are kept going even if there are very few applicants for them. After all, the dons teaching the course are around anyway, engaged in their own specialist and highly reputable research. What this means is that while it can be murder to get into Law, there are few barriers to the students wanting to do Sanskrit, or a language mix including Czech (with Slovak). Here, a bright applicant willing to broaden his horizons might well be greeted with open arms.

Why don't more state school students go for courses like these? The answer lies in the information available. Neither Oxford nor Cambridge will tell you, for instance, what the acceptance chances of a candidate applying to do a particular language course are. Instead, the success rates listed are overall ones, based on all the degree courses run by an individual faculty. This was fine when a candidate could always call on a cousin or family friend who had been to Oxbridge and knew what was on offer there. Alas, times have changed and, without such key data, how can a student from a non-academic background possibly decide?

Families also like to know about the practical value of courses. Without this information, parents may not feel that they will be spending their hard-earned cash on something worthwhile. Actually, when it comes to languages, it's a case of no worry. They are amongst the most popular degree subjects in the eyes of top employers. However, while French remains useful to diplomats, business now loves Spanish, Chinese and Russian.

All these facts, of course, are exactly what public school teachers, who are usually Oxbridge educated, have at their finger tips. They are aware that relatively few people apply to do a combination of German and Turkish, or Arabic and Portuguese, even though these courses require only a prior knowledge of the European language. They know the success rates for Egyptology at Cambridge, and the chances offered to their particular students by the existence of so many Oxford courses involving Classics.

These teachers will also tailor their suggestions to the individual student by explaining that Materials Science (once called Metallurgy) at Oxford is not as academically demanding as Engineering and Materials, that Land Economy at Cambridge is less of a tough intellectual slog than Economics. They are aware that Cambridge Theology turns out graduates interested in comparative religion, while Oxford Theology suits potential vicars, and that very few eighteen year olds aspire to become either of these things.

One of the main reasons such a disproportionate number of Oxbridge students come from their kind of schools is that they apply to a far wider range of courses than state school students do.

Public school teachers also realise that being flexible about your degree subject does not make for a disappointing outcome. Many of their students return to recommend their course to others, not only for intellectual satisfaction, but also on career grounds.

This does not, of course, mean that a student should completely disregard her own instincts in order to get in. If you hate languages, don't apply for a course requiring full-body-immersion in two of them. If you hate scientific research, looking at flow charts all day could make you feel sick. Most students, though, do not have preferences quite as strong as this and a little open-mindedness can be very rewarding indeed.

If you are wondering whether you should consider a course which is in no great public demand, the answer is probably yes. Do look at previously unconsidered options like the mysteries of Assyriology and, if they even vaguely spark your interest, skim through one of the relevant course textbooks listed on the faculty website. The excellence of Oxbridge teaching often makes a not (as yet) loved subject a highly stimulating experience.

Equally importantly, the student will still have access to the lively intellectual scene which characterises Oxbridge. Not only do students mix socially by college rather than by course, but the brightest often attend lectures in a subject other than their own. There is also nothing to prevent an interested science undergraduate from joining many of the Oxbridge arts societies and vice versa. More than one lost Engineering student has found his spiritual home on the university's drama stage.

So, you should certainly take a close look at non-school subjects. If a course description baffles you even after you explored the relevant faculty website, try to discuss it with a teacher or look at some introductory text in the library. By all means do a further search on the net, but remember that it is awash not just with facts but with the outpourings of aggrieved individuals: a key word like Archaeology will bring up several specialist magazines, but also dozens of personal websites in which students criticize their course. You might well have a completely different experience. At this stage, a student needs proper direction and the confidence to be broad, rather than narrow in his choice.

PICKING FOR A CAREER

The psychologist and ability expert Joan Freeman discovered that very bright children can find it especially hard to make career choices. To a quick, thorough mind, Latin and Persian, or Maths and Medicine, can seem equally manageable and attractive. Even ambition is not necessarily a good guide. Your son may want to become a successful, well paid young professional, but teenagers outside the educated middle classes often know too little about real jobs to link university learning with the work people do. The gifted sixteen year olds interviewed by Professor Freeman thought that bankers handle money, or that chemists hand out medicines at Boots.

Knowing more about the reality of work helps pupils to make better choices. It is useful to realise that a banker, for instance, benefits from knowing about politics. He might have to decide where money should be kept, and a bank's investment decisions will have to take into account political developments. City institutions also need science graduates to evaluate business plans and mathematicians to devise financial products.

Then there is the historic precedent. Britain was, for hundreds of years, ruled by white men with an Oxbridge degree often known as "Greats". The idea behind this was that a politician needed a good grasp of the moral principles taught in Classics courses – if only to disregard them. Today's politicians are more likely to have done Politics, Philosophy and Economics (PPE), which elderly dons call "Modern Greats", a course only available at Oxford.

If you are after an academic reputation, it helps to know that this does not depend on the subject an Oxbridge don has specialised in. Cambridge Celtic is taught by people who are no less world renowned than those teaching French or, say, history at the same university. By choosing a less popular course, your son is likely to get personal, undiluted attention from some of the best minds in the field.

Parents doubting that their son has the potential to become a don may not be convinced of such a course choice. Aren't Celtic, Oriental Studies or Medieval Languages peculiar interests which lead nowhere? Surely, a solid, familiar subject like Maths or English is a far safer bet? You want your son to have a career, after all, not to be on the dole.

Luckily for the lovers of deeply obscure Oxbridge courses, this is not so. For instance, Oriental Studies degrees built around complex, demanding subjects like Japanese, Chinese or Egyptology, appeal to top employers in finance or law and supply Britain with a steady trickle of ambassadors. So do Classics, perhaps because they really involve moral judgements or perhaps because so many people in a position to offer highly-paid jobs got a First in them and still feel deep loyalty to the subject. Classics graduates make the Mafia look like a loose-knit group.

In short, by choosing his degree subject, your son is not automatically embarking on a "till death do us part" relationship with Norse or Chemistry. He might remain faithful if he becomes a teacher or lecturer. Otherwise, his degree course will have served as a kind of mental fitness gym in which he can practise unloading cartloads of jumbled facts, writing reports that need to be ready by dawn and having polite, informative chats with people he never met even over the most disgusting sherry.

What about the business world, though? Cambridge Economics may well sound less useful to a budding tycoon than Business Economics, a subject widely offered elsewhere. The world-famous Cambridge course will, in fact, cover this aspect alongside others, but will stress the subject's theoretical base and its historic and political context. Once a student is able to produce sound essays on all this to sharp weekly deadlines, many employers will assume that he can learn how to actually trade in bonds or beer cans at work.

Oxbridge Economics is not all about making money either. Exploring the causes of poverty may be as important as pointing the way towards wealth. The groundwork for the British welfare state was laid in Cambridge by the economist John Maynard Keynes.

Lastly, we must tackle many an English student's secret dream, that of becoming a writer. Don't you need an English degree for that? Well, actually no. Some experts even argue that you might be better off finding something to write about instead.

You can certainly remind your budding literary star that neither Jane Austen nor Charles Dickens, George Orwell, Virginia Woolf or Doris Lessing had any university education. Of Oxford writers, Evelyn Waugh, who celebrated its upper class students in Brideshead Revisited, did History at Hertford. Shiva Naipaul did Chinese at University College, John Le Carré did German at Lincoln, Julian Barnes did French Lit. at Magdalen and Marina Warner did Italian at LMH. Salman Rushdie read History at King's, Cambridge, and J. G. Ballard Medicine at the same college.

Other famous and prize-winning literary authors are non-Oxbridge: Pat Barker read International History at the LSE, London, Anita Brookner did her degree at the Courtauld Institute of Art and Hanif Kureshi did Philosophy at London's own King's

College. The poet Linton Kwesi Johnson has a sociology degree from Goldsmiths' College, London.

So, don't be too narrow in your choice. All Oxbridge degrees, especially if they are "good", which means a First or an Upper Second, will open up a wide range of interesting careers.

WHAT NOT TO DO (ABOUT COURSE CHOICE)

Quite a few parents, delighted at the thought that their son or daughter might indeed stand a chance of getting into Oxbridge, will now be tempted to impose their own dream. More often than not, this is for their daughter to become a medical consultant or for their son the family's first-ever lawyer. There is no denying that these are indeed satisfying and financially rewarding careers. They might even happen if your teenager is very smart and hard-working and actually fancies one of them.

If he'd rather do History or English, though, forget the idea. Telling the boy about the sacrifices you have made by keeping him at school and saving for his tuition fees is unlikely to make him change his mind. Nor will constant hints about the pleasure it would give his dear old gran to see him in a doctor's scarlet graduation gown. Today's young men pick their own colour schemes and careers.

But let's say your more soft-hearted daughter obeys your command, drops her plan to do Oxbridge Philosophy and applies for the "sensible" subject. All well? Unfortunately, not. Medicine and Law are highly competitive fields. Admissions tutors look not just for innate ability, but for genuine, bubbling, information-packed enthusiasm. Faced with a sullen, wistful teenager secretly pining for her abandoned pet subject, they'll rapidly move on to the next candidate. So, there goes the poor girl's Oxbridge dream – and yours.

This is not to say that, in the case of Law, you need to totally give up hope. Many lawyers reach the profession by following up a first degree in another subject by a conversion course leading to a quali-fication called CPE (Common Professional Examination). This involves the cost of an extra year's study, but is an entirely respect-able route in: not only are there always too few good Law graduates for the legal profession to choose from, but solicitors' firms and barristers' chambers actually welcome the variety of intellectual approaches other graduates bring along. Most importantly, science and engineering graduates in particular have the kind of expertise that can be highly useful in court.

You might also find it reassuring to know that even if your girl scoffs at this option, your dream of having a lawyer in the family need not go into the dustbin yet. The Open University offers an excellent Law course, open to applicants of all ages. All it takes are a few undisturbed hours a week, perfect for a parent whose children have flown the nest...

WHAT IS BEST WHERE?

What subject, though, is best studied where? Well, as a start the old saying that Oxford is best for arts and Cambridge for sciences is hopelessly out of date. Oxford regards itself as tops in Medicine, while Cambridge points to its excellence in Maths. Both have world-famous English departments. In real terms, there is little to choose between them. The Government assesses the quality of teaching and research at British universities and regularly lists Oxford and Cambridge among the top three in these fields, which means both have extremely high general academic standards.

What about the best colleges, though? Well, since each of these famous universities is made up of colleges, it is fair to assume that no individual college will be completely useless (we'll deal with the Oxbridge college, a mysterious beast with some very odd feeding habits, in the next chapter). Not every college will take students doing every single subject and you must therefore work out which one offers what from the university prospectus. A college not offering your degree course subject may still accept you, which is nice if you have picked it for its great church organ or badminton court. However, you will then be taught by academics who are fellows of other colleges, while the staff of your own college will take little interest in you.

Experts will tell you that some colleges are the best in the world for some subjects, for instance Trinity, Cambridge, for Maths and Magdalen, Oxford, for Classics. While this is probably true, it is most important for the ambitious postgraduate student seeking to become an expert. An undergraduate might not worry about this or might have other priorities: different colleges specialise in very different aspects of a subject, which means that a student interested in Human Geography will get the best tuition at one college, but someone more interested in Physical Geography is better off at another.

How do you find out where to best study your preferred subject area? The answer to this question was once jealously guarded by private school heads who dined in their old Oxbridge colleges several times a year and kept up with developments. Nowadays, all you need to do is go into the Cambridge Geography course website. This will tell you that many of the fellows (lecturers) who specialise in Physical Geography are at Sidney Sussex, while others specialising in Human Geography are at Emmanuel (www.geog.cam.ac.uk/ people/academic.html). That's college choice sorted.

On the other hand, if your teenager is open-minded and likes to explore new directions within a subject, any college that enjoys a good academic reputation will do him fine. Many students I met had picked a college without worrying too much about its course specialisation and none regretted the result. It can be thrilling to discover aspects of a subject you never knew existed at school.

In other words, the option is either to look quite thoroughly into the subject angle taken by specific colleges or to be fairly relaxed once you've made a general subject choice and go with the flow. In either case, you will end up in a place that has a library, a lawn, a supervisor with a doctorate and a wardrobe without any decent coat hangers.

This, however, takes us to the subject of Oxbridge colleges, which is dealt with in the next chapter.

6
College daze

One of the decisions Oxbridge candidates are asked to make as part of their application is which college they would like to attend. Once upon a time, this was a simple matter. Writing in the "National Review" of October 1906, an anonymous public school headmaster issued this firm advice:

> A parent who asks "which is the best college at Oxford" means "where would my son fall in with the most desirable companions." If your son is a clever boy, send him to Balliol. Even if he does not appear clever, still send him to Balliol, as that is where any latent abilities which he may possess will be drawn out. But if you cannot, will not or do not send him to Balliol, why then send him to New College, Christ Church, Magdalene, Trinity or University (College), and he will have every chance of spending two or three, or even four, completely happy years.

Nearly a hundred years later, the bit about sending a clever boy to Balliol remains pretty valid. But there are lots of other places at Oxford and Cambridge which that boy (or girl) might like to consider for happiness and intellectual stimulation, as well as to improve their entrance prospects.

How do you, though, choose between fifty-nine different Oxbridge colleges? As the college system hardly exists outside Oxbridge, this question can flummox even university educated parents. To make matters worse, there are quite different places called Trinity, St. John's, Pembroke, Magdalen(e), Jesus, Corpus Christi and St. Catherine's at both Oxford and Cambridge.

As a result, some candidates would rather not pick at all. Both the Oxford and the Cambridge prospectus make clear that this is perfectly OK. All students need to do instead is to submit an "open" application. This will leave the decision as to which college, if any, their application will be passed on to the university itself. But is that wise?

It can certainly be tempting. As some dons will point out, almost every college now contains some undergraduates who had ticked this option. However, you need to know that open applications have traditionally been far less successful than targeted ones. The reason for this is unclear. Perhaps colleges do like to be chosen or perhaps candidates who shrink from such a choice come from schools academically less geared than others towards Oxbridge.

Certainly, sending your application form to the university rather than a specific college should not be taken as an obvious way out. It does work, but mainly "for excellent candidates with exam scores in the top percentile marks", as one admissions tutor put it. In other words, if what you have to offer is more mixed, pick your own college.

One way to do this, of course, is by putting down a name at random. Another, traditionally suggested in the Oxford prospectus (and echoed in the Cambridge one), is "not to worry too much about choosing a college," as this is mainly about "your living environment". To the uninitiated, this could suggest that the size of the snooker table in the student common room is all you should care about.

Candidates might want to take this advice with a large pinch of salt. For a start, not all colleges take students for all courses. Also, the most academically renowned ones have vastly more applicants but not necessary more places. Their interview questions, moreover, can be considerably harder. And while at least arts candidates invited up by Oxford may be seen by two colleges, Cambridge ones are not. A Cambridge college faced with a good candidate it nevertheless does not wish to admit will merely put her on a university-wide shortlist (the so-called Pool). Very few Pool candidates do, in the end, get an interview elsewhere.

Most importantly, each college has its own ethos, preferences and, to some extent, admissions policy.

Such details are never spelt out, but a college which describes itself as "exceptionally informal" or stresses its students' varied social and educational background is really saying that it would love to find yet more smart applicants from modest homes. This information can narrow your choice, while still leaving you with a decent shortlist.

LOOK AT THE FOUNDATIONS

One way to understand what real options you have is through a potted history. Oxbridge colleges started off as separate monastic foundations in the 13th century. Religious scholars gathered there to study philosophy and theology, as well as to train clergymen. To fund themselves, they also took up training pious students in law and, later still, less pious ones to become gentlemen. Great minds beavered away at great works along-side this job for a good few hundred years, but college scholarship gradually declined. Some colleges became little more than finishing schools for any 14 to 18 year old boy whose father could pay. By the early 19th century, standards within the two college clusters which made up the universities of Oxford and Cambridge varied shockingly. Their better academics often did not teach and in some colleges bored students fought or vandalized halls to pass the time. Lord Byron arrived at Trinity Cambridge with a live bear and complained: "College improves in everything but learning, nobody here seems to look into an author, ancient or modern, if they can avoid it."

When it became clear that the more academic universities in Germany, Belgium and France had overtaken Oxbridge in reputation, there were calls in Parliament for British standards to be raised. Changes followed, but as they were up to individual colleges, they did not produce identical results. Instead, colleges evolved into three distinct types.

At Oxford, Benjamin Jowett created a "nursery of public men" as Master of Balliol. The college picked the most intellectually hardworking students and turned them into civil servants, diplomats, politicians, colonial governors, judges and law lords. Trinity College, Cambridge, a centre of mathematical learning which had produced Isaac Newton, was bitten by the science bug and began funding research and laboratories.

Other college masters emphasized character development through sport. Identifying with the Athenian philosophers, they saw college as a place to watch "our young barbarians at play", which meant having lots of jolly sporty chaps and the odd classics scholar. Training clergymen was now a minority pursuit.

Colleges did not have to account for their choice to the university, because they lived on their own endowments and the fees they charged. Like local councils making up a town, they cooperated at times, but more often defended their independence tooth and claw. The subjects a college taught, how it taught them and whom it chose to teach were its own business, and each had its own Royal Charter to prove it. Some Oxbridge colleges taught nobody at all.

An endless series of reforms, sometimes imposed by the Government but more often by the colleges themselves in order to pre-empt greater Government regulation, have narrowed college options. The reward has been Government funding. Public money allows Oxbridge to spend about twice as much per student as other universities because it tops up the funds most colleges have accumulated over the centuries from benefactors and property investments. The result is that Oxbridge students, as well as dons, enjoy a stunning environment. Most study and dine in priceless antique surroundings and relax in beautifully kept gardens closed to the general public. Even first years get their rooms daily cleaned by college servants. One Midlands student told me he felt like a lord at his Cambridge college when told he wasn't even expected to lick his own stamps (porters there frank all students' mail), but this shows a slightly warped view of peers' privileges.

The price of reform has been a degree of standardisation. Today, all colleges must comply with Government teaching standards, equality laws, health and safety rules, etc. Out went poorly qualified, non-publishing academics and in came lots of women students. Ethnic minorities, taken as one group, must also be represented, at least if enough of them can be persuaded to apply. Accommodation too has improved. The damp, medieval student rooms, so cold that older graduates recall sleeping in their coats, have been replaced by spacious, electronically equipped bedsits.

Oxbridge colleges, though, remain a mixed bag when it comes to levels of academic success, atmosphere and social composition. Pupils asked to list their preferred college on the application form therefore need to find out as much as they can before picking up their biro. They should certainly disregard the advice given by both Oxford and Cambridge that these places are all alike and so students might as well leave the section blank if they're unsure. This hands the choice to the university, which may push such applicants towards a less renowned college. Measures are being taken to counter this trend, but a 2004 Oxford study revealed that nearly all self-selected "open" applicants were allocated to four of its colleges.

But what can your poor confused daughter, stuck with two parents who stubbornly insisted on earning their living from an early age, do instead? Take her time is the most immediate answer, but below are some methods people use to arrive at the right choice.

ASKING FORMER STUDENTS' ADVICE
If you are considering a college, it is tempting to ask the opinion of someone who went there. For people who don't move in Oxbridge

circles, this is often a teacher, the family doctor or a clergyman. Elderly chaps with fond memories of Oxbridge tend to wax lyrically about the unique character of their college and its unique features, telling you categorically: "Sidney Sussex is the only place to be. Nowhere else has such a jolly crowd, once threw a chap into the Cam for wearing the wrong bow-tie."

On the other hand, quite a few who went there from disadvantaged backgrounds have very bitter memories of their college as a place of loneliness, braying public school boys and no respect for hard work. I was struck to discover that several of the working class students I interviewed turned out to have a father or uncle who was accepted by Oxbridge, but dropped out because he absolutely hated the place. Forget the fun of the Footlights: there were no Swinging Sixties in Oxbridge and, a generation ago, some college boys still wore plus fours. The younger students I met almost didn't go because they were put off by such accounts.

In the end, all were extremely glad they had gone. The Oxbridge of the 21st century, a place where women and state school pupils make up half the undergraduate intake, works even for students who don't know what plus fours are (for those who care: they are knee length sporting trousers). Some quaint college customs, like the annual May Ball, remain unchanged. Some dons still like to say grace in Latin. Some students are still very much richer than others and strangle their vowels. A surprising number know how to jet-sky. All Oxbridge students, though, now wear jeans and communicate by that unique social leveller, the text message.

This is not to say that college life is a vision of perfect harmony. You can still become a hate object, only it will not be for your strong Yorkshire drawl but for pinching other people's chocolate mousse from the fridge. Old men's tales are not a reliable guide to the Oxbridge of today. Its colleges have strong, not always lovable individual traits, but none remains the idle public schooler's haven or the working class student's nightmare of yore. So, you might as well choose your new abode by whichever positive features are most relevant to you.

PICKING BY ACADEMIC REPUTATION

The general fame of a college, often based on the writers, scientists, TV historians or Kremlin spies it has produced, is no reliable guide to what it can offer the undergraduate.

Brilliant minds regularly pack their bags for the stratospheric salaries of Princeton or Yale. Dons become bestseller writers and decamp to the Georgian mansions of Hampstead. And even if they keep living opposite your side of the quad, they will probably be far too eminent to teach greenhorns like you.

Academic reputations certainly need to be date-checked. Trinity College, Cambridge, proudly reveals on its website that it has won more Nobel prizes than France, and a little research will reassuringly tell you that the last time it indeed garnered one of those prizes was in 1998. On the other hand, some colleges still base their reputation on educating a famous philosopher, poet or scientist who has been dead and buried for well over a hundred years.

There is, however, a league table of colleges, which tells you at which Oxford or Cambridge college students get the best grades. The better the grades, so the theory goes, the better the teaching offered there. Traditionally, the top half makes up a kind of academic college elite, so here are the respective lists for 2007.

There are some problems with relying on this information alone. As a start, the Norrington table, thought up by a 1940s don while in the bath, is largely based on how many Firsts the students of an Oxford college obtained, with little weight given to the next-best degrees, Upper Seconds. The same is true of the Cambridge version, the Tompkins table.

The difference between the top and the 30th ranked colleges can be a mere handful of Firsts here and there, which can radically change the table from year to year. Pembroke College, Cambridge, which topped that university's 2002 table, for instance, was seventh in 2001 (but should not be confused with Pembroke College, Oxford, which was 25th). Balliol took the top Oxford place in 2001, but found itself tenth in 2002.

Another problem is that Firsts can also be the result of careful student selection. A college which picks all its candidates on the basis of great intellectual promise, ignoring singing skills or rowing stamina, will find itself higher up on the table, whether or not its teaching is brilliant. Degree subjects can affect the outcome as well. In colleges offering mainly Engineering, a subject that can attract less academic candidates, 35 per cent of graduates may get Lower Seconds or Thirds. Very few Oxbridge English or History graduates do.

Still, this gives you some idea. If a college is somewhere in the top half, it will be harder to get in. On the other hand, once admitted, a really bright student should be in her element. So, if you are dreaming of an academic career or want to spend three years in the presence of truly brilliant and influential minds this is what to go for – at least in the humanities. Aiming low may feel less risky but that does not always make it wise.

Changes have also been made. In 2009, Oxford introduced a new admissions scheme designed to make applicants' success less dependent on college choice. This allowed for promising arts (but not science) candidates to be interviewed at two colleges. A student

---

COLLEGE TABLES

Cambridge Colleges 2008	*Oxford Colleges 2008*
1. Selwyn	1. Merton
2. Emmanuel	2. St. John's
3. Trinity	3. Balliol
4. Gonville & Caius	4. Magdalen
5. Magdalene	5. Christ Church
6. Churchill	6. New
7. Jesus	7. Queen's
8. Christ's	8. Jesus
9. Corpus Christi	9. St. Hugh's
10. Pembroke	10. Lincoln
11. St. Catherine's	11. Corpus
12. Downing	12. St. Anne's
13. Clare	13. Keble
14. Sidney Sussex	14. Oriel
15. Trinity Hall	15. Trinity
16. Queens'	16. Wadham
17. Robinson	17. Hertford
18. Peterhouse	18. University
19. King's	19. Exeter
20. St. John's	20. St. Peter's
21. Fitzwilliam	21. Brasenose
22. Girton	22. St. Edmund Hall
23. Murray Edwards	23. Mansfield
24. Newnham	24. Harris Manchester
25. Homerton	25. Pembroke
26. Hughes Hall	26. St. Catherine's
27. Wolfson	27. Worcester
28. Lucy Cavendish	28. Somerville
29. St. Edmund's	29. St. Hilda's
	30. Lady Margaret Hall

might even be offered a place by a college she never applied to. Cambridge applicants are still only seen at the college of their own choice, but might attend several interviews there, conducted by different dons. However, until the new, fairly complex arrangements are shown to improve the odds, students should try and pin-point the most suitable college.

College choice is slightly less crucial in the sciences. The 20th century growth in scientific knowledge forced Oxbridge to centralise. Many science students now treat their college as what one professor I spoke to called "a bed and breakfast establishment." Rather than sitting all day hunched over a little Bunsen burner in their college, they will work in one of the new physics or chemistry laboratories built with millions of pounds of taxpayers' money. These faculty labs are shared by students from the entire university. Much of the students' progress is assessed by staff working there, although tutorials will still be held in their own college.

So, if your chemistry-mad son ends up at Cambridge, but not at Trinity, his college of choice, do tell him to cheer up: it does not mean he won't make professor, invent a new wonder drug and/or win the Nobel Prize.

PICKING BY STUDENT TYPE

Pupils unsure whether Oxbridge can really want someone like them often try their luck at the colleges with the highest state school intake. These can be easily pinpointed by looking at the university website's statistics page and are, consequently, engulfed by such applicants. As a result, many have to be turned away.

If your daughter really wants to get into Oxford or Cambridge, she might, in the current political climate, be wiser to look elsewhere. It is the more middling colleges with the most conservative entrance policies which are being leaned on to change, so let her target them. One of those castigated for always picking candidates who happen to be fourth generation Oxbridge might love to snap her up. The college will, of course, be doing so because it values her intellectual gifts, but accepting her will also save it from having its knuckles rapped by a nervous university administration.

But how do you find out which college is on the prowl for students like your girl? The answer is that there are two ways. One is by sussing out who might be particularly keen to change their intake. Every so often, a news story appears about a college criticized for having too few state school pupils and this sometimes is followed by a wider recruitment drive. This does not mean that you need to scan the education press for Oxbridge stories every day. Colleges seeking to change their intake proportions tend to be extremely pro-active. If a college keeps adding to the Access initiatives listed on its website, bombards your daughter's inner city school with information and welcomes the girl on her Access visit like a long lost friend, it is what is called by dating agencies "ready to commit."

In practice, this means it intends to take perhaps a dozen pupils like her and it would therefore be a good idea to get an application in, even if she is not sure of getting three As.

Another way to check for promising colleges is the traditional "minor public school house master's route" to Oxbridge: if a college is small, poorish, far from the town centre and low down on the relevant league table, tell your boy to make a beeline for it.

The natural prey of such a college is the rural private school chap who rows, has been in the cadet corps and plays the bagpipes. As a result, it will have far fewer really bright candidates than the rest. Relegation to the bottom of the league constantly threatens this college, and in these days of "Widening Access" even applicants from bog-standard comprehensives are welcome if their presence can avert this fate. They no longer need to be male or middle class, but it helps if they are all-rounders with a good singing voice.

Another default choice are the four original women's colleges. Low down in the academic league tables because they are relatively poor and few of their dons are eminent enough to set university exams, they can't afford to turn away too many applicants. While New Hall and Newnham in Cambridge are still single sex, Somerville and St. Hilda's in Oxford would welcome more really bright males. Before you opt for such a college, though, read the chapter on Oxbridge women.

A final option that should not be dismissed out of hand are Oxford's Permanent Private Halls, colleges established and run by religious groups. Some teach only theology, but Regent's Park, which is mixed, and St. Benet's Hall, which is all male, also offer some secular courses. Their students need not share the college faith and dons sometimes take a special interest in disadvantaged students. Regent's Park, which was founded by Baptists, works closely with black pupils attending inner city schools.

Applying to such a place also gives you a unique advantage: while students may generally pick only one college, a PPH may be listed as a second choice, thereby doubling your admission prospects.

BUT WILL SHE BE HAPPY THERE?

Some colleges can be hell for some students. Many a young Oxbridge feminist has been furious to discover that her lovely college gardens are infested by rugby players barking sexist ditties and trying to bear hug every passing girl. A quiet, non-drinking male student will loathe to share his JCR with teams of drunken rowers listening to what one such wretch described to me as horrible Welsh Indie Rock. If you want to avoid these experiences, don't pick Oriel College, Oxford or Peterhouse, Cambridge. These are the favourite haunts of sporty boys from small public schools.

If, on the other hand, you combine academic interests with a real talent for a major college sport, you'll find a warm welcome in such a place. Don't worry about your background; a winning rugby team knows no class distinction.

This is not to say that you will feel the same way. Your rugby mates may, after all, be pretty brainless and only got in because their school coached them to the hilt. Even in this day and age, a well taught "young barbarian" can still melt the heart of a sporty admissions tutor. So, while your college mates will be half-heartedly aiming for a third in some undemanding subject, you might be trying to pick up top professional skills and a good degree in between games. Such misfits have spoilt the university experience of quite a few male working class students. Female ones tend to cope. Perhaps girls just get on with life.

Some colleges can, on first sight, seem far more scary than others, but don't assume that the grandest places are the ones you'll feel most uncomfortable in. A good example is Oxford's by now much mentioned Balliol College. This has age, beauty, money and a stunning academic record, yet works very well for articulate state school students. Here a sharp mind really is all that counts. What also helps is the presence of a large number of foreign students, mostly from continental Europe. Thanks to a blissful ignorance of the British class system and its linguistic quirks, this group somehow defuses the tension between the two English camps.

In fact, most Oxbridge students, whatever their background, display a remarkable affection for their own college. As long as the place actually has a substantial state school presence, even people from non-university backgrounds tend to cosily settle in. Fears about being among all those terribly posh kids often fade as soon as students meet. Very few privately educated students have parents who are aristocrats or millionaires. So, don't be automatically

put off by a college's reputation as popular with public school crick-
eters or piano-playing southern girls. There will be some such
students about, but they might well be nice, and outnumbered too.

Having said this, a good social life in your college is undoubtedly
harder to build if you are black or from a solidly working class background. Breaking into a group of students who may have known one
another from age six (which can be true of comprehensive school
girls from smart urban areas, as well as for public school boys) sometimes does feel like mission impossible. And you'll be more tempted
to give up, convinced you are being snubbed, if you're the only girl
from Moss Side or an Afro-Caribbean boy from Liverpool.

More often than not, such fears are unjustified. These people are
just used to hanging out together. They also tend to study different
subjects and so will gradually grow apart. By the end of the first year,
students usually have far more in common with those struggling
through the same enormous reading lists than with their bosom
buddy from nursery school. Their best friend now will be the
person they share their tutorials, seminars or college microwave
with. Others bond over drama, student politics, football or darts –
though if you're really shy, getting past the bonding process can
feel like a long wait.

HOW TO BE HAPPY

Happiness at Oxbridge is often a function of understanding what you
are meant to do there. The answer is certainly not just "get a degree".
Instead, dons vaguely mumble about wishing you to explore both
different ideas and different activities in the company of your peers.
Foreigners are often best at translating such waffle. In his wonderful
account of how he made his way from a Burma guerilla camp to
Trinity College, Cambridge, Pascal Khoo Thwe says that being
there was not simply about competing; nor was it just a means to
an end:

> It was a place where you were given the gift of an "interval", a
> time of leisure, where you did not have to make up your minds
> about your beliefs, and learned as much from conversation as
> from lectures and books ©.
>
> (*From the Land of Green Ghosts* by Pascal Khoo Thwe, Flamingo,
> 2002)

Annie, a giggly Danish friend who came to stay with me after
doing a placement year at a very famous Oxford college, put the

same thing rather more simply: "They have all these funny clubs and societies where students meet. At first I couldn't understand why, but then I thought it's a bit like Legoland: you're meant to play with all the little houses, not just to swot. The university put them there as a kind of practice for grown life, I think."

So, try and persevere in finding new playmates. Beth, a nurse's daughter from Northern Ireland recalls that she walked into Fresher's Week at Hertford College, Oxford, shaking with nerves, but forced herself to think: "Excellent, here's 115 potential new friends."

It worked for her, but if your college is really useless at supplying friends, remember that there is always the university. Just treat the college like a plush but rather boring hotel and join the university's student union, drama group or choir. Talk to people in your faculty lab, offer to write for a university mag, volunteer for charity work or political campaigns. There are over 10,000 people roughly your age and ability in the place. Surely, you are not so unique that you have nothing in common with any of them?

This is not to deny that college life does stink for some. In fact, I have spent many hours over the years listening to former students who have been utterly miserable. Until the mid 1980s, this was almost entirely a matter of class: the tone at Oxbridge was set by a wealthy, privately educated majority of students and those without their kind of manners or money had to be quite assertive to survive. Also, quite a few of the older college dons were horrible snobs or misogynists.

But we're talking about your parents' or even grandparents' generation. If an Oxbridge student is constantly unhappy now, there may well be other factors. Often, these are personal, and it is worth knowing that student counselling and health care are pretty good. Both Oxford and Cambridge have come to accept that students can be badly thrown by events happening elsewhere: it is hard to settle into college life when you've learnt that your best friend is now sharing a hammock with your former lover in Goa, the family dog is sick or your father has left home to have the op and become a lap dancer.

Alternatively, a student may just be doing the wrong thing. One exceptionally bright working class student tracked by Professor Freeman in a study of gifted children had been used to being always top of her class. Finding herself surrounded by people who were at least equally smart, her response was to rush back to her books. Rather than enjoy the company of her intellectual peers, she tried to out-work them until she collapsed with exhaustion.

Depression can also be the result of a student not acknowledging that she really needs more cash. Which brings us to yet another way of choosing a college.

PICKING FOR FINANCIAL SURVIVAL

Today no student drops out of Oxbridge due to genuine poverty. The poorest have full university grants, as well as loans designed to cover the basics. Many also receive a college grant, bursary or scholarship.

Older, richer colleges, though, can be rather more generous, and this can affect how well you do academically. A student needing to improve her French language skills because she is studying the subject, but has never been abroad, will have no trouble securing a travel grant from one of the older colleges. These may also offer substantial bursaries for book purchases. College rents there may be kept low by subsidies and students will usually be able to live in for three years, rather than move into more expensive private housing after the first year.

In addition, there are many other types of bursaries, often funded by grateful former students. Some are essentially a cash prize for a good essay on a specific topic dear to the donor's heart. Others are designed to fund small scale research projects. All colleges make provision for helping needy students, but the older the college, the wealthier it is likely to be and the more generous its help. For instance, the average hardship grant in 2002 was £560 at Oxford's ancient Christ Church College, but only £45 at the far newer Keble College up the road. If many students at a college are well off, moreover, there will be little competition for such grants.

So, the poorer you are, the more you might want to apply to a grand old Oxford college like Merton, enjoying an annual endowment income of £2 million, or to Christ Church, which earns a whopping £4.5 million a year from investments alone. Another wealthy Oxford college, St. John's, used to own so much land in the 1930s that people claimed you could walk from Oxford to Cambridge without ever leaving college property. (The Cambridge equivalents of these rich old colleges are Trinity, Gonville & Caius and Corpus Christi.)

There is, of course, another and even more crucial consequence of a college's wealth: it will be able to attract the best, and therefore most highly paid academics – albeit sometimes in exchange for a promise that they won't have to teach beginners. Its libraries too will be better stocked and they may have a smaller students per tutor ratio. Wealth and academic glory often go hand in hand, at least within Oxbridge.

PICKING BY SYMPATHY

Are you a thoughtful, confident talker from an academically oriented, high achieving, well resourced school? Did you gain top marks in all your exams so far, and are your teachers predicting the same for your A2s? Have you won the Maths Olympiad or published a book? If even one of the above profiles fits you like a glove, you stand an equally good chance at any Oxbridge college.

Most Oxbridge candidates, of course, have more modest achievements and many get in nevertheless. The trick is to target the right kind of college. Students from ordinary comprehensives, especially, may want to do a bit of research first. What you need to know is that dons at the most ancient, highly–ranked and visually stunning colleges tend to ask the most difficult interview questions.

This is because a college that combines all three of these qualities can hand-pick its students from an almost infinite supply of applicants. It will still have a state school intake of around 50 per cent, but a high proportion will be grammar school kids or the offspring of other academics, educated at a clutch of top comprehensives. College dons can be quite a cohesive group, seeking similar academic standards and traits.

Certainly, some "three star" colleges prefer candidates already used to verbally juggling a large and varied body of knowledge. Even if their interviewers "move students out of their comfort zone" by asking questions outside their field, years of intellectual juggling do confer some advantage. Let's say you are a brilliant but less intensively taught candidate from an inner city school: being asked to discuss a totally unfamiliar subject may feel pretty scary. You've left your comfort zone by merely walking through a late medieval gate.

Fortunately, attitudes vary even among the most seductive colleges. According to *The Cambridge Reporter* of April 2009, comprehensive school applicants to Cambridge enjoyed a success rate of 76 per cent at King's and of 73 per cent at Sidney Sussex in 2008. Both of these are very old, brainy and fancy places. Meanwhile, down the road, such applicants had a success rate of just 45 per cent at

St. John's and 48 per cent at Clare. Similar data are not available for Oxford, but do note that state school applicants to St. Edmund Hall have a 9 per cent higher success rate than independent school ones, while at Jesus and Magdalen it's the opposite.

If you're determined to get in, please, do not conclude from this tale that you must pick a redbrick college from the bottom of the academic league table. Pupils from state schools often underestimate their abilities and there are comprehensive-friendly dons at even the grandest colleges.However, if you'd like to improve your odds, it may be best to focus on a college that that is not too old, too smart *and* too palatial.

PICKING FOR POWER

While Oxford and Cambridge like to present themselves, at least to the general public, as purely scholastic institutions, they are also something quite different. Politicians, industrialists and journalists will regularly make the weekend pilgrimage to their old college, rather like a medieval lord would visit his fiefdom's learned abbot or a 19th century Jewish industrialist his wise old rabbi.

This is not merely a sentimental journey. While sipping port from cut-glass goblets in a college's panelled dining room, the Oxbridge men – rarely women – who run the country will discuss public affairs, form alliances and take crucial decisions. They will also graciously mix with a few promising undergraduates brought by their tutors. This (to the justified fury of non-Oxbridge graduates) is where to pick up news of top jobs coming up, of Government reshuffles and of business plans that may shake the finances of ordinary people.

But which colleges hold the power key? The answer used to be that there were two: Peterhouse, Cambridge, which produced much of Margaret Thatcher's various Cabinets, plus Magdalen, Oxford, the intellectual cradle of most Prime Ministers. To this had to be added All Souls, a postgraduate college which raised editors for *The Times*.

Former Prime Minister Tony Blair was educated at St. John's, Oxford, and Jaqui Smith at Hertford, but time are a'changing. Gordon Brown went to Edinburgh, Harriet Harman to York. This is not exactly to say that Labour is solidly redbrick. In 2008, its Oxford educated Ministers included Lord Mandelson (St. Catherine's), Lord Adonis (Keble), Yvette Cooper (Balliol) and her husband Ed Balls (Keble, again). Brothers David and Ed Miliband had both been at Corpus Christi. Labour's Cambridge graduates included Andy Burnham (Fitzwilliam), Shaun Woodward (Jesus) and Patricia Hewitt (Newnham).

Even the reputation of Magdalen, Oxford, as the cradle of political leaders is not unchallenged anymore. Of the 2008 Shadow Cabinet, George Osborne, William Hague and Dominic Grieve were indeed educated there, but David Cameron was at a smaller Oxford college, Brasenose. Michael Gove and Pauline Jones were at LMH, while David Willetts was at Christ Church. Tory Shadow Ministers educated at Cambridge include Chris Grayling, (Sidney Sussex) and Ken Clarke (Gonville and Caius).

So, any Oxbridge college can kick-start your political career, though it helps if you also get elected President of the Oxford or Cambridge Union. This, as said earlier, is the university's main debating society – not to be confused with that champion of under-graduate interests, the students' union. Anyone is free to become a member of OU or CU by paying the membership fee, if necessary by instalments.

PICKING FOR BEAUTY

Budding aesthetes in flowing silk scarves will have no problem picking their perfect college: it has to be St. John's, Cambridge, with its Bridge of Sighs spanning the river Cam, or Christ Church, Oxford, with its Tom Tower, Christopher Wren's masterpiece. While other colleges spoilt their appearance by adding on nasty modern fripperies such as labs and snack bars, both remain pure examples of Britain's Classical architecture. There can be no more perfect backdrop for the photo the aesthetes plan to email to their world-wide chat-group on English life.

On the other hand, one future architect I met confidently opted for Robinson College, Cambridge, a 1970s redbrick structure. An out-standing example of the modernist approach seeking to mix clear lines and varieties of shape, it is much loved by its residents, mainly future research scientists and veterinary surgeons. Robinson is also unique in Oxbridge by having one feature perhaps more conducive to beauty than anything else: students' en suite bathrooms.

7

Accessing Oxbridge

What can make a student decide against applying to Oxford or Cambridge at the last moment, sometimes even after he has found a course he really likes, is not what he knows about these places, but what he thinks he does. One 2002 survey, for instance, found that many comprehensive school pupils put the number of Oxbridge undergraduates from state school background at below 10 per cent. The actual figure, in 2008, was 59 per cent at Cambridge and 55 per cent at Oxford.

Others have heard strange and deeply off-putting rumours. One boy proudly told his father's boss of his university plans, only to be told "Cambridge? Well, it wouldn't have been my thing. Do they make you wear them jackets with the long tails only in class or do you have to wear them to the shops as well?" (For the record, Oxbridge students wear jeans during the day, and dark suits or two-piece outfits to formal occasions. It is Eton pupils who pre-pay for a lifetime of privilege by wearing the naff tailcoats at school.)

Schools deal with Oxbridge during careers advice, but this can mean anything. The sixth form head may well give your son a detailed pep talk, based on his own Oxbridge years or on a teacher's workshop attended at one of the two universities. Such a talk will help a pupil understand what is special about studying there, as well as cover entry requirements, subject options and the tutorial system. At best, it will also address the most common fears: "Can I afford it?" and "Is it for people like me?"

More likely, though, your son will have the following experience:

Teacher (slightly rushed as she has to explain university choice to 90 first-generation higher education applicants before tea): Well, John, you've had excellent GCSEs and your AS level work is going well. Have you considered Oxbridge?

Pupil: No, not really.

Teacher (brightly): Well, you might want to. Anyway, let me know what you decide. You might also find a leaflet on the sixth form notice board, unless someone has taken it down. I'll check the deadline for Oxbridge applications if you're keen.

Pupil (keen to end this obvious waste of time): Sure.

The above conversation, reported to me by quite a few people, is the end of many a promising Oxbridge career. How, though, can your son, who has never given a moment's thought to Oxbridge or, worse, tried to find it on the map, work out whether he wants to spend three of the most important years of his life there? One obvious answer seems to lie in a family visit.

WHAT NOT TO DO (ON A SUNDAY)

Having seen the odd colour snap of your son's potential university, you may think that it is enough to let the place speak for itself. Just set aside a Sunday afternoon, check out the train time table or pile into the car. Surely, walking through a pretty town like Cambridge or Oxford will help the boy make up his mind?

I once tried this myself, with my goddaughter. A 17 year old with body piercings and a prediction of top A-levels, she needed only a bribe of double pocket money before agreeing to tag along. While her mother and I then gushed over every gothic building and ornate bridge before settling down to a traditional cream tea in a wood-panelled shop, she sulked on an iron bench outside one of Oxford's most famous colleges. It was raining and, as this was term time, strangers were banned from entering colleges or libraries, even for a quick glimpse. On the drive back, the girl summed up her views: Oxford was boring and old, as well as weird, three of the worst traits in her value chart. She put Sussex at the top of her UCAS list as soon as she had walked through her parent's front door.

A disaster? Not quite. She had some regrets in her student days, feeling she would have been more challenged at Oxford, but ended up with a First and is now a young financial journalist. Her best friend, who did choose Oxford, has yet to settle into the perfect job. Best not to get too worked up about university choice.

How else can you help your son or daughter to make up their mind? Luckily, you don't need to. There is a glut of publicly funded projects designed to do just that.

ACCESS, OUTREACH AND ALL THEIR FRIENDS AND RELATIONS

Public concern that too many students still come from the same class background has generated a veritable supermarket of widening access initiatives. Most of the Oxbridge-linked ones are funded directly by the government and England's Higher Education Funding Council (HEFCE) which between 2000 and 2003 alone spent around £2.4 million a year on three projects, called Aspirations, Summer Schools and Widening Participation.

Oxbridge also draws applicants from the various projects aimed at promoting higher education among inner city pupils, which are funded by the Department to the tune of £63 million per year.

The result has been a myriad of university projects under ever-changing names. Most, but not all, of Cambridge Access activities are now run under the Widening Participation label. Part of Oxford Access has become Outreach. Excellence in Cities, the government scheme which used to run an Oxbridge link-up, has been re-launched as Excellence Hub under the umbrella of another outfit called Aimhigher.

These initiatives which, for simplicity's sake, I shall call Access, are aimed at a wide range of targets, from to FE students to children in care and from mature students to ethnic minority pupils. They are also run by a variety of bodies. Admissions departments, university faculties, colleges and student unions have projects of their own, aimed at encouraging specific groups of potential students. Education trusts run separate schemes.

Some of the most imaginative Oxbridge projects are student-led, and the enthusiasm which these young men and women exhibit for their university is so great it makes you think of those bright-eyed moppets in Disneyland ads. Many talk with almost touching gratitude about the life and opportunities given to them.

So, how does your teenager find out whether he, too, might want to try for Disneyland? The answer is that he can do so in a dozen ways and, even better, without cramping his style. Initially, the idea was that teachers would suggest Oxbridge schemes to suitable pupils, but this has now changed. Finding that many overstretched schools did not respond, Oxbridge has started to encourage individual pupils to book themselves in. Those interested in what Cambridge university has on offer will find most details on the Target Schools, Widening Participation or Open Days websites listed at the end of this book. Oxford's main Access projects can be tracked down in the same way.

If you're a student interested in a particular course, say Law, you may want to phone the Law faculty of Oxford or Cambridge directly. This will lead you to discover that they not only hold an annual "Law conference" in which sixth formers explore the subject, but may also have a Law lecturer giving talks in your town. Below you'll find a selection of what else is on offer.

A TASTE OF OXFORD

Oxford runs some 100 open days each year, targeted at different groups and aimed at dispelling different anxieties. Many involve students chatting to visiting school kids about university life in terms of workload, nightlife and general atmosphere. Oxford also organises events in towns which have traditionally sent very few students. Both open days and the more course-oriented information days may include workshops on the admissions process for visiting teachers. In addition, many colleges run a school visiting scheme in which Oxbridge students from state schools tell pupils about their university experience.

The assumption behind all this is that state school students don't apply in large enough numbers because they feel shy. The events are designed to break down myths and stereotypes about the university being a posh place and replacing them with a vision of Oxford as a world in which students from all backgrounds enjoy life in a "work hard and play hard" sort of way.

In this spirit, questions on open days are often taken by a working class student. If you ever wondered what it's like for a girl from a mining town to share a tutorial with someone who misses her horse, here you will find out: apparently, it is absolutely fine, because she might well share your enthusiasm for philosophy and Garage. And if she doesn't there are, literally, thousands of other people to make friends with. Most Oxbridge students, like the horse lover and you, will have gone to state schools. (Surprised? Given the current level of school fees, few parents can afford to buy their privately-educated daughter a horse.)

Oxford staff unhappy about the weak knowledge base of many state school applicants are also slowly coming round to the idea that some actual teaching may be needed. This has led some colleges to offer potential applicants e-mentoring in certain subjects. Others now run master classes, offer online lectures and broadcast academic debates in science and arts subjects. All these mind-expanding initiatives can be accessed via the Oxford website.

What isn't on offer is explicit help in preparing for the Oxbridge interview, but even so these are useful projects because they are open to all. Although its student organisers advertise events by writing to all schools and FE colleges in February, no teacher involvement is required. Pupils whose school has not organised a day trip for them can book themselves in directly through the website of the Oxford University Student Union (OUSU), http://www.ousu.org/.

A GLIMPSE OF CAMBRIDGE

Cambridge admissions staff and student groups run projects similar to those at Oxford. There are open days, enrichment days and discovery days (see schools800@admin.cam.ac.uk), visits designed to counter misconceptions and conference-type introductions to specific degree courses. Some events are specifically aimed at students attending academies or access courses, rather than comprehensives, grammars or private schools.

Inspire too funds initiatives that bring disadvantaged pupils to Cambridge in order to raise aspirations. The idea is to familiarise them with unfamiliar university subjects such as Philosophy or Engineering and to offer some information about the application process.

Cambridge is also involved in running special events for students and parents in poor inner city neighbourhoods. Speakers aim to convince pupils that the university welcomes applicants of all sorts and offers them a useful education. Some information about course contents may be included and there is ample time for questions and answers. Even larger events, open to all Year 12 students, are held in football stadiums to widen their appeal.

Actual teaching is still rarely offered to visiting pupils, but they are offered a wide range of academic experiences. Some of these build on the knowledge gained from the university's excellent learning sites, now covering English, Science and Classics. Others are based on a more innovative approach: some colleges now run events at least vaguely linked to a popular book or film. One recent taster lecture offered by Magdalene College, Cambridge, was on "Angels, Demons and Ghosts in the Middle Ages".

For what's on offer this year, check out the Open Days web page in the university's online prospectus.

SUMMER SCHOOLS

A further inroad is provided by the summer schools run annually at both universities. Many of these are organised by the Sutton Trust, an educational charity which encourages able sixth formers from a low income, non-university background to aim high. Places go to "plausible applicants for university places with a minimum of five A/A* grades at GCSE".

Sutton Trust events last five days and aim to introduce participants to non-school subjects such as Medicine, or to the university version of other subjects, through talks and workshops carefully tailored to their age group. This is combined with sightseeing and various leisure activities.

These much praised events are run by Oxbridge academics and are completely free: the Trust covers all travel to and from the venue, food and accommodation and also trips and activities. Pupils can apply directly to this scheme, but are advised first to visit the Trust's website, http://www.suttontrust.com.

In addition, Cambridge and Oxford play host to summer schools targeted at mature students, ethnic minorities and pupils at FE colleges. Most come under the umbrella of the *Inspire* scheme and offer pupils a week in the academic world, including sessions about costs, degree subjects, college societies and the prospects of graduates. The scheme is restricted to specially chosen schools so as to ensure that only disadvantaged pupils benefit.

Shorter stays can offer valuable insights into the most avidly fought-over course subjects. Law and Medicine weekends allow pupils to find out not just what such a course would involve, but also what qualities and skills each of these departments seeks.

COLLEGE INITIATIVES

Quite a few individual colleges at Oxford and Cambridge also run their own schemes, either in cooperation with *Inspire* or under their own *Target Schools* label. Some of these are focused on areas of low educational attainment. Jesus College, Cambridge, which has a partnership link with Newcastle, organised a 2003 visit by seventy Year 10 students from the town to the university.

Other Cambridge Colleges are working with specific local education authorities in deprived areas. For instance, St. Johns' College has a scheme in Lambeth and Clare College in Tower Hamlets, while Sidney Sussex and Fitzwilliam are active in Greater Manchester and the North West. For pupils wanting to take the initiative, many colleges also hold a free open day to which anyone who has booked can come.

Some initiatives are based on a more scatter-gun and at times rather defensive approach. When Brasenose, one of the richest colleges in Oxford, was publicly criticised because its state school intake was (just) below half, its Warden responded in *The Guardian* of 26th January 2003 by revealing that it was now involved in no fewer than 51 events aimed at recruiting state school pupils.

So, if your son likes the sound of an Oxbridge college, the best way forward is for him to check out its website or the university website's Open Days page for a suitable event. Chances are that there is more than one and that someone is actually being paid to make him feel welcome.

Both Oxford and Cambridge students also run "shadowing schemes" in which interested pupils can follow an undergraduate around for a couple of days. The visitors get to sit in on lectures and tutorials, as well as visit a student pub, in order to find out how that mysterious creature really lives.

This approach can be immensely reassuring. Apart from proving to the young visitor that many of the turreted buildings contain not just libraries and labs but also state-of-the-art bars, cinemas and snooker halls, talking to a student guide can allay deeper anxieties. The guide may reveal that even Cambridge has a branch of HMV, point out those local businesses which give skint undergraduates part-time jobs and, by his very normality, suggest that most Oxbridge students are neither geniuses nor geeks. To become a Cambridge shadow, go to the Cambridge University Student Union website, www.cusu.cam. Potential Oxford shadows should email admin@targetschoolsoxford.com.

Teachers sometimes have to push their pupils hard before they will set foot on Oxbridge soil but it's worth doing. To be gently introduced to a new subject by a brilliant thinker in their field can be a life-changing experience, even if the student does not end up at Cambridge or Oxford.

DOES ACCESS WORK?

The honest answer is: some of it does. Projects involving a visit to Oxford or Cambridge are definitely worth doing. This is because they enable hundreds of pupils each year to spend time in a very different, rather beautiful world at someone else's expense. They also introduce a proportion of them to brain-tingling new fields.

This does not mean that Access is the answer to every bright sixth former's prayer. A student overwhelmed by the range of events being offered needs to know that some are much more useful than others. Attending a course-related summer school or weekend conference is more likely to get you in than just going on a "shadowing" visit. Also, the longer you can stay, the better. This does not mean, of course, that he who sleeps on a sheet marked "college property" has got admission sorted. He may, however, return with a clearer picture of the knowledge gaps he needs to fill, pick up a clutch of useful new terms and get used to the fussy way in which academics ask the most simple questions.

Any Oxbridge visit, though, will give you some advantage should you be invited back for an interview. Walking up to those ivy-clad towers and stained glass windows next time should feel less like approaching Dracula's castle and more like returning to a place of nice memories like Blackpool or Benidorm. And a relaxed interviewee is more likely to impress the admissions tutor.

The hometown events held outside the university may be less trouble to get to, but they lack this psychological hook. Your daughter might come away eager to apply but seeing Oxbridge for the first time at the interview could still put her off. Still, a confident, very well taught pupil can certainly further improve his odds by attending a local talk.

Do Access projects ensure that "the brightest and best" succeed? This is more doubtful, despite the great effort put into them, especially by the unpaid student volunteers. One reason is the total absence of talent spotting. You may have a young Isaac Newton in the family, but nobody at Access is in the business of finding out. Although university lecturers are involved in many events and may spend up to a week with a small group of pupils, they are not expected to even guess at an individual's ability. The Access brief is, above all, to encourage applications.

This means that while your son might be a deep thinker asking super-smart questions in his summer school, no formal note has to be taken of this. So, when it comes to having his application considered, he is in the potluck bowl with everyone else. Rumour has it that the odd don may quietly suggest to a particularly impressive participant that he should perhaps consider an application to her college, but this actually is against the rules and as far as it goes.

The opposite approach is taken by America's most prestigious academic institutions. Over there, the top universities' talent scouts visit schools and summer camps not to encourage the most doubtful kids, but to identify the most talented ones. The latter are then asked whether, subject to passing their SATs, they would honour the university by becoming one of its students. Which situation would you rather be in?

The main flaw of Oxbridge Access, though, is the underlying assumption that the problem lies with the pupils themselves. The schemes, I was repeatedly told, were necessary because state school pupils "are hesitant to apply because of low self esteem". So, the stated aim is to give them the confidence to apply – not to ensure that more state school pupils actually get in. Access does not even have a numerical target when it comes to raising the proportion of state school entrants, rather than just the number of applicants, to a more representative level.

When I asked Access officials if widening participation might not also require a change in the current entrance procedures, the response was embarrassment. People emphasized that they were not campaigning for any such thing, heaven forbid. Both paid Access staff and student volunteers insisted that entry remains a matter entirely for the university's admissions department. They had no views on whether the system was fair or could be improved. Pupils' university choice was all that mattered – and was clearly the only thing they could influence.

So, Access concentrates on broadening the field of applicants. Colleges keen to admit more state school pupils, and especially more working class ones, now have a much bigger pool to draw from. Many take advantage of it. Access cannot, however, force a specific college to abandon the idea that Winchester public school is the main source of intelligent human beings nor curb its enthusiasm for fresh-faced kids from genteel country towns. Colleges are independent bodies or, to put it disrespectfully, college admissions tutors are a bit like horses: you can take them to the water, but you cannot actually make them drink.

Government expenditure of some £10 million on Access in the four years leading up to 2003 had little impact. In fact, the proportion of state school students entering Oxford actually dropped by two per cent that year. Cambridge acceptance figures for this group rose by the corresponding percentage, but the cart remained stuck. By 2005, only 53.4% of new Oxford undergraduates came from state school backgrounds, down 0.4 percentage points from the previous year. At Cambridge, the corresponding figure was 56.8%, which was a little better, but still 0.1 percentage points down.

What this means is that the two universities' annual intake had been made up of roughly 55 per cent state school students since 1999. As the benchmark figure which the government had set for Oxbridge is 75 per cent, progress could fairly be described as non-existent.

Public criticisms of this state of affairs made by politicians and education journalists (including this author) have now begun to change the picture. In 2008, Cambridge proudly announced that the proportion of UK state school students admitted by the university had now risen to 59 per cent. Oxford revealed a somewhat more modest rise to 55.4 per cent. Whether either of these improvements was due to Access or just reflected a policy decision by admission heads to alter the intake proportions is impossible to tell.

WHY ACCESS IS WORTH DOING

Despite their undoubted flaws, Access projects, which vary greatly in focus and scale, work for some teenagers. Merely attending an Access event will gain your son some brownie points if he decides to apply and he might well do so because Oxford or Cambridge now seem less alien. The rest depends on brains, careful subject and college choice, good interview preparation and a bit of luck. Reassured that Oxbridge is the place for them, boys and girls from urban comprehensives and rural council estates handle the entrance process right and get in.

But how many do? There are no official data about the success rate of pupils attending the big Oxbridge Access events. It is not even clear what proportion decide to apply after attending. Sutton Trust schemes run in Cambridge in 1999 resulted in nearly a third of participants getting in. Students running a smaller, more socially focused scheme, which includes expert talks on general interview skills, told me that between 3 and 5 per cent of their pupils were now Oxbridge students. Of those attending a medical summer school, for which all participants had been intellectually cherry-picked, 10 per cent, or five out of fifty, were accepted.

In other words, while such figures give applicants some hope, they don't exactly amount to a cast-iron guarantee of success. So, don't let your teenage whizkid get too fixated on the idea of spending the next three years doing PPE in a manor with its own tennis court. He needs an attractive second choice, just in case. Greater certainty would be nice, but it may have to wait until Oxbridge yet again alters it entrance quotas or adopts an entrance process that works equally well for all.

8
The paper trail

The most crucial thing to do, if you'd like to study at Oxbridge, is to actually apply. This involves submitting a batch of forms, some but not all online. You will need to do all this in good time. Don't even dream of leaving the job to the night before the deadline. Try to paste up or photo-copy everything you plan to send. This way you can write draft versions first and also mark what documents or information you still have to ferret out.

Oxbridge candidates usually have to supply four separate bits of information, five if they are applying through the *Cambridge Special Access* scheme for disadvantaged students. There is a further online form for students required to take a pre-interview test either at an approved centre or at their school.

Daunting as this may sound, most of the information requested is perfectly straightforward: what you are being asked for are relevant personal details. Surely, somebody in your family remembers your date of birth? The exam details requested are also simple enough.

Candidates still at school don't usually battle alone with their UCAS application forms. Once you have looked at yours, do approach a teacher or careers advisor to help you with the factual bits (this is not a job for parents). External candidates will have to assemble exam information from the records they have kept.

Still, there is quite a lot else to do, and we'll go through it bit by bit.

FORMS TO FILL IN
Oxbridge until 2008 expected candidates to complete a separate, university-generated form in addition to their UCAS form. However, both Oxford and Cambridge have now abolished this, for UK students at least. What this means is that you can now apply to all the universities of your choice through the standard UCAS form.

Still, to be considered for a university place, you need to comply with a whole series of information requests:

1. UCAS Information

The first thing to fill in is the main body of the UCAS form, in which you give your personal details and list all the university courses you have picked. You can list up to five courses, but if you are applying for Medicine, Dentistry, Veterinary Medicine or Veterinary Science, this drops to only four. Most of the information requested on the form is of a pretty general kind and advice on how to fill it in can be found on www.ucas.co.uk. If you are on your school's Gifted & Talented Programme, make sure to tick the relevant box.

2. The UCAS Personal Statement

The UCAS form, which changes slightly each year, also requires you to provide two longer bits of writing. One of these is your Personal Statement. This is your very own promo, in which you are trying to sell yourself as the kind of student any course leader might like. Are you hard-working, imaginative, a born linguist or a lover of abstract thought? The resulting document, which should be upbeat, persuasive and perfectly spelled, must adhere strictly to the word limit set.

The best way to achieve this is to write crisply, without labouring your points, and to back-up your claims with examples. You don't need to use old-fashioned language in order to communicate with an old university, but make sure your grammar is correct. Oxbridge candidates need to be a little creative in terms of style, so don't just adapt the dull Personal Statements found on the internet. This is especially important if you are applying for an arts course. Try to describe yourself in your own voice. This can mean a lot of rewriting at the draft stage, so set aside a few evenings for it.

While one common way in is to describe how you approached a school project or A-level topic, keep in mind that more is required here: top universities look for clear signs of independent academic activity. Evidence of this can be work you have done on an A-level topic beyond school requirements. Being able to also list an intellectual interest of your own, especially if it is relevant to your university course, makes you look even smarter. This can be an aspect of physics, a form of poetry or medieval warfare.

Now tell the reader what inspired this interest and how you are pursuing it. What are you hoping to understand and what have you already learned? Which books, excursions or maths problems have thrilled you? Do you have any career plans yet?

Hobbies which have some bearing on your university plans should probably be mentioned next, but treat this with some caution. If you're into scuba diving, for instance, a future science interviewer may well ask you to explain the physical laws which make this possible.

Voluntary work, leadership activities and honours you achieved also belong here, so for heaven's sake don't forget that you are involved in the Maths Olympiad. Try to point out what skills you have developed as a result and don't be too modest: describing your academic side does not count as showing off.

Some factors mentioned can be personal: medical students, for instance, are often drawn towards this career by an illness in their family. Mainly, though, the personal statement is a chance to create a positive (but not arrogant) academic profile of yourself. This can be made up of quite diverse elements, though every university loves a reader. When mentioning books, make sure you give the correct authors' names and titles.

It is also sensible to include some reference to your home circumstances if they affect your work. Parental unemployment, poverty, homelessness or the need to care for an invalid relative are in this category. Try to avoid vague phrases if you would like to convey the personal consequences. Writing that you spend much time helping your parents tells the interviewer nothing.

Stating instead that you help out on weekday afternoons in the family's Chinese takeaway or each Saturday at the supermarket suggests that you are conscientious in your commitments and have achieved your present academic record against considerable odds. Such information will not demean you in the eyes of the university. Staff really do look for a good mix of candidates and I have met Oxbridge students with backgrounds like these.

So, anything you spend lots of time on might be worth putting in your UCAS form and if it's a bit unusual and memorable, the better. Don't be swayed in your efforts by some recent rumours. While the head of admissions at Cambridge, Geoff Parks, let it be known in May 2009 that the personal statement would no longer count towards a candidate's academic assessment, he was much misunderstood.. Cambridge (and Oxford) dons still read all statements and often base interview questions on what they find.

Do, however, beware of exaggeration. Having seen a TV film about George Stephenson does not yet qualify you to state that you are passionate about engineering. Above all, don't mention that impressive-sounding book you were planning to order ages ago. You won't get round to reading it in time for your interview and fibbing will do you no good. Oxbridge dons have had centuries of practice in teasing out the truth.

3. The UCAS Open Reference

The next bit of writing your completed UCAS form must contain is an Open Reference, which is a recommendation from a teacher, tutor or head. This should mainly be a thumbnail sketch of the pupil's qualities, but should also include information on relevant outside interests.

The referee should certainly not only provide a summary of work done at school. She must also make clear how any qualities mentioned are reflected in the pupil's independent academic work. The idea is to impress all the universities listed, but also to ensure that Oxbridge sees the applicant as outstanding and suited to its learning style.

If the student has succeeded in his career so far against personal odds or great poverty, but has not referred to this himself (many disadvantaged students take hardship for granted), this should also be made clear. Generally, a candidate requires more than a cautious endorsement along the lines of "he is a good student and we recommend him". His tutor or head has to be a strong advocate for his cause and a few superlatives like "one of the best" will not go amiss.

Pupils are entitled to see this entry and can even make suggestions, if only to ensure that the Personal Statement and the Open Reference do not repeat the same points. If an Open Reference is particularly tepid, I do feel the candidate deserves an explanation. The referee might be quite right about his academic potential – or quite wrong about the kind of student Oxbridge, especially, might be looking for.

I would certainly not drop the idea of applying there at this point, unless strong reasons were given to me. Because the Oxbridge interview counts for so much, some clever students do get in with a less than brilliant reference.

The Open Reference should also describe the school. If it is not an average comprehensive, some details should be provided on its educational status and the nature of its intake. If a school has the kind of problems that are likely to affect student performance, all universities will want to know.

It is important to spell out anything of relevance quite clearly here, above all that there is a good match between subject choice and a student's gifts, interests and work habits. (Applicants who have picked different courses at different universities may be asked why. Oxbridge, for one, likes to feel that the course you have chosen is the love of your life. Any dithering between the respective attractions of Maths and French can get you dismissed as a wrong 'un.)

So, what are Oxbridge admissions tutors looking for? Well, it depends partly on the individual, college and course, but quite a few of them agreed that the kind of Open Reference which would make them feel particularly well-disposed towards a student might be a variety of this.

OPEN REFERENCE SAMPLE

John is a very bright and inquisitive student who takes an active interest in physics well beyond the requirements of the school syllabus. His classroom work has consistently been above A-level standard and truly outstanding at times. The GCSE and AS level marks he obtained were among the highest in his year. Project work John has undertaken has impressed the staff as well-planned, imaginative and thoroughly researched. He is also involved in an online project by young people trying to set up their own science website. John is the kind of autonomous, interesting pupil we do not see every year.

Moreover, John has maintained this standard despite difficult economic circumstances. Unemployment within the family has required him to take on weekend work. This suggests that he is focused and determined, as well as bright.

Ours is a rapidly improving school, which has just been upgraded to become a Special Language Academy. Most of our intake comes from the local neighbourhood, which is one of the most deprived in London. 50 per cent of our students qualify for free school meals and an even higher proportion (70 per cent) have English as a second language.

---

4. Candidate's Work Sample

A university interested in a candidate may also want to see one or two samples of her work in the subject she is planning to study or a related one (which can mean History, if she is applying for a course in PPE or Oriental Studies). This sample can be a completed project, an extended essay or a piece of work done in class during a 45 minute test. Although the school can send any of these, admissions tutors like you to include class work. Its advantage, they feel, is that one can be sure no one else has been involved in producing it.

If you are able to send an extended project undertaken to gain an A* grade, this is even better.

5. Special forms for disadvantaged applicants

Teachers supporting Cambridge applications by disadvantaged students should fill in the Cambridge Special Access Scheme form, http://www.cam.ac.uk/admissions/undergraduate/apply/forms/ csas.pdf. There used to be an Oxford equivalent, the Oxford Application Support form, but this has now been abolished and teachers should provide relevant information in their Open Reference.

Further personal information will be requested from students by either Oxford or Cambridge if their UCAS application is being considered. This is done through the new Supplementary Application Questionnaire sent out by the university.

6. Application forms for pre-interview subject tests

These online forms need to be filled in and sent off by applicants before the UCAS form. Students hoping to study Medicine at Oxford or Cambridge or Veterinary Medicine at Cambridge need to apply to the BMAT assessment centre at which they'd like to sit the test. Details can be found on www.bmat.org.uk.

Candidates applying for Law at Oxford need to register for the LNAT test before filling in their UCAS form. This test too is taken at a special centre, but you can access the registration system through the LNAT site, www.lnat.ac.uk. Cambridge no longer uses the LNAT and in 2009 replaced it with a test of its own. Details can be found on http://www.law.cam.ac.uk/admissions/ cambridge-law-test.php.

Cambridge Maths candidates need to take the STEP test (http:// www.admissionstests.cambridgeassessment.org.uk/adt/step), which is now administered by a new education company, *Cambridge Assessment*. Candidates should register for it at an examination centre or their school.

Students taking the Cambridge Thinking Skills Assessment Test (TSA), need not pre-register, as they will take the test during their interview. However, those taking the Oxford Thinking Skills Test (TSA) need to register at a test centre administering it or at their school. Information on both TSA tests can be found on http:// www.admissionstests.cambridgeassessment.org.uk/.

Not all of this is free. UCAS is charging a £17 processing fee and candidates sitting the BMAT or LNAT need to check their websites for the amount applicants have to pay. A UK student genuinely unable to afford test fees can ask the university to be reimbursed.

Students also need to be aware that rules about pre-interview tests and the course subjects that require them frequently change. They might even be replaced by one single entrance exam one day. Meanwhile, though, applicants must read the test details on the Oxford or Cambridge website with great care.

CONQUERING THE PAPER TRAIL

This large list of requirements means that even the most motivated candidate requires a fair bit of assistance from her school. Private schools often manage the whole process for their pupils, right from explaining the forms to editing candidates' draft Personal Statements. Comprehensives which regularly send pupils to Oxbridge also often have a routine in place that smoothes a determined pupil's path. They direct candidates towards the right forms, offer advice on what they might write and ensure that the tight deadlines are met. One such school even arranged for a pupil with unemployed parents to have his processing fee paid out of public funds.

The most disadvantaged candidates, though, also often attend the least Oxbridge-oriented schools, and this is where the system breaks down. Even those few student run Access schemes which offer guidance on the applications process cannot change the fact that teachers may be unsure about what to write, or students unused to filling-in forms. The good news is that Oxbridge, which used to argue that the paper trail was essential to attract "non-traditional candidates" has now taken this problem on board by abolishing some forms. The bad news is that the introduction of subject tests has generated others.

Rereading all those forms, it certainly struck me as amazing that thousands of young people every year managed to return them at all. Even more amazing is that so many of them handled the process skilfully enough to be offered a place. Perhaps this is a measure of the qualities possessed by Oxbridge candidates (one admissions tutor certainly thought so) but, more likely, it reflects the sterling support provided by so many schools. What this book enables you to do is to maximize the value of that support, or to get by without it, in case it is not there.

9

What not to wear to the interview (and other worries)

Having received the completed paperwork, Oxbridge does a month of sorting. As long as your teenager has very good GCSEs, AS grades and A-level predictions, or did very well at a pre-interview test, he is likely to be asked up for an interview. Contrary to popular belief, the majority of candidates are.

While pretending that interviews are cool, a student will be thrilled, as well as panicked by this development. You may want him to get on the net immediately and track down the cheapest fare to Oxford or Cambridge, but he has more urgent matters to resolve. The first of these concerns his appearance.

What to wear for the interview can seem like a trivial question, but if both of you are nervous about the event you might be pushed into expenses the family can ill afford. So, forget that Paul Smith suit which your son says is a must-have for the great day. Hardly anybody wears suits for the interview anymore. If the admissions tutors who will interview him really cared about designer clothes, they would be working in a place with far better salary cheques than Oxbridge.

Even the message sent by a certain type of old clothes is out of date. Among the sixth formers fidgeting as they wait for their interview, there will invariably be one confident young man dressed in his father's frayed, greenish-blue tweeds, with the label of the best Cambridge tailor stitched into the silk lining. Unless, however, he also has a lot between the ears, he too will not necessarily get in.

This is not to say that clothes don't matter at all. Turning up in dirty, scruffy gear, with mud-covered shoes indicates a lack of respect for the institution you are supposedly keen to join. So, smart casual is the order of the day. This means jeans are OK but should be in a healthy state, an ironed shirt might be preferable to a T-shirt and if it has to be a T-shirt, let it be plain. Anything imprinted with an even mildly obscene message is absolutely out.

The same basic rule, of course, applies to girls. They don't have to wear skirts, suits or dresses any more, but it probably does no harm to look nice. This does not mean showing masses of bare skin. Even the most heterosexual male don will take this as a sign of desperation.

Gay men, whatever their usual style, are wise to avoid looking wildly camp at their interview. It will only get you typecast as one of those idle, tiresome chaps seeking to relive Brideshead, Evelyn Waugh's great homoerotic novel, set among upper class students in 1920s Oxford.

A light jacket might usefully complete the outfit of someone applying for Medicine or to one of the posher colleges, such as Magdalen, Oxford, or St. John's, Cambridge. Clean hair, needless to say, is a must. I would not go into a panic about nose rings or even tongue studs at this point. Students sporting them can be seen in a few medieval quads, so clearly they are not, in themselves, a cause for rejection.

Lastly, it is crucial that once these basic principles have been absorbed, you leave the choice of interview gear to your daughter or son. It's no good sending someone off to an important interview sobbing: "I look like a prat."

MANNERS

Most people teaching Oxbridge entrance include a smattering of manners. This usually means things like sitting straight, looking (at least occasionally) at the interviewer and speaking clearly, rather than mumbling. Most academics I have interviewed swear blind that manners don't matter one bit. What they are looking for is talent, and if talent bites its nails, that's OK with them.

I am not so sure these academics are telling the whole truth. Obviously, saying "may I sit down", rather than just sinking into the nearest chair is no longer an adequate entrance qualification. Equally obviously, a young Maths genius scratching his back as he rattles down perfect formulas, explanations or equations is rarely shown the door.

However, if your child is not a genius but is still rather bright, then sheer pleasantness may well tip the scale. After all, the interviewer will have to spend at least an hour per week in a small study with the applicant. This is a less attractive proposition if she cannot easily hear what the boy is saying, if she risks being showered with dandruff or if he does not show her any respect.

THE HORRORS OF FISH

One of the key anxieties I have heard expressed are about table manners. Interviewees eat their meals under the medieval eaves of the guest college's often very impressive dining room. One girl recalled her horror when served a whole Dover sole at her first dinner there. How on earth was she going to get this dead body into an edible state?

She need not have worried. The dinners are not a test of whether you'll fit in, just a way of meeting other students. Of course, if your son takes the opportunity to get drunk and abusive instead, it might be assumed that he is not interested.

Still, for the sake of reassurance, you might want to pass on the basic rule: treat the fish like a travel bag to be unzipped; cut round the edge, throw it open so you have two fillets, one of which should have the skeleton attached to it. Lift out the skeleton with knife and fork, put it on the side of the plate and start eating, preferably with your mouth shut.

And, by the way, the slightly deformed looking bits of cutlery next to your plate are the fish knife and fork, to be used much like the other kind. If there are several knives and forks are laid out, start with the ones at the outer edge, working your way inwards, course by course. The same rule applies to the row of shiny wine glasses to the right of your plate.

Conversely, Oxbridge dons keen on wider participation might also wish to learn something new. Fish is eaten by most of the population in the form of easily dissected, breadcrumb covered fillets without bones. Perhaps the hall menu in interview week could take account of this fact.

10

What to expect at the interview

Having resolved the big issues, like whether a micro-skirt qualifies as smart-casual and whether someone living on prawn crackers can define herself as a visiting vegetarian, your jittery daughter can now address herself to secondary matters. In other words, she can start wondering what on earth, Oxbridge actually wants her to go up for. Is the interview just a grown-up conversation?

To many non-university parents it seems logical that being such a grand place, Oxbridge has summoned their teenager primarily to see whether she will fit in. They will consequently advise her to be on her best behaviour and, perhaps, "to treat these great professors with respect".

If you are a teenager, you are likely to interpret this to mean that you must not talk too much, not query anything you will be told or, heaven forbid, disagree explicitly with any, however, objectionable statement. It also suggests that you should sound as posh you can and not dangle your legs in those hideous, freshly polished new shoes. The prospect is dire enough to make you want to miss the train up on the appointed day.

In fact, the purpose of your forthcoming visit is something completely different, so just forget this advice. The word interview is a misnomer which can trip up even the most talented students from non-university backgrounds. What awaits you is a verbal ability test, supplemented in a few subjects and colleges by a short written test, set by the interviewers. Only candidates for the most popular courses also sit a proper, scientific exam, devised by outside experts. It is very much easier to get into Oxbridge once you know what to expect.

Most British universities no longer routinely interview potential students. Only those whose record is defined as "borderline" are still invited in for a chat. That tense half-hour in which a terrified 17 year old, who had probably never talked to adults outside her immediate family before, faced three men in corduroy trousers sitting behind a shabby wooden desk bit the dust in the 1970s. A friend who started his academic career then and is now a sociology professor at a popular university, recalls it as a supremely pointless exercise. "What on earth do you ask somebody applying for a subject they haven't done at school?" he had asked a fellow interviewer. "Beats me," was the reply, "but we always pick the girl with the longest legs."

Oxbridge, though, has an almost religious belief in the magic of the interview. Combined only in some courses with a test devised by education experts, it is meant to establish the candidate's ability to think. Few state school candidates, of course, get this far without such an ability, but displaying it while balancing on a 16th century armchair which keeps tilting backwards can be a different matter. Not all of us spontaneously do our best thinking among the oak-panelled set of a period film.

So, how do you cope, apart from by reminding yourself that you are there because Oxbridge was impressed by your potential? The answer will be obvious to every pint-sized boy scout: be prepared. Find out as much as you can beforehand.

DOING THE GROUNDWORK

Before setting foot in Oxbridge, it is wise to do yet another bit of light reading. Start by skimming through the essay you sent and your personal statement, so you're prepared to talk about anything mentioned there. Look at the university prospectus again, then recheck the course details given on the faculty website. You want to know where you are going and why.

Applicants should also find out in advance what exactly the structure of the interview will be. As every college can choose its own, this can vary considerably. Take two Cambridge candidates: if your daughter applied to read History at King's, she will have to sit a written test at her interview. Her classmate, interviewed for the same subject at Jesus, may get only oral questions. If the invitation or prospectus does not tell you what to expect, it is perfectly OK to ask the college by email.

Next, it helps to know that "the interview" may consist of up to three separate conversations. A candidate is usually interviewed by the admissions tutor teaching the course applied for in her college room. A second tutor may be present, especially if the candidate has mentioned a personal interest in an unfamiliar field. For instance, a History tutor expecting a candidate who has done a project on

Northern Ireland may bring in an expert on the Province from another college. An English tutor specialising in Victorian poetry might ask an expert in modern American literature to sit in on the interview with a young Alice Walker fan.

An arts candidate invited up by Oxford may from 2009 be seen by two colleges. If neither is keen, he may even be passed on to a third one. This does not necessarily reflect a low opinion of the lad. Tutors and colleges often have very specific approaches and they like candidates to fit in with them. Science candidates are only seen by one college, though this can mean attending several interviews.

A prospective Cambridge student is seen only by the college of her choice, or by one picked for her by the university if she submitted an "open" application. She may have two interviews there, occasionally three. Should the two sides not hit it off but the girl still manages to impress, she'll be put into a "pool" of shortlisted candidates. If another college with places to spare is keen, it will fish her out for a further interview.

Traipsing around between colleges or waiting for one's turn to be seen can be a nerve-wracking experience. So, try and remind your daughter before she leaves that her success does not, in fact, depend on her interview performance alone. The results of any pre-interview tests will certainly count. So will a good open reference from her class teacher, especially if he does not just praise her school work but also broader qualities such as motivation and a willingness to read beyond syllabus needs. The teacher should also mention any obstacles she had to overcome during her schooling.

If your daughter has attended any Access event, even if it was just a morning visit during an open day, this again will count in her favour. Attendance is interpreted as a sign of commitment, yet another quality Oxbridge dons like to encounter. And if she actually visited the same college she is about to be interviewed in and made a good impression there, even better.

Lastly, a good personal statement, crisply written and packed with details about her own interests and achievements, will direct questions towards areas in which she can shine.

TALKING THE TALK

Most interviewers start off gently with small talk unrelated to the course, often while your son is still in the waiting room. This is not the moment to show off, but to connect with a stranger by exchanging feather-light bits of information. The first question, especially if the interviewer is no creative genius, might well be: "Did you have any difficulty getting here?"

All your son is expected to do in return is to keep the ball rolling. "No," by itself, is a conversation killer. "No, but it's quite a long journey up here from Sunderland, what with half the points system not working," will do fine. Such an answer allows his conversation partner to ask questions about the boy's home town, his school or the state of British railway engineering. His answers will help to make him a real person to the interviewer.

Do tell your son not to fret too much about his answers at this stage. Anything said to him while he is still taking off his coat is unlikely to be a test.

Once everyone is seated, talk will rapidly shift to scholarly matters. Interviews have become less rambling and more academically focused, but neither of the academics present is likely to dwell on the candidate's A-level syllabus. Instead, he may want you to talk about a school essay sent in or about coursework. Questions will centre on your research, the independent reading you did and the problems you encountered. Not only does this gives you a chance to show how you think, but it confirms that the document was really all your own work. Remember to mention what it is you enjoy about the course-related subject!

Another "easy" question sometimes used to kick-start the actual interview is: "Why did you choose this college (or Oxford)?" Fortunately, the traditional answer, "Daddy spent such a wonderful three years here" is no longer good enough. Still, it is probably best to avoid total honesty, if that would mean saying: "Because you're rich enough to give me a decent hardship grant."

A better idea would be to suggest that you had heard that it was best for a specialist field which you are becoming interested in, say Medical Physics or Civil Engineering. Candidates who have done their net research might even add that their interest in this field was prompted by a piece in New Scientist, contributed by one of their own dons. Remember, you can find this inside dirt on the college website!

Be cautious about bringing up your own ambitions here. Magdalen College, Oxford, has indeed educated most British Prime Ministers, but "because I want to run the next government" is still the wrong answer. While this might be true, your university chances will be far better if you focus on the academic training the college can offer. True, Magdalen has unbelievable connections and an old boy network that seems to run the world, but to mention this would be rude, proof that you don't understand the subtle strategies needed for political careers.

There is a further reason, of course, to talk about academic work, not networking: your future dons are human beings. They like to spend their time with people who enjoy their teaching and give something back, rather than regard their tutorials merely as stepping stones to power.

In any case, such questions mark the end of the warm-up. After that, things tend to get rather pacey. Transmogrifying into a more paunchy, less well-dressed version of Jeremy Paxman, the interviewer will start checking what kind of things, in or outside your field, you can understand, explain or make sense of. Now, question might follow question, without any feedback about whether you hit the spot.

This style can be quite disconcerting for some candidates. State schools have in the last two decades gone out of their way to communicate with students in ways that build confidence, rather than just implant knowledge. They emphasize the positive, try to be soft on delicate young egos.

Many Oxbridge interviewers, on the other hand, believe in the rapid fire approach, in tough questioning not interspersed with any reassurance or praise. After all, they have scores of candidates to see within a couple of days. By pressing on, they hope to quickly discover hidden strengths, expose weaknesses, get to the core.

This is not the moment for a candidate to feel shy. No intelligent guess or opinion is likely to harm her chances of acceptance. What matters is to take a stand, then back it up by giving good reasons or facts. Often, she will be invited to apply familiar theories or principles to new areas. A History candidate, for instance, might be asked the following question: if the appeasement of Hitler was a bad thing in 1938, would we now be right to appease North Korea's dictator?

Fortunately, the girl is not expected to issue the final ruling on this world-shaking matter. The interviewers are trying to extend her understanding of the subject by their questions, not trip her up. A promising candidate will be happy to speculate on whether the theory behind the first scenario might be effective in the second. The skill the interviewer is fishing for here is an Oxbridge favourite: lateral thinking, known to members of the computer generation as "mental cut-and-paste."

It is also important to realise that candidate and interviewer are playing a subtle game. A Politics tutor, for instance, might choose to put forward a quite outrageous proposition: "Could it not be argued that dictatorship is a natural form of government suited to many nations?"

A young candidate might seriously consider walking out at this point in horror. Are these ghastly old fogeys the people she had considered studying with? Best to suppress this emotion. This is not the time to run, but to hold your ground. Chances are, the tutor is merely playing devil's advocate. He'll want to hear why she would disagree, and will expect logical grounds and/or concrete examples. She is being invited to play intellectual tennis and should hit the ball back hard but politely.

Scoring a point here means showing that one would be responsive to this kind of teaching, has respect for its learned practitioners, is articulate and keen enough on the subject to have done some independent reading. The interview is a selection test for the ability to do academic work. Could this candidate, the interviewer asks himself, benefit from tutorials, engage in dialogue, contribute to college life?

WINNING STRATEGIES

While your son has no control over what questions he will get or how they are delivered, there are strategies he can adopt which will greatly improve his answers.

The first of these is to make sure that you have understood the question correctly. It's OK to ask for it to be repeated or rephrased slightly, if necessary. Don't spend too long wondering about the perfect answer, but it is best not to rush in either: often a question will contain subtleties that require a bit of reflection. And don't panic if you really do not know one answer or get it wrong: this alone won't fail you.

The second strategy is to always remember in what context you are being asked a vague or unrelated question, seemingly plucked from the sky. One example is: "Could you imagine the country doing without TV?"

If you are hoping to do Computer Science, you are probably expected to take this as an invitation to describe the various ways in which electronic signals can travel through air. If you are aiming at a politics-related course, say PPS or PPE, on the other hand, this may be the moment to talk about the role of television in education or about the shaping of public opinion instead. There is almost never a single correct answer here. A good answer, though, will connect the question to the course and allow you to display any knowledge you have.

The third strategy involves not being too set in your ways, a sin some of the smartest applicants are prone to. Not all of human behaviour can be explained through the writings of Karl Marx, Sigmund Freud or Virginia Woolf. Equally, great historic figures are sometimes revealed by later historians as liars or wimps. Great scientific theories, which seem to explain everything, turn out to be incomplete and are superseded by others.

So, temper your views with a good dose of scepticism. If your daughter has been holding forth on the evils of capitalism, it may be a wise thing for her to end with something like: "On the other hand, poverty might have a whole number of causes, and I'm really keen to learn more about those."

Much of this, it should be clear from the examples given above, applies not just in the arts, but also the sciences. While scientific facts are of a more definite nature and interviewers expect you to know the basic ones, you also need to be aware that assessments can change. This means you could get a question along the lines of: "What is wrong with Watson and Crick's views on DNA?"

THE APPLIANCE OF SCIENCE

A concern for the implications of scientific developments is often seen as essential. If a Natural Sciences candidate claims that her main interest is biology, for instance, she might well be asked her opinion on the possible consequences of genetically modified organisms (GMO).

Again, no ultimate judgement is expected of her. What she needs to show by her answer is that she has enough of a sound factual basis to speculate intelligently, as well as a grasp of the most important scientific principles. The idea is to apply these principles to the new information put in front of her, to notice connections, or differences, or rules.

Again, too, it is crucial to elaborate. The ideal answer to any question, no matter how short, will be long enough to show that you have a solid grasp of the subject, a positive hunger to learn more and a healthy awareness that certainty can be an elusive thing, even in science. Thinking aloud here is a good idea: this way, the interviewer can appreciate how you arrived at your answer.

Some science subjects require a very hands-on attitude and this too should affect what you say. In Engineering, for instance, a willingness to apply the knowledge you already possess in Maths or

Physics to practical problems marks out the right candidate. If asked a question that starts with "Is it your sense that it would it be possible to ..." don't ever think about answering yes or no. Instead, try to suggest an experiment that might work in response. If you have ever conducted a relevant one and can describe it, even better. The point is not to offer a perfect solution, but to show that you are willing to grapple with a problem.

Science interviewers, whether they are vets or physicists, also share a general appreciation of certain traits. High up among those is a numerical bent. So, don't just put all your answers into words. Instead, show your awareness that figure analysis is often a good way to tackle even a non-mathematical problem.

This need not be a scary prospect. Often, it just means doing mental calculations based on estimates, or suggesting a simple statistical inquiry. At other times, a verbal question may be best answered by scribbling equations, calculations or general diagrams on the nearest pad or board. But do talk about what your scribblings might mean; don't just assume that they are self-explanatory.

THE NEW EXAMS

To give applicants yet another way of proving they have brains (and to allay public concerns), Oxford and Cambridge have since 2002 introduced pre-designed, written tests for some of their most coveted courses. What this means it that tutors can no longer decide whether to put an applicant to their college through a paper-test of their own during the interview. While some of the course tests (Medicine and Law) have been devised by external ability experts, others (in subjects such as Maths and Economics) were formulated by Oxford or Cambridge dons themselves. Each tries to establish whether a student has the intellectual aptitude for a specific field. Tests taken in advance of the official interview date matter more because only half of those taking them, those who do reasonably well, may be offered an interview at all.

Oxbridge likes to stress that as these are not simple knowledge tests, preparation is unnecessary. Still, candidates sitting an exam for a science course, for instance, need to be at ease with their GCSE Science and Maths. And while an AS-level in Critical Thinking grade does not count as an Oxbridge entry qualification, it offers good practice in logical thought, a quality sought by most Oxbridge dons. While this kind of thought comes naturally to many bright students, frequent engagement with logic-based questions can greatly speed up your replies. You'll find lots of examples in Mensa: *How to Excel at IQ Tests*, edited by Robert Allen (Carlton, 2002). There is more general advice in *How to Pass Advanced Aptitude Tests* by Jim Barrett (Kogan Page, 2002).

Don't worry too much if you really cannot work out an answer: the tests are meant to be hard. A few questions may defeat even a brilliant student. As these are long papers, though, it pays to work reasonably fast. How much they will count for, exactly, neither Oxford nor Cambridge will say.

LEARNING TO WRITE

What also helps you write good test answers is familiarity with their style. A puzzling format or wording can completely throw a nervous student, so always check for sample papers available online.

You may also need practice. Many students, having down-loaded a sample paper, then merely skim it for a few minutes, or mentally speculate on the answers. This is rarely enough. Try to check whether you can write responses of the right length and within the right time. This is not a skill you will suddenly acquire during the test.

Practice matters most for Oxbridge tests involving short essays. Many state schools no longer set classroom essays and their students can lose marks over this. What they have been taught is to write extended essays which require detailed, laborious pre-planning. As a result, some spend most of the time stipulated for their Oxbridge test filling pages with outlines and key points. The result will be an unfinished essay or one barely started. If you have only 20 or 30 minutes, it's better to keep things short. An outline consisting of one paragraph and half a dozen key, one-line points, at very most, will allow you to move forward.

An essay is also the place to showcase your analytic mind. This is not as hard as it sounds. In a subject such as geography or history, for example, it means that you should make clear three things when dealing with anything from a subterranean earthquake to a Highland uprising: why it happened, what difference it made and what were the consequences. Again, keep it short!

11
Becoming a great interviewee

Many of my readers will, at this point, throw up their hands in despair. How can a smart but inexperienced teenager possibly cope with such a complex scenario? Do those dons really expect a 17 year old from a comprehensive to shine in a kind of discourse they never have at home?

The answer is, of course, that it is much harder for those from non-academic backgrounds, and for the quieter kind of young person. Nor can you expect much help from Access. Only one of its myriad projects offers Oxbridge interview training. Some of the scheme's organisers say that this is because to do so would be unfair to other applicants. Given that almost half of those accepted will come from private schools which lay on intensive training, this seems pretty odd. Other Access staff argue that what matters more is to raise pupils' low self-esteem. The interview, from this perspective, becomes a minor obstacle, rather than the decisive event in the application process.

State schools can be very good at bridging the gap. The most crucial thing a school can do at this point is to provide enough inter-view practice. At some schools, sadly, the sole Oxbridge applicant, already feeling edgy about going on this jaunt, is matched up for one brief mock interview with the school's sole Oxbridge-educated teacher, who may not have been back to his old university for 20 years. This rarely goes swimmingly, leaving the candidate more anxious than before.

State school teachers who regularly send students to Oxbridge are adamant that three interviews, each of them followed by detailed feedback, are the minimum it takes.

Feed-back should be given not just on what to say, but on how to say it. One young Oxford English graduate, now teaching at a London specialist school and proud of sending a steady stream of students to her old college, is clear about what is required. "My students," she says, "are encouraged to practise the long, explanatory reply, rather than the brief, correct schoolroom answer. This can involve speculation, examples, even an admissions that the girl does not know enough yet about the subject to be certain she is right. I also tell them that it's fine to question something that has been said, as long as you are willing to make clear why."

The teacher admits that if a pupil comes from a culture in which openly disagreeing with your elders or betters is just not done, this can seem an almost insurmountable challenge. Still, talented pupils faced with a sympathetic interviewer somehow do occasionally bring it off. "Of course," she added, "it might be fairer to allow our students to acquire such skills in their Oxbridge years."

Another state school teacher, educated at a northern university, concentrates on ensuring that her well-taught Modern Languages students are relaxed enough to display their abilities. Having visited Cambridge several times, not just on an Access day seminar, she can honestly assure candidates that "people like you" are already there. She also encourages them to feel that the visit to Oxbridge is already a special treat, a reward for their hard work.

Yet another teacher, an Oxford educated scientist, tries to keep up with scientific work done in the two colleges which he directs pupils towards. This helps him to recommend papers they can read in order to show that they are interested in the "cutting edge" approach taken by their chosen college. He also prides himself on knowing Oxford well enough to always pick one particular feature of the place, college or course that will appeal to the individual applicant. His pupils, as a result, manage to display genuine enthusiasm at the interview.

Not surprisingly, given the quantity of ground covered above, only a handful of state school teachers manage to do all these things in between marking, classwork and smoothing the path for six dozen university candidates applying elsewhere. The number of Oxbridge students going into teaching too has been steadily dropping, so pupils from urban comprehensives, in particular, cannot rely on their teachers alone.

How, then, can your state educated son walk in with a realistic hope of success? After all, being lively, brainy and enthusiastic in the presence of some terrifyingly eminent older figure does not come naturally to any teenager.

WHAT NOT TO DO (BEFORE THE INTERVIEW)

One temptation at this point, for some parents at least, is to assume that determination will do the job of preparation. In other words, if the lad will only understand just how important Oxbridge entrance is to them, they feel, he will study as hard as he can beforehand and concentrate as hard as he can on the day. Surely, this is enough to swing things?

One young man I talked to was actually told by his father, as they walked to the train, that as he was his parents' eldest son, the family's entire fortune depended on his interview. The poor man was not alone in making Oxbridge entrance a life-or-death issue: one girl recalled that her mother, a single parent who had been forced to leave university due to money troubles, spent weeks saying that she would be absolutely gutted if her daughter did not get in.

Unfortunately, telling your teenager that you don't know how you could possibly live with the disappointment is the worst possible thing to do. She needs to be at least tolerably calm to succeed, but can't be if you keep upping the stakes. Instead, the wretched girl is almost certain to panic on the crucial day and fail, crushed by a responsibility far too great for someone young.

THE DO-IT-YOURSELF INTERVIEW

Instead, it is best to concentrate on honing general interview skills. The interview is, above all, a talk between a teenager and a strange (in some cases, very strange) adult, so one of the most useful things you can do is to ensure that the experience is not totally new to your son.

But who can he talk to? With the demise of the extended family and the growing fear of "stranger danger", many children reach 18 without ever having talked to an adult who is not their teacher or parent. How you can solve this problem depends on the stage you're at. A young child likes to chat in a safe place. So, invite a neighbour in for tea or take the boy along when you go to the tax office, doctor's or physiotherapist. Then encourage him to answer the friendly questions these strangers might ask. The crucial thing here is to let the boy speak, not to butt in and answer on his behalf.

Later on, send him on a play scheme, to summer camp, to a youth club or to Sunday school if you can, any place in which he will have to interact with people he hasn't known all his life. Older teenagers gain more that just confidence from an engagement with the community. Preparing a church service and picketing a multinational are equally good for mixing generations.

Sleepovers at same-age friends' homes are great confidence builders, too. You'll be amazed how many candidates spend a sleepless first night at Oxbridge, freaked out by staying in a bedroom not their own.

Academic talk will seem far less daunting after such enrichment activities. They may well pay off, as long as your son has done enough general work, of course, and is prepared to follow the route outlined by this book, as well as his own good sense.

While there is no way of accurately predicting Oxbridge questions, he can limber up for the interview by doing a few practice runs. This does not necessarily mean setting up a whole trial interview; even just preparing for a likely kick-off question can be worthwhile, because this will prevent him from going blank at this early, scary stage and in those unfamiliar surroundings.

But how do you prepare? One way is by writing a brief profile of yourself. What are your university-geared interests? How are you pursuing them and what made you consider the course? Was it a book (remember its full name), an article or some fascinating programme? What key insights did you gain from it? Did it lead you towards any further research? Candidates need to know their subject, say dons, but should also be clear about their motivation and interests.

This information need not cover more than a quarter of a typed page or around a hundred words. Now, read it out to yourself, then take the three key points, write them on a scrap of paper and, drawing only on these, try to tell the whole story smoothly. Then do it without any notes. The point here is not to become word perfect, but to make sure you know what you want to say and are used to speaking up.

Another way to prepare is by assuming that your interview will be entirely subject based. This will generate quite a different type of starter questions: what is history (or a virus, or thermodynamic flow)? How does it impact on us? What makes it so important? Try to ensure that your answers touch on the subject's complexities or problems.

Try to sound confident – and to feel it. There are good reasons for this. You've been invited to attend an Oxbridge interview because of what you have achieved so far, and your potential educators want to know more about how you think and what you might be capable of. They are already teaching students from backgrounds like yours.

GROWN-UP TALK

In an ideal world, you should practise your mini monologue on an adult, perhaps a neighbour, careers adviser or family friend (not your mother, who might feel too involved and will only make you tense). This could be a good time to visit your old cricket coach or your aunt. Alternatively, the bathroom mirror will do.

Parents determined to help should know that practice for more detailed interview questions is best integrated into normal conversation. What you need to offer, most of all, is a sympathetic ear. While some expert knowledge would be nice, it is not absolutely essential. Your limited familiarity with the subject currently occupying that teenager's brain can even prove a positive advantage.

Being asked "So, why are cells so important?" will enable the girl to contextualise her knowledge. "What problems will this make for the government, you think?" is a question that will allow a student to formulate his political ideas after you have watched the news together. "How do you figure these robots work?" subtly challenges a potential engineering student. You can then both consult www.britannica.com/eb/article-9063935/robot.

What matters most here is that you pose open-ended (not yes-or-no) questions and listen politely to what the student has to say. You can now add a follow-up, starting with "But what about...?" This approach will not just build verbal fluency, but also foster a broader, more complex world view. Don't, however, interrupt just because the girl has stopped talking for a moment. This is her show. Moreover, a bit of silent reflection before finalising one's point can pay off at the interview.

DIGITAL LEARNING

Despite their often stern demeanour, dons conducting an interview do not perceive themselves as interrogating students but as debating with them. But what if you have done no debating before? Well, the next best thing to a real-life, fast-paced intellectual debate is a recorded one. Top of the range are the *Today* programme and *The Moral Maze* on BBC Radio 4 (www.bbc.co.uk). BBC2's televised *Question Time* (found online via BBCi) is hectic and sharp. To discover a calmer, but more academic debating style, listen to one of the archived radio programmes of *In Our Time* (http://www.bbc. co.uk/radio4/history/inourtime/inourtime_archive_home.shtml). Here, a student can learn what our best minds disagree on, from imperialism to the impact of Tolstoy on the British novel. She can also get a sense of how real academics argue their points A weekly dose of this could turn a timid talker into an intellectual bulldog.

Once a student has concluded that highbrow arguing can be fun, it is time to see how Oxbridge interviewers do it. Students who attended one of their conferences held in major towns may have had a taster session, but for those who didn't, all is not lost. Clips of interviews, albeit mocked up, can now be found on both universities' websites.

While your own experience may turn out to be very different, as each interviewer has her own style, the clips can be helpful. Most importantly, they familiarize students with the very adult, formal terminology many dons use. A question starting with "What is your sense of..." or "Can you imagine a situation in which..." is not meant to scare you into silence. Instead, it seeks to elicit both subject knowledge and your views.

Not just are you meant to answer at some length, but your answers may be challenged. Could there be other outcomes or interpretations? The interviewer may also check you're aware of your subject's general principles or rules. Keeping up your end now can be tough, but an able, truly interested student tends to manage, or so Oxbridge dons believe.

Lastly, it pays to know that some of the worst advice you can follow will also be found online, or rather in student chatrooms. Out there, privately educated students whose entire school life has been geared towards Oxbridge regularly beseech others to eschew all interview preparation. Behaving naturally is all that counts, these anonymous friends insist - and it got them in. Sometimes the persuader is genuinely unaware that years of intense coaching by teachers who speak just like the interviewers do aided his Oxbridge success.

BECOMING A SPECIALIST

Having decided what you might say during the first few minutes of the interview, you may wonder how to prepare for more specialised questions. Should you jot down yet more detailed notes? Well, it's best to have your school Physics or the rules of Spanish grammar at your fingertips, but cramming works only up to a point. There is no way of second-guessing the interviewer. She might, in any case, want to hear you talk about a subject area or topic you never studied at school.

Still, if you have expressed an interest in evolution in your Personal Statement, it is as well to double-check what issues keep popping up in the literature. This will mean you can offer an informed opinion when confronted with a question like: "Should all living species be preserved?"

Arts admissions tutors in particular like to discuss topical issues, so it can be worthwhile, yet again, to read at least a quality Sunday paper in the months before the interview. Look out for relevant articles written by experts, which will be on the features pages, as well as for news. The most useful ones will have headlines asking things like "should we go to war?" or "should we give up the Pound?" before laying out the pros and cons of the case.

It helps to expect different types of questions. "Talk about biological success," for instance, is scarily open-ended, but this does not mean you are being asked to go on and on. Just list what you think might be its key features and then, if you feel confident, venture an opinion on whether the term is meaningful at all.

Often you'll need to decide quickly whether you are being asked to establish a fact or express an opinion. If the interviewer is fishing for facts, then try to respond in that vein. If it is your opinion which is being sought, don't just state it but give reasons too. This shows you are capable of analysing things. You'll get extra brownie points for making clear what you base your answers on: is it a theory, an observation, a principle or a book you have read?

Now give some thought to how you lay out your stall. A good answer is not a ramble. It will be fairly concise, which often means between two and four sentences long. Many interviewers also like you to use qualifying terms such as "perhaps," "in some circumstances," or "on the one hand" (don't forget the other!). So, draw up a few sample questions, no matter how far fetched, do a quick think and practice using these phrases as you write five line replies.

Lastly, what can keep you calm is not to expect the interview to have a steady rhythm. A tutor will briefly spot-check key points but may want to dig out every single fact you know about others. So, when your turn comes, be prepared to launch into a long, detailed reply, only to be interrupted after a few words.

The point of all this is not to try and have a stock of perfect answers ready, but to avoid being thrown by the way in which your interviewer talks. While a sound factual basis matters, of course, so does an awareness that questions may take you outside your field or beyond your subject knowledge. As long as you have those and practice the Oxbridge answering style, you are bound to come across well.

On the other hand, don't bother learning how to speak without your own perfectly normal accent. This is not a test about whether you can pronounce your h's. One or two former candidates have said that their voice suddenly sounded out of place to them at the interview, but they still got in. It helps to remember that nobody on earth sounds quite like an Oxbridge admissions tutor.

Instead, you want to sound keen, thoughtful and open to new ideas. The standard advice from Oxbridge publications is to "be yourself" but perhaps it is a more a case of being you "with added value." There are other options too. One very shy science candidate, whose textile worker parents had moved to Britain from Bangladesh, decided that she would field all questions by imagining she was the cool and smart Carol Vorderman. Reader, it worked for her.

THE BOOK

What, though, is the strongest factor which swings the interview for a candidate? Dons are unequivocal: it is his willingness to analyse, combined with some lateral thinking.

The successful Oxbridge candidates I talked to were just as unequivocal: it was "the book." Each of them had read (and mentioned in their Personal Statement) an adult work relevant to the subject they were applying for. By putting their subject into a broad, intellectual context, the book had enabled them to understand the questions and answer clearly. Reading only photocopied magazine articles or the key chapters of books produced far poorer results.

This is not to say that the candidates had necessarily read the same book, or the same kind of book, even if they were applying for the same course at the same college. The more determined ones had indeed patiently worked their way through a first year university textbook, in the case of science candidates something with a title like Modern Organic Chemistry or Advanced Physics.

Others had had their enthusiasm kindled by a more specific study, and below are some examples, again in the science field. Popular among biology fans were: *Genome* by Matt Ridley, *The Making of Memory: from Molecules to Mind* by Steven Rose, *Trilobite* by Richard Fortey, *The Lying Stones of Marrakech* by Stephen Jay Gould, *The Darwin Wars* by Andrew Brown or *The Human Brain: A Guided Tour* by Susan Greenfield.

Aspiring physicists had read: *QED* by Richard Feynman, *The Physics of Star Trek* by Laurence Krauss, *Chaos* by James Gleick, *Mr. Tompkins in Wonderland* by Russell Stannard and George Gamow, *The Restless Atom* by Alfred Romer or *The Physics of Ball Games* by C.B. Daish.

Aspiring engineers listed: *The New Science of Strong Materials* by J.E. Gordon, *The Engineer in Wonderland* by Eric R. Laithwaite and *Heat Engines* by J.F. Sandford.

Those interested in astronomy and cosmology read anything by Stephen Hawking.

Science: A History 1534-2001 by John Gribbin was popular for its broader sweep, but interests could also be developed with the help of a good biography, such as *Marie Curie: a Life* by Susan Quinn, *Einstein* by Banesh Hoffmann, *The Periodic Table* by Primo Levi or *Genius: Richard Feynmann and Modern Physics* by James Gleick. A more spiced-up, fictional version of the scientific life, centred on ethical problems, was found in *Cantor's Dilemma* by Carl Djerassi or *The Swarm* by Frank Schatzing.

Even certain plays could make you a more interesting science interviewee. These included: *Copenhagen* by Michael Frayn, *After Darwin* by Timberlake Wertenbaker, *Arcadia* by Tom Stoppard, *The Life of Galileo* by Bertold Brecht, *The Physicists* by Friedrich Durrenmatt and *An Experiment with an Airpump* by Shelagh Stephenson.

Young mathematicians trying to bridge the yawning gap between A-level Maths and the Oxbridge version were helped by *Alice in Numberland* by John Baylis and Rod Haggarty, or read *Thinking Mathematically* by J. Mason. Those sitting the Cambridge STEP papers also need to work through *Advanced Problems in Mathematics* by S.T.C. Siklos, an OCR collection. They might then want to read *Dr. Riemann's Zeros* by Karl Sabbagh for fun.

Law candidates new to the subject's formal language and issues often have a go at *Learning the Law* by Glanville Williams (but warm up first by reading the weekly Law supplement published by *The Times*). Alternatively, books like *Eve was Framed* by Helena Kennedy, which deals with the courts' treatment of women, can prompt an interest in a specialised field.

In other arts subjects, and especially in languages, history and philosophy, the range of "useful" books varied so widely with candidates' personal tastes that there is no point in even giving examples.

A brief word about English Lit.: its candidates need to be the most voracious readers. Here, a familiarity with novels, plays or poetry well beyond the school syllabus is absolutely taken for granted. Avid fiction readers need to show a taste for a specific genre and must have some clear favourites. If your son claims to love Magic Realism, for instance, the interviewers will expect a list of such novels read (four's a good score, two will not do), plus, perhaps, some interest in their structure or social context. Real show-offs also try to understand Terry Eagleton's *Literary Theory: an Introduction*, or at least the first two chapters.

Interviewers for most Oxbridge courses are delighted to encounter a well-read candidate, which does not mean that you should be trying to impress them with a long list of half-digested famous works. In most cases, mentioning that you have read a relevant book or two will do fine. It does not always need to be an academic work; detailed popular science books written by experts certainly count.

For students keen to start at the deep end, both Oxbridge prospectuses now list books recommended by departmental dons. This is a new and positive development, but most works are taken from undergraduate reading lists and thus too difficult for sixth formers. You might want to give one of them a try, but don't drop the idea of an Oxbridge course just because you cannot make sense of it unaided!

What the interviewer will try to do is establish whether the candidate has reflected on the tomes he has been consuming. The lad will be expected to voice an opinion based on his reading, make comparisons, mention what problems he encountered and show signs of lateral thinking.

A good bookworm, in other words, is a selective bookworm. Candidates who "skim" lots of material may have a wider range of facts at their disposal, but the best books teach you to connect.

BREEDING A BOOKWORM

So, the wise parent does not assume that never looking up from one's homework is the key to getting into Oxbridge. Discouraging hobbies and restricting a pupil's reading to school textbooks, as some well-meaning, non-university educated parents try to do, can produce a very dull candidate and make family life hell.

By the A2 stage, most teachers have produced a university geared reading list, but until then a wild dash through world fiction or a solid diet of electronics textbooks can work equally well. As long as it has a spine, its presence on top of that pile of dirty washing in your son's room is probably a good thing. All sorts of books, serious or funny, novels or nonfiction, highbrow or lowbrow, will broaden your son's outlook and introduce him to unfamiliar ideas, places and words.

How, though, can you support this expensive habit? The point is, you shouldn't even try. If your daughter is a serious reader, she will go through far more books than you could possibly buy. Instead, make sure that she acquires the library habit early on. Take her to your local children's library, let her pick her own books and go to the counter to have them stamped. Back home, establish a corner where only library books live, so they will never get lost. A working bedside light is not just a convenience but will protect a bookworm's eyes.

If she seems to lose interest after a while, consider that she might have outgrown the children's section, even if she is only ten. Ask the librarian for a map of the grown-up shelves. Then suggest that you might both potter around for a bit in what she thinks is the most interesting looking section. At this point any section, whether philosophy or photography, will be fine. And if your local council tries to "rationalise" library services by closing your local branch, tell them what you think – then campaign for the opposition.

YOUNG OXBRIDGE

If your family's potential Oxbridge student has a younger sibling who shows similar ability, here are a few practical suggestions. You don't need to be brilliant or highly educated yourself to implement them. If the child has a good mind, the following strategies will help him on his way.

1. Let him experiment with his pile of bricks without rushing in to help and without sneering when things go wrong.
2. Tell him it's all right to say "I don't know".
3. Encourage him to ask "why" or to say "can you explain".
4. If you can't answer his questions, suggest that you both look for answers in a book.
5. Don't always interrupt what he is doing. It is important to eat, but it can also be important to finish drawing a picture.
6. Listen to his opinions with respect. He might be wrong, but has probably thought before speaking.
7. Ask his opinion about films, teachers, the state of the world.
8. Ask for advice. By ten, a child should know quite a bit more than you do about computer use, video-setting or recording CDs. By 15, he is probably lightyears ahead of you when it comes to the facts about hair dyes, online travel booking and modern music.
9. Encourage him to give his opinions and advice clearly and politely.
10. Teach him that there may be more than one right way of looking at major issues.

Encourage your daughter to ask for advice. Once she has worked out what kind of books she likes, it's OK to ask the librarian or a subject teacher for suggestions. Only if the books have just come out or have been stolen from the shelves (a regular event in our local library) should you think of buying. Book tokens make excellent, lightweight presents and show that you trust the girl to make her own choice.

If your daughter gets interested in a subject via a TV documentary, she might want to read the book of the series. Before you buy it, though, encourage her to skim through to check whether it really expands on the subject, or just offers bits of recycled text in large print plus lots of film stills.

Dramatised fiction, on the other hand, will more directly lead to top quality books. The only problem of discovering a great story in this way is that the TV version remains in the mind. So, before talking excitedly at her interview about Dr. Zhivago and how the star-crossed lovers managed to escape at the end, your daughter had better crosscheck what happens at the end of the book (the hero dies).

THE PITFALLS

No amount of reading can fully prepare you for the interview, and neither is it meant to. One of the key ideas behind the Oxbridge interview is the precise opposite: to discover how well a candidate will cope when faced with the unexpected. Elderly dons still fondly quote the first lines of Rudyard Kipling's poem, *If* – in this context. Oxbridge, so they imply, wants you:

> If you can keep your head when all about you
> Are losing theirs and blaming it on you,
> If you can trust yourself when all men doubt you
> But make allowance for their doubting too,
> If you can wait and not be tired by waiting,
> Or being lied about, don't deal in lies,
> Or being hated, don't give way to hating,
> And yet don't look too good, nor talk too wise...

Well, this is an impressive list, and the ability "to keep your head" was mentioned even by many dons without reference to the poem. The quality would certainly have been useful for picking a Victorian district officer who would be ruling over half of Burma or some pre 1948 Indian state with a million inhabitants and no other Queen's representative within 500 miles. Why it should be quite so crucial "to keep your head" for a future Music or Biological Science student, though, is anyone's guess.

Questioned about this by *The Independent* (1st October 2000) Susan Stobbs, the veteran director of admissions for Cambridge Colleges, said somewhat defensively: "We are not trying to catch people out. But our courses move very fast. We need to see that students can pick up and develop ideas fast."

Younger Oxbridge academics can be quietly critical of this. One female science tutor from a comprehensive insisted (off the record) that guiding a student through a set text, however complex, was a totally different process. She thought it wrong to put already intimidated young people on the spot and certainly never adopted the tactic herself.

Still, certain, often elderly admissions tutors continue to go for the If-approach in a big way and like to make sure the candidate feels surprised.

Often this is just a peculiar seating arrangement. One successful candidate recalls being made to sit at the far end of a very long table, while the interviewer sat at the other end, almost invisible in the gloom. Another one described how her two interviewers positioned themselves at opposite sides of the departmental office, so she could not look at both of them as she talked.

More disconcerting can be a swap between two related subjects. Sue, a grammar school girl who was hoping to read Chinese, found herself interviewed by someone actually teaching Thai, and was asked to apply her (as yet very basic) understanding of Chinese grammar to a line of Thai writing. As the two languages are closely related and she had followed her yoga-teaching mother's advice to do relaxation exercises before the interview the girl, somewhat stumblingly, managed to comply.

Tess, a comprehensive school pupil from a non-academic family, had applied for the Anthropology and Archaeology course after reading an article about a Japanese anthropological project. She was shaken when she found that her interviewer was an archaeologist. Her total ignorance of his subject, she felt, meant she did not stand a chance against "cleverer" applicants. Shrinking back into her seat, which was miles from the tutor's, she whispered: "I don't know a thing about this." However, when reassured that this was OK and invited to speculate, she decided she had nothing to lose. She is an articulate girl, and her off the cuff suggestions on how one might study a dead, rather than a living culture got her in.

Another popular tactic is the prolonged silence, which can be used in various and sometimes disconcerting ways.

Tim, a terribly well-read candidate, was faced with an elderly interviewer who failed to greet him, settled into a distant window recess and after several minutes barked "talk about your own subject" in his direction. The young man launched into an account of what he, out of nervousness, called Astrology, though he meant Astronomy. He quickly corrected himself, but felt so embarrassed he lost his thread. He stumbled on, expecting to be told when to stop, but instead was allowed to go on. When he eventually ran out of things to say, the interviewer maintained his silence. After what felt like an eternity but was, as the candidate later realised, only quarter of an hour, he was told that he could leave.

Grace, who had applied for Modern History, had the opposite experience. She had mentioned in her Personal Statement that she was the leader of a Brownie pack. One of her interviewer's first questions was about the founder of the scout movement, Robert Baden-Powell. Shaken, she admitted to having never heard of him, and prayed that they would move on to another subject. Instead the tutor gave her a little lecture about the famous man, which took up most of the interview. He then asked a few questions to check she had understood. However, the main thing she was expected to do, she realised after a moment, was to nod enthusiastically.

(Unlike the prospective astronomer, the Brownie leader got in. What can we conclude from this? Probably only that external factors, rather than the interview itself, determined the result: she was a Shropshire working class girl with top grades and a perfect mix of brainy interests and sporting skills, while he came from an already overrepresented public school.)

A more tricky approach can be deeply unsettling for vulnerable candidates.

Maher, an applicant from a poorly rated comprehensive, did well in his written science test, although he felt that had he been less nervous, he would have started faster and done even better. But faced with a plummy-voiced interviewer whom he found hard to understand he clammed up. He had never sat in a room with such precious old furniture before. Being fairly dark-skinned, he also wondered whether the fact that the interviewer made him sit at the end of the room was a put down. Did the professor not want to sit next to a dark-skinned person? Or did he think that he, Maher, smelled?

Or take Joseph, who came from a struggling urban sixth form college. He had applied to do a course based on Spanish, his mother tongue. When his interviewer explained that she did not actually teach the language, Joseph's first thought was: "So the Spanish tutor can't even be bothered to see me." Hurt and confused, he refused to play the game. He gave short, terse replies to any factual questions put to him and when asked what he thought was the most exciting aspect of European culture, he just mumbled: "No idea." He had, in fact, worked as a Saturday cleaner for a small record company that promoted regional music and was interested in its work, but felt that mentioning his lowly job would demean him in Oxbridge eyes.

Both applicants were rejected, which came as no surprise to them. Their respective teachers, though, were absolutely furious. Each of the boys had been carefully hand-picked by his school as a highly talented student.

So the result of such an überclever approach, although perhaps designed to transcend subject coaching and create a more "level playing field", is often counterproductive. It is bad enough being in an unfamiliar environment with someone speaking in a superior accent without being asked about a subject one knows nothing about. Almost invariably, the applicant's residual doubts about whether this venture into other people's world was a good idea will click in. The suspicion that he is undergoing a deliberate humiliation, rather than a fair test, may paralyse a student intellectually, so that he might fail.

12

Paying to shine at the interview

There is one obvious way to make the Oxbridge interview a cinch rather than a nightmare: this is to go there from the right school. While creating Oxbridge entrants used to be a mission restricted to a few public schools, fee-paying parents now expect this from every private establishment. They also tend to obtain it, and not just in terms of the intensive, small class teaching by qualified staff which the schools officially emphasize. One such establishment, once mainly known as a supplier of officer cadets to Sandhurst, includes in its weekly time table for Oxbridge entrants amongst other things:

- a 40 minute tutorial in which pupils go through old Oxbridge entrance papers
- A short essay on verbal interview questions pupils were asked in the past
- Verbal interview training
- A talk on an interview-related course subject given by an expert
- Half hour talks given by pupils on their own academic interests
- A problem-solving session
- Guidance on how to research a project to be mentioned
- "Six of the best" book club sessions in which pupils discuss with a teacher the half dozen books pupils are expected to have read in the holidays etc. etc.

The effect of all this has been to create what one young ex-Oxbridge lecturer now teaching abroad referred to as "a Sparkler", meaning a candidate who shines brightly at his interview, but might or might not soon fizzle out. The Sparkler would deliver all the "right" answers from the start. Asked why he picked his course, for instance, he would launch into a little monologue which suggests that he embodied all the qualities and skills admissions tutors were fishing for. To show you what this means, here is a (mildly satyrised) version of the Sparkler's performance:

"Well, I thought a lot about it before deciding. I was very impressed with your general academic reputation, of course, especially in Historic Anthropology (my housemaster told me about it), but I became really interested in the family structure of medieval Provençal villages when I went to the local museum near our French holiday home and found some old land records (actually, the careers teacher recommended that I go there, having steered me towards this unfamiliar subject, because he knows that two fellows here specialise in it). I am currently reading *Provençal birthing rituals* by Dr. Deepthought who is teaching here. It is absolutely fascinating.

Actually, I was so keen I started a Provençal Society in our school, and one of my friends has already become a member (after, that is, I agreed to join the Latin Grammar Society he founded so it could go on his Personal Statement).

Then, of course, there is the recreational side. Your team usually wins the inter-collegiate rugby final (my PE teacher translated the prospectus reference to 'lots of Rugby Blues' for me) and I am quite a keen forward scrum myself (actually, I find rugby terrifying, but it was mandatory at my boarding school and the headmaster claimed that playing the game went down awfully well with Oxbridge. I'll drop out of matches in the first term)."

Evidently eager, motivated and academic, the Sparkler seems to be the answer to even the most sport-hating don's prayer. But is he? The answer lies in the mixed intake of most fee-paying schools. While some parents opt for private schooling because they hope it will stretch their bright, fast-learning child, other parents see it as a way of giving a slow, under-achieving pupil the best chance in life.

So, a Sparkler could be anything. The best Oxbridge entrance training makes it impossible to tell whether you are dealing with a gifted youngster who will excel once on the course, or a carefully tutored but middling pupil who will struggle to keep up once his support system is gone and will finally leave, having barely scraped a Third.

Now contrast this with the (again mildly satyrised) answers given by another candidate, when asked why he chose the college:

Fred: "Well, I was told it was not too high up the league tables, so it might take more state school pupils. I wasn't too sure about this place at first, what with most of the buildings being so old, but apparently the student rooms are in a new block, so I figured that would be alright."
Interviewer: "Anything else?"
Fred: "Well, of course that I could do Archaeology here. I got the idea from seeing 'Raiders of The Lost Ark', and then I read a magazine article about what archaeologists do in FHM. My local library also found me a book that was mentioned there, even though I had to wait for three weeks, but it was really interesting. Not quite as good as history, mind you, which is what I like best at school. I even got to read out my holiday essay on Scottish war songs on local radio. Only Oxbridge History is supposed to be really difficult to get into and so my teacher suggested I settle for Archaeology instead. I'm halfway through the introduction he lent me. There's quite a bit of history in your course, isn't there?"
Interviewer: "You could say that. But archaeology is still hard work and requires excellent time management. Do you combine your reading with anything else? Rugger? Rowing?"
Fred: "Not really. My mate and I used to bum off for a fag when the rest got on the minibus to the sports centre at the other end of town. And we don't have any rivers in Luton. Mind you, I've heard that you got your own full size football pitch here. Would it be OK to have a kick about later on?"

Well, who sounds more like a potential Oxbridge student to you? The answer is not quite as clear-cut as it seems. A handful of colleges do have an intelligent, motivated, honest student like Fred. What makes the huge parental investment in school fees seem worthwhile, though, is that so many admissions tutors, including state school educated ones, still go for the Sparkler.

While Oxbridge is not unaware of this problem (first raised in the 2003 edition of this book), no satisfactory solution has yet been found. Interviewers now ask fewer personal questions and sport counts for rather less, but the language used by dons and the knowledge base expected can still trip up ordinary students.

INTERVIEW TRAINING

So, what options do parents have if they cannot afford the fees that would transform Fred into a Sparkler? Until the appearance of this book, which was put on this earth to do exactly that, the answer has been precious few.

The cut-price option has, for the last decade or so, been a bit of interview training offered by an Oxbridge graduate doing home tutoring while he waits for his dream job, or a few extra sessions tacked on to a private A-level course in some private college. Alternatively, such training can be bought, in the form of about a week's coaching plus general guidance, from a small number of outfits specialising in this field.

Oxbridge absolutely hates these paid interlopers. Mentioning that interview training courses were now held in Oxford itself, one powerful admissions tutor told me with almost a hiss: "I am appalled to think that some genuine colleges here would agree to have their premises used by such people."

Anthony Smith, the President of Magdalen College, Oxford, went even further when he described the staff of one interview training company whose success in placing pupils had been much in the news as "just a bunch of grasping, meddling, money-grabbing young men" (*The Times*, 29th May 2003).

This is a quite extraordinary reaction. After all, the headmasters of most private schools are welcome guests at the dreaming spires. So, if a man who charges parents £10,000 a year to (amongst other things) get pupils into Oxbridge is regularly invited to dine at the dons' high table, why is the chap who offers to do this for a more affordable sum, between £250 and £1,000 a throw, treated as socially below a pimp?

There are two possible answers to this. One is that interview training companies, or at least those which work on the basis of a no-win-no-fee basis, will only accept the kind of students who would get in anyway and therefore, as Magdalen's President has also suggested, "make their money out of parents' social anxiety about Oxbridge."

This would indeed justify the Oxbridge disdain, if it were not for one thing: some dons are claiming the precise opposite. Far from agreeing that all those evil, venal young men always get their pupils in, they insist that interview training never works. They are convinced that they can always spot its signs (unless, presumably, it is done by a private school) and that this leads them to dismiss the candidate's own abilities.

In other words, just a tinge of snobbishness about the kind of training which is acceptable, as opposed to the kind which is not, might be a more likely explanation.

But if you buy, will you get value for your money? You certainly might. While interview training cannot impart a knowledge of facts, it can help a student decode the often mystifying questions asked by Oxbridge dons. Ways of neatly structuring your answer may also be taught. This may be enough to shift the balance in favour of a bright, well-taught applicant from a non-academic home.

The crucial thing is to watch out for the problems. One is that an outfit which prepares lots of students for Oxbridge during a very short time may blur their individual style. This can make it too obvious that a candidate has been coached.

And if parents only pay the interview trainers if their son or daughter gets in, that target can end up overriding others: pupils might be subtly encouraged to lower their sights in order to improve their entrance chances, for instance by considering less competitive fields than Law or Medicine. Alternatively, they might be directed away from the most academically renowned and hardest to impress colleges, in favour of the old "housemaster's route" outlined earlier.

The less popular a candidate's course and college choice is, after all, the more likely the candidates are to get in and the interview trainers are to get their money. The result of such a strategy could be an unsuitable course, or a miserable time at the wrong college and a career that does not live up to one's expectations.

However, there is no sign that any of this is happening, on the whole. Instead, students who had paid interview training are often delighted with the results. If there is a real problem with interview training, it lies elsewhere. Many parents cannot possibly spare several hundred pounds, never mind several thousand, just to help a top university recognise their teenager's ability.

13

Grading the interview

Oxbridge students tend to be very positive about the interview process. After all, it enabled them to join "the brightest and best" in their delightful mini-world. Unsuccessful candidates, who went into the interview cold, are often more bewildered than cross. "I just couldn't work out what they wanted from me," was a phrase heard more than once.

Outside experts can be more critical. Ability expert Deborah Eyre insists that identifying those who will benefit most from a top academic education is an expert job. As the director of NAGTY (now superseded by Y, G & T), she set up an enrichment programme based on first establishing prospective students' intellectual profiles on the basis of a whole portfolio of evidence, including a battery of scientific tests. The Oxbridge interview, to her, is "a very unscientific way of testing ability, made even more arbitrary by the variation in practices by individual admissions tutors and colleges".

Much of this is due to the fact that dons used to be given no formal preparation for interviewing at all. They could ask a candidate whatever they liked and, if the spirit took them, with both eyes shut. After protests from a humiliated interviewee in the 1990s, it was agreed that interview talk must not be offensive, but there was no rule against it being obscure. Only the admissions tutors to the Oxford medical course were somewhat restricted; their questions had to cover specific areas, listed on a task sheet. How to cover them, though, was up to the interviewer.

Having fiercely defended this policy for decades, Cambridge started to coach newly appointed admissions tutors a few years ago and Oxford announced in September 2008 that all its interviewers would now be trained. Still, the secrets of accessible behaviour seem to elude some of them. In December 2008, one bright student I had mentored was placed opposite three men in black gowns who stared at him for 30 minutes with fixed grins, while bombarding him with very formally worded questions. The young man, who lives on one of London's scariest housing estates, found the scene so disconcerting he could not display his skills. He was not offered a place, but other students I knew who were interviewed at the same college did well.

The interview, then, remains a bit of a tombola; those candidates who get in and those who don't may have totally different interviews despite university guidelines.

Professor Eyre is also concerned about the distorting effect public school training has on interview outcomes: "What we see is that children in the private sector seemingly over-achieve. They are trained up to the limit of their potential, then groomed to come across as exceptional, whether they are that or not."

Nor is she happy that the blame for failure is, so often, attributed to a lack of self-esteem. "Some interviewers," she says, "are overbearing, and some young people just do not like to be interrogated. They find the encounter unattractive, whatever their ability."

Another problem has been pointed out by Joan Freeman. "The talented are not a homogeneous group," insists Britain's veteran expert on this group. She wants interviewers to be aware that a gifted young writer and a gifted young scientist will behave quite differently, and individuals within each group may do so too. The "brightest and best" can be dozy or sparkling, quick witted or ponderous.

No testing system is entirely value free either, warns Professor Freeman. This is true of the Oxbridge one, as well as of the standard IQ test and the American-type SAT. The shorter a test is too, the more the values of the tester will affect the outcome, and the Oxbridge interview is often very short indeed.

The new aptitude tests introduced for specific courses have also failed to reassure some experts. The Schwartz Report of May 2004, commissioned by the Government, warns that preparing and travelling to additional tests can interfere with a student's classroom work. Deborah Eyre feels that having subject tests that also vary from university to university "makes life more difficult for the student, parent and school". A set of generally accepted ability tests might, both suggest, work rather better.

Foreign academics, while admiring the intellectual glory of Oxbridge, are amazed at its entrance process. Graduates of top US universities like Harvard and Princeton, or of the Paris Sorbonne, are renowned within international organisations like the UN for their analytic minds, articulacy, lateral thinking and all the rest of the Oxbridge wish list, but they have not been entry-tested for any of this. Instead, a great university seeks to gradually develop these great qualities in bright applicants.

This is why American universities grade all applicants by a standard academic ability test, the SAT, which is regarded as fair, though you can bone up for it. The candidates with the highest scores are offered places in the most highly rated institutions. Applicants to even the most renowned French universities need only to have done well in their baccalaureate, an extended form of A-levels.

A VIEW FROM THE STAFF ROOM

How does another group, the teachers, feel about Oxbridge entrance? One group of sixth form teachers I spoke to were clear about the problem faced by large schools like theirs, with a mixed and often disadvantaged intake. It is not just that they cannot possibly provide the intense interview training offered elsewhere. Oxbridge also wants a candidate who is positively bubbling with enthusiasm about his subject and is actively pursuing it beyond syllabus requirements.

Now, although comprehensives seek to get all their bright pupils into university, "Oxbridge qualities" are a minority trait and pupils exhibiting them too publicly risk trouble from their peers. Winning a prize, or even choosing to compete for one can, in some schools, set the bullies on you. So can speaking up too much in class or knowing so much more about various subjects than your classmates do. Not until the A-level years, when these pupils are taught separately, does the classroom really become a place in which it feels safe to show off intellectually, or even to openly pursue unusual hobbies.

If a pupil has an articulate, educated family, this will balance outside factors and no damage is done, said the teachers. For many bright comprehensive school pupils, though, the interview becomes a place where they are suddenly expected to do what instinct told them to carefully avoid: show wild enthusiasm for their subject, be quickwitted and sparkle. The deliberate underplaying of their abilities perfected over the years now backfires. They undersell themselves.

To illustrate the outcome one teacher quoted the feedback he had received after the rejection of an outstanding pupil interviewed at a Cambridge college. The boy, the admissions tutor wrote, "got an A for his written exam, is serious and passionate about his subject. Unfortunately, he was nervous at the interview and overly defensive."

148

The head of the department, who had sent seven other pupils to various other Cambridge Colleges that year, all without success, quoted similar feedback from the university. His candidates, he was told, had been too tense and not fluent or expansive enough at the interview. To this was added the usual sop: "We had so many very able candidates this year."

A teacher at a more successful school nevertheless concurred with her colleagues. Oxbridge was clearly trying to broaden its intake, but there were still "social" entrance qualifications. Far too much, she felt, hinges on a pupil's ability to sustain a long, clever verbal exchange with a well-spoken, highly educated adult.

Oxbridge success must not remain merely the responsibility of schools, insisted the experienced teacher: "There is a need for a Joint Working Party made up of dons and sixth form heads in order to work out what precise qualities Oxbridge colleges can reasonably seek. It also needs to consider how entrance can be made a fairer process, given that some of these qualities just cannot be fostered in a large, mixed ability state school."

WATCHING THEM RUN

Recent changes in the interview process could be an attempt to fore-stall such intervention. Questions have become more subject-centred and an admissions tutor can no longer single-handedly grill two dozen students in a day. Now there are usually two interviewers present, both to guard against prejudice and against the exhaustion that might cause the talents of the last poor soul ushered in to be overlooked.

But will that be enough? Contrary to popular belief, it is not just outsiders who are wondering. Writing in the *Times Higher Educational Supplement* of 13th January 2006, Oxford don Alan Ryan questioned the weight attributed to verbal interviews compared to written tests. "What students do at university is write", argued the Warden of New College. "What they get a degree for is performance in examinations. You'd have thought that the way to decide which applicants to accept is to see how well they do what they will do at university. If you were picking a team to run in the Olympics, you wouldn't interview them about running; you'd watch them run."

14

Going for it

Despite all the criticism voiced of it in recent years, the interview remains the most crucial part of the Oxbridge entrance process. Most dons insist that although it may not be totally value-free, it is essential to help them find the right students for their unique face-to-face teaching system. Those found today include a (slight) majority of state school students, some from very poor backgrounds. Passing the interview means that you will be offered an internationally coveted university place, subject only to the kind of A-level results most candidates can expect.

To a bright teenager setting out for Oxbridge, these points should provide enough reassurance to carry her confidently past those manicured lawns, shiny iron gates and freshly painted stone walls into a room full of people wearing bicycle clips. Parents still toying with the Valium, though, may want a slightly more detailed summary, which goes roughly as follows:

> That the interview structure does not compare like with like there is no doubt. There is just too much difference in pupils' academic and social background. Equally, there is no doubt that it does pick up on real talent in all sorts of candidates, and that many interviewers genuinely seek to broaden their course intake, albeit in oddly unscientific ways. Even if there is prejudice among some, this cannot be allowed to determine general outcomes. While the university bench marks set to expand the proportion of state school students have never yet been met, they must be striven for. The alternative could be a – regularly threatened – cutback in Government funds.

As a result, interviewers can be surprisingly nice, and those whose fierce or peculiar manners flummox outsiders are gradually being reined in. Responding to criticism from headmasters, one admissions tutor argued that the treatment of applicants had been "a great deal more savage" in the past.

It should also be said that while some candidates find the interview nerve-wracking, others actually enjoy the rapid verbal to-and-fro and get an unexpected thrill from being able to show off their mental skills. For many a junior thinker, there is nothing quite like a famous senior thinker's quick, almost imperceptible nod of approval after a good reply.

Leaving you for the 9.43 train, your son should therefore take heart. Not only is Oxbridge committed to taking someone like him, but you and this book are on his side. Guided by the information given on these pages, he need not feel at a disadvantage compared with posher and seemingly more confident students. Quite of few of them will fail, because even the most meticulous coaching and the greatest familiarity with ancient buildings is not a substitute for a well-focused brain. If you are blessed with the latter and have followed this book's advice, you stand an excellent chance.

The important thing is to be both optimistic and prepared. Confidence based on wise choices, well-planned school work, selective reading and an understanding of the interview process begets Oxbridge success. So does the realisation that much of this is just a game with mirrors, played by clever young people and sometimes not so smart older ones. You can join this game and win, if you understand the rules and draw on all available help. There is nothing spontaneous about the Oxbridge entrance process, and you need not comply with that absurd claim.

ONE FOR THE ROAD

If you have come this far, you have probably absorbed enough information to get through the interview, or to prepare your teenager for it. Still, just in case it all seems too much, here is a basic summary in the form of ten simple commandments:

Rule 1: Be prepared to answer questions about your interests, activities, subject, course or college choice.

Rule 2: Accept that you might not be asked about any of this.

Rule 3: Treat the interview as a conversation in which ideas are thrown back and forth, not a quiz session with correct answers.

Rule 4: Say not only what you think but also why you think it.

Rule 5: Give longish, considered answers.

Rule 6: Speculate, compare and explain.

Rule 7: Don't expect the interviewer to tell you whether you were right or wrong.

Rule 8: Express curiosity and a willingness to learn.

Rule 9: Don't be too dogmatic: the more you know about the world, the less certain things look.

Rule 10: Don't panic if you are being asked about a topic you have never thought about: this is not a disaster, but merely a way of giving you a chance to improvise.

Or just try to remember one phrase in which a state school headmaster I knew used to sum up the interview to his pupils: "The interview explores the ability to reason and to support an argument with constructive thought – and the skill of thinking on your feet."

15

Oxbridge Medicine

Parents and students often view the medical degree courses offered by Oxbridge as the most glittering of all prizes. In this, they are both right and wrong. They are right, because Medicine is the only Oxbridge degree which almost guarantees you a job, and a well-paid, prestigious, and often highly satisfying lifetime one at that. As one young doctor I interviewed put it, it was great to be in a profession which combined science with human interaction: "You get up in the morning and you don't know what will happen. The joy of medicine is that your bleeper goes and your day changes."

However, people are wrong in that Oxbridge Medicine is not necessarily a better route to professional glory than a degree from, say, Newcastle. While Medicine involves a huge amount of academic learning, the success of a medical career depends first of all on a doctor's work record. What matters is how skilled you are in practice and how well you get on with colleagues. As a result, students rise to the top from any good medical school. The bright, enthusiastic (and privately educated) young doctor I quoted above was, in fact, rejected by Cambridge, but is, nevertheless, shooting up the career ladder. His friends, who made it into Oxbridge Medicine, have similar, but not actually better jobs.

There is, of course, something special about Oxbridge Medicine. Penicillin, the drug that continues to save millions of lives each year, was developed at Oxford in 1940 by two men, Australian medical scientist Howard Florey and a German Jewish asylum seeker, biochemist Ernst Boris Chain (although the compound had been discovered in 1928 by Alexander Fleming, who worked and trained at St. Mary's Medical School, London).

Cambridge can take credit for a more theoretical discovery. In 1953, Francis Crick and the American James Watson decoded the "double helix" structure of the DNA molecule, which carries the genetic information from old cells to new ones, in a Cambridge lab. Few individual discoveries have so quickly ushered in so many fundamental advances in so many fields, from genetics and evolutionary theory to biochemistry and medical research. Today's students attending the Oxbridge courses have yet more reasons to feel privileged. They don't just enjoy some truly brilliant staff and labs, but also have the opportunity to mix daily with contemporaries involved in quite different academic fields, which makes for a vibrant social and intellectual life. Medical students elsewhere tend to live, study and party within the far duller confines of a teaching hospital.

As a result, the competition is fierce. Oxford and Cambridge, which run similar entry systems, get up to seven applicants for each place. (In most other subjects, the proportion of applicants to places is four or three to one.) After years of bitter criticism over their selection procedures, these have been greatly restructured. No longer can a bright young chap expect to get in thanks to what older medics quaintly recall as "trial by sherry".

Medicine is, in fact, one of the very few Oxbridge subjects which has had a long, proper entrance exam, in addition to the interview, for several years. This was sat by applicants to all colleges. Each of the two universities, though, had its own exam, devised by its own medical faculty staff, and each exam was designed to test not so much an applicant's background or IQ as their aptitude for this particular course.

However, there was concern that both exams favoured public school pupils because of their broader level of knowledge and special coaching, and so both have now been scrapped. A more ability-based, pre-interview exam, the Biomedical Admissions Test (BMAT) was introduced in November 2003 for medical candidates applying to Oxford, Cambridge, University College (London) and Imperial College.

So, how do you prove that you have what it takes?

The answer lies in grasping that Medicine at Oxford and Cambridge is more theoretical than elsewhere, at the start at least. Beyond this, many aspects of the courses offered by the two universities differ, though. In order to provide a potential student with helpful details, we'll zoom in on the Oxford course below. You'll find further information about it in the university's online prospectus.

Students considering the equally renowned Cambridge course will find some of this relevant, especially as far as the entrance test is concerned, but also need to check out the Medicine pages of the Cambridge prospectus, again available online.

THE OXFORD MEDICAL COURSE

While Cambridge likes to stress the patient-centred nature of its course, Oxford puts a strong emphasis on research. The Oxford course "suits the academic mind", as William James, the Dean of Admissions at its Medical Faculty, puts it. A high proportion of Oxford medical students will not just become consultants, that is medical specialists, but will combine patient care with medical research. Some will spend most of their professional lives in the computerised labs of hospitals, pharmaceutical companies or medical schools.

Tutors therefore look for the qualities that any good medical researcher needs, qualities like curiosity, persistence and an ability to accurately connect facts. A good bedside manner and a taste for the operating theatre dramas seen in medical soaps also help, of course, but are often taken for granted. This is not the place to emphasize in your personal statement that you like working with people.

Oxford also teaches medicine in the most traditional way. While some top universities move their students' knowledge forward through a problem-centred approach, for instance by taking them through all possible causes of a bad headache (Manchester, Liverpool) or by a systems-based one, for instance by teaching students "all about the lower limb" (Edinburgh), the Oxford curriculum is taught discipline by discipline. Students gradually work their way through anatomy, physiology, biochemistry etc. In their first two years they may (unlike Cambridge students) hardly see any patients. So, any reference to your enthusiasm for the theoretical sciences and not just the practice of medicine will go down well.

On the other hand, Oxford students are not expected to absorb this demanding curriculum by spending most of their time in large lecture halls or doing mainly practicals. Instead, their course is tutor-based. This means that a medical lecturer will work through the material with two students, sometimes even one to one. There is a huge reading list, but the mass of books can be absorbed because their contents is filtered through personal discussion. Tutor and student may remain together for up to three years.

All this personal attention does not just allow students to take in large amounts, it also enables them to follow their personal interests with encouragement from their tutor. There is a flipside, of course. A student really needs to be brave enough to ask questions, speculate on answers and risk being wrong.

As William James puts it: "This suits some people, but students who like to have their knowledge neatly laid out for them may not like this approach. Nor will those who like only applied science."

UNIVERSITY PLACES

For a subject which has generated so much public debate, Oxbridge medicine is surprisingly small. Oxford admits only 150 new undergraduates a year and Cambridge 280. Their postgraduate medical courses open to students with top science degrees are even smaller. Each university fills about twenty places a year.

GRADES

Top grades are essential for Oxbridge medical candidates. What this requirement means at GCSE level is mostly As and A*s. The number of GCSEs which an applicant must offer varies: privately educated pupils are expected to have close to the maximum number taken at their school, often ten or eleven, while state school pupils might be acceptable with eight. A disadvantaged candidate may impress if she has GCSE grades well above those generally obtained in her year.

AS-level grades too need to be high and when it comes to A-levels, candidates absolutely must have predictions of three As. There is no allowance made here for an applicant's type of school. A student from a successful comprehensive in some middle class suburb and a student from a struggling inner city one, where hard-pressed staff lack the time to coach individuals for top grades, will be judged on equal terms.

A-level requirements are not totally rigid. While an Oxford applicant must offer three A-levels, one of them in Chemistry, the second one may be in either Maths, Biology or Physics. The third A-level can be an arts subject such as English and sometimes even in a "soft" one like Psychology. Apparently, Oxford medical students with an English A-level get better medical degrees than those with A-level Physics.

(The rules for Cambridge medical applicants are different. They need A-levels in three out of the following four subjects: Biology; Chemistry; Physics and Mathematics. Moreover, the A-level grades obtained must be A*AA.)

General Studies, as has been pointed out elsewhere, does not count as a real A-level at Oxbridge, though William James admits that it is rather helpful when it comes to answering test questions involving verbal reasoning.

In practice, a college tutor might make a promising applicant a lower grade offer in a handful of circumstances. This happens if he or she has recently changed schools or, perhaps, lost a parent. But there is no special allowance made for being working class. The reason that used to be given for this was that information about students' families was not available to universities anyway. Now that UCAS will at least tell universities whether an applicant's parents went to university, both Oxford and Cambridge have said that they will not make any use of this. The reason given is that such information is uncorroborated data, i.e. unreliable.

THE ADMISSIONS TEST

The formal test for admission to the medical faculties of Oxford and Cambridge is identical, as already said. Called the Biomedical Admissions Test (BMAT), it lasts for two hours and is taken by students about a month before their interview at their school or some other approved centre.

Part one of the test assesses what is defined as aptitude and generic skills, that is the skills enabling a student to solve problems, understand arguments and analyse data. There is much emphasis on logic and on the ability to think in numbers: can that girl or boy handle a simple set of figures applied to a real world situation? Candidates might be given figures for incidences of multiple sclerosis and for the altitude of towns, then asked to interpret them. Questions often require you to look at graphs or test results.

(A word of advice here: when interpreting a graph, candidates should watch out for the difference between a medical cause and a correlation. A cause explains an illness, a correlation just means that the illness exists alongside another factor, causal or not. Candidates are meant to note the connection, but not jump to conclusions. For instance, Aids in the western world, largely correlates with male homosexuality. However, homosexuality does not cause Aids.)

Part two seeks out the scientific mind. While no medical knowledge is expected, candidates now need to be armoured with the background facts of GCSE science, including Physics and Maths. An interest in basic structures, such as cells, often comes in handy.

Part three is essay based, and a student trying to guess at likely topics may want to prepare for something like "Does politics determine health?" The writing tasks set are designed to explore whether the candidate understands a concept, can express herself, see both sides of an argument and offer some sort of analysis. This part of the exam is marked by the individual university, which makes it the place to hint at your aptitude for its particular course.

Sample questions and more details can be found on the exam website, listed at the end of this book.

THE MEDICAL INTERVIEW

A few weeks after the exam, Oxford applicants progress to the next stage. Once they have been put up by the college of their choice and dined in its hall or cafeteria at its expense, they sit their first interview there. This is followed by another one at a second college. The initial interview can be with any science don, but the next must be with a practising clinician (meaning a doctor who actually sees patients, rather than a medical researcher).

Interviewers now may ask what and how they like, although they have a score sheet they must fill in afterwards for the central medical faculty. The score sheet, designed to establish whether a candidate's intrinsic qualities can carry her through, is a fairly recent innovation, even more recent than the written test. It seems designed to ensure that individual tutors cannot go totally wild in their preferences for tall public school boys or sharp-witted Scottish girls.

Like the centrally devised and marked test, the score sheet also tells the outsider something important about Oxbridge: while their dons will always argue that its admissions procedures are as perfect as can be, they will somehow manage to make them just a little fairer and less idiosyncratic when there is enough outside pressure.

So, what can you expect to be asked? The warm-up question could be about anything, but quite often involves your reasons for choosing medicine. You may then be asked about your work experience. It is fairly essential for medical candidates to have worked, though it can be paid or unpaid, in a hospital or elsewhere. Any volunteer scheme involving handicapped people will go down fine. It will also count if you have cared for a relative at home. Medicine is hard work, and interviewers are looking for tough people, for "grit and determination."

Talk about how you adjusted to your work environment, and what relevant things you noticed there: the observation or non-observation of health and safety rules, pollution or shift work all have medical implications.

Much of the time allotted to each interview, though, might be spent answering specific questions. Many interviewers go for the

158

"show and tell" type. You might be shown a simple graph or a picture of some body part and asked what this might be. The question is not designed to test whether you have done your school work (which is assumed) or whether you have read lots of extra stuff (which is helpful, but not crucial). The interviewer is not checking what you already know, but whether you can use data, make sense of information.

This means you are being invited to make an intelligent guess and to spell out clearly how you arrived at it. So, the right answer would be something like this: "This is a heart, judging by the shape and the valve, no, actually, the valve is at the bottom, so it could be a kidney. It is, isn't it?"

You might still be wrong, but you have shown that you have grasped the process of arriving at the truth.

The opposite of an intelligent guess, adopted by some panic-stricken candidates at this point, is the stupid guess. After a long silence (bad if you only have 20 minutes to impress the tutor) one desperate candidate, I was told, finally whispered: "It could be a penis." Asked to explain why, he replied crossly: "I don't know, I'm just guessing."

Was he prepared to guess again, asked the tutor. "Not much point," he snapped, clearly regretting that he had ever taken up the invitation. As you may have guessed, he was turned down.

So, the ideal medical interviewee is someone willing to think, and to think aloud. She should also be calm enough not to panic if she doesn't know something. She should be willing to try and analyse the data put in front of her, in other words, to make sense of and combine bits of data. It also helps greatly if she understands what kind of information you might get from a graph.

Much of a candidate's interview success is due to attitude. Be willing to engage with the questions put to you, even if they are about something unfamiliar. Don't go into disaster mode if you get something wrong – candidates are often accepted even if they do. Be prepared to have more than one try and, above all, don't keep mum.

Basic good manners also help, though this need not mean upper class speech. Again, don't make assumptions about Oxbridge only wanting posh students. The grander the college, the more likely it is these days to need a few working class applicants to stave off public criticism. So, don't mumble "I don't know, we didn't do that stuff at my school," if you are stuck. Instead, say "I don't

159

know a lot about spinal vertebrae, but I'd really like to find out more, also for family reasons: my father's has a lot of problems with his spine because of his job as a warehouseman."

Allow for the fact that the interviewer herself may well have gone to a state school. Accents do fade over the years. While there is no point in worrying about your own accent, "you need to be a bit formal," as one Medicine interviewer put it. What this mainly means is wearing a jacket, using polite phrases like "would you like me to" and, of course, not smoking without first asking permission.

There are also a few human qualities that go down well. Cheerfulness is tops. Medicine will give you traumatic experiences and encounters with people who need reassurance. It also involves lots of exhausting teamwork. So, no tutor wants to take a young Victor Meldrew.

Modesty can be another useful trait. Interviewers really do hate arrogant candidates who seem to believe that they have a right to get into Oxbridge just because they are smart. Almost all candidates are.

Lastly, this is one subject in which the otherwise rather imperial demand that candidates must be able to "think on their feet" may well be justified. After all, that is what doctors faced with a new patient or a new slide of some diseased organ do every day. The fancy name for this, done on the basis of lots of knowledge, is "diagnostic skills".

HOW DOES ALL THIS PAN OUT?

Well, after their two interviews, candidates can spend the rest of the day kicking their heels, being intimidated by the seeming confidence of Oxbridge students and wondering how people living in such a beautiful place can have such atrocious dress sense.

Meanwhile, a bit of academic horse trading goes on. Each college will rank the candidates it has seen in order of perceived ability. A college with too many top ranked candidates might pass on some of them to another college less impressed with those it has seen. If that happens, the "traded" student may be called in for a further interview. Not all colleges have the same ideal candidate in mind, so quite a few of those recalled will get in nevertheless.

After that, all the selectors meet to coordinate their offers. These will be based on three equally important factors. One is a calculation based on the candidate's GCSE results: all candidates may have grade

As, but what matters is how these measure up to the results generally achieved within the candidate's own school. In other words, getting three As in a school in which nobody else did gives a candidate that special edge.

The second factor are the BMAT results, which will be with the central medical facility by now. Here, no allowances are made for a candidate's school or background.

Lastly, the score sheet produced by the college as a result of the interview makes up the last third of the evaluation.

As a result, some 150 candidates will receive the offer of a place at a specific college, conditional on them getting three As at A-level. Another 16 or so will get an "open offer", which means that their college cannot yet be specified. Where they will go depends mainly on the candidates dropped because they did not get the required grades.

So, how fair is the outcome? Well, it is not as bad as the Laura Spence story suggests. In 2002, two years after the working class school girl from Whitley Bay was rejected by Oxford, the university received 51.5 per cent of its applicants from the state sector and 34 per cent from private schools (the other 13.5 per cent are foreign students etc.). Almost exactly one fifth of each group (20.8 per cent) got an offer. Since the state school group was considerably bigger, this meant that its students would make up the majority of Oxford medical students.

What about other categories, though? Well, the picture is uneven. In recent years, the Oxford medical faculty has consistently admitted a slightly higher proportion of women and of students of Asian origin than there are in the general population. It has, however, an unrepresentatively low proportion of Afro-Caribbean students and male students of working class origin. The official explanation for these last two facts is that Oxford is not a regional university. Black and working class students, I was told, generally prefer to study close to home.

There is another explanation, of course. These two groups of generally very poor young people taught in poorly equipped schools will find it hardest to obtain the qualifications required to get an interview and so will not be encouraged by their schools to apply. Also, working class boys with the right grade predictions may lack the formal manners that carry you through. They are likely to be gruff rather than polite, macho rather than carefully balanced in the way they express themselves. While these are useful qualities in their current environment, they might well shed them in a different one – university students almost invariably do. By judging them purely on what they are at this point, the Oxford medical selection system does not work for them.

The same problem, despite slightly different selection criteria, exists at Cambridge, as one story shows. A sixth form head at a London comprehensive situated between two large housing estates bitterly recalled to me how he had sent one of his very best students to a medical interview there. The teacher had spent a lot of time encouraging the boy to take this frightening step and had carefully picked a college the school had some links with. The applicant, who came from a large working class family, was rejected nevertheless. When the teacher asked for an explanation, he was told that the main problem had been "nervousness in the interview, a lack of ability to hypothesize, expand on points, a lack of verbal articulacy and of interview skills."

Working class girls generally do better in the interview, though it is not clear why. Perhaps being polite and formal comes more easily to them or perhaps the interviewers are more sympathetic towards a timid girl than a sullen boy. It is hard to tell.

DOES COACHING WORK FOR MEDICINE?

Tutors admit that quite a few of the students they see have probably been coached for the interview, but feel that it would be unfair to reject a good candidate on those grounds alone. One tutor actually suggested that such preparation did, after all, suggest a commitment to the medical profession.

Some coaching is informal. Quite a few candidates in both the state and the private sector are doctor's kids and will have had a chance to talk through likely questions at home. Alternatively, a doctor friend, relative or neighbour might be roped in.

On the formal side, many schools in the private sector also run a brief course, usually called something like "how to get into medicine", which is especially geared toward Oxbridge. In addition, private schools also run science societies which may discuss medical research or explore health related issues.

Well-off state school parents can also buy in help. As a start, some private AS level revision courses now offer interview training for a range of subjects, including medicine (by A-level revision time, it is too late for this). There are also numerous companies specifically offering Oxbridge Entrance training in science subjects, including Medicine.

Do interview training courses work? One of the medical dons I spoke to insisted that he "could not believe that the organisers of such courses could possibly deliver on their promises." Others felt certain that they would be able to spot a candidate who had been coached. They also seemed unreasonably sure that they had not encountered such a candidate yet.

Some short courses primarily introduce A-level students to aspects of medical practice. Teenagers whose parents can afford the £200 fee learn about medical terms and diagnostic practices, get guidance on the university admissions process and have a mock interview. One such outfit, called *Medlink*, even let them treat Harvey, a state-of-the-art dummy, for a variety of conditions. Although a strong grasp of science is far more important for Oxbridge success, such an immersion process may enable a bright candidate to "talk the talk" and meet the requirements set out above.

What, though, can you do to help a talented child with a genuine interest in Medicine if you cannot afford any of the above? There are, in fact, quite a few things:

1. First, get your teenager yet again in front of his computer. He needs to look at the internet archives of *The Guardian* or *The Independent* (which are free) or the more detailed one of *The Times* (which levies a small charge) under words like "public health", "cancer", "disability","Aids" or "swine flu". This should throw up articles on key issues, as will a trawl through *New Scientist* or *Scientific American*. Ask him to pick out half a dozen recent pieces and read them through. What are doctors' main concerns? Which specialist deals with what medical problem and how?
2. Encourage him to think about the moral dilemmas faced by today's doctors, sometimes as the result of scientific progress. He'll find lots of articles and radio programmes dealing with those under "medical ethics".
3. Help him to make friends with medical statistics. Buy a simple statistics textbook which gives examples from real life. Your son need not understand everything inside (and should not panic if he doesn't), but it will help him to get used slowly and in his own home to seeing graphs etc. as information givers.
4. Persuade your son to borrow *Gray's Anatomy* from the library or look at the illustrations online (the text will be too hard). He may have done this in human biology before, but has probably forgotten what our various components look like. Checking out

enlarged online photographs of molecules or cells so he learns to identify the various types can also be of some help.

5. Find out how medics think. All sorts of medical writing can supply the reader with very useful insights: The *Man who Mistook his Wife for a Hat* by Oliver Sacks will serve your purposes no less well than *The Invisible Enemy: A Natural History of Viruses* by Dorothy H. Crawford. For a broader grasp, the insider tip is *The Logic of Life: Challenge of Integrative Physiology* by James Black, C.A.R. Boyd and D. Noble (note down the author's name, not just the title, as there is an economics book of the same name).

6. Ask your GP if your son can shadow her. Then encourage him to take the opportunity to asks her questions, which makes the experience doubly useful. He will not just learn about the practice of medicine, but also practice talking to medics.

7. Encourage the lad to arrive at his college the night before the interview, even if you live relatively near. Medical interviews are intense and it is not a good idea to walk into yours breathlessly after getting up at 5 a.m. and standing for two hours on a train. Far better to have an exploratory stroll first and meet other applicants.

These points should cover just about everything done in "entrance training courses" for potential medics, except for the treatment practice. Candidates are not expected to have treated anyone before.

At both the beginning and the end of this process, you must also do something else. You must get across that Oxbridge, in fact, does want some candidates from a quite ordinary, non-medical background. So, your son has nothing to hide and should try to mention his origins. If we ever get a regulator determined to ensure a fair distribution of university places, of course, Oxbridge might suddenly discover great promise in more young people like him.

16

Other ways of healing the sick

Medicine, especially in the era of the TV serial, offers bright young people an almost irresistible dream. The dreamer, dressed in a crisp white coat, is bending over a pale, rapidly fading patient. He then straightens up, furrows his brow and proceeds to deliver a brilliant diagnosis or to prescribe the perfect drug. The patient recovers in a jiffy and is full of gratitude. Colleagues standing near the doctor glance up at him (or her) with total admiration (or unbridled lust).

Waking up from such a dream can be tough but is often inevitable. Medical applicants, despite their sharp minds and top science A-levels, have some of the lowest UCAS success rates. Oxford admits only 14 per cent of them, Cambridge around 22 per cent. Competition means that most will not get any of their four university choices. Reaching for another, last-minute option, perhaps abroad, can be unwise. Some medical courses are not accredited in the UK, so their graduates cannot work here.

Fortunately, a sixth former determined to heal the sick has another, equally attractive option: pure science. This is because when it comes to finding out what ails people or to curing them, those who lead the field are often not doctors at all. They are scientists working in a great variety of disciplines or in cross-disciplinary ways.

By opting for a career in Chemistry, Biology or Physics, the young idealist can improve the well-being of patients all over the world. She can also earn an excellent salary, become world famous and, sometimes, even wear a white coat. Given the range of medical problems still in search of solutions, the opportunities are endless.

Despite this, a bright student's prospects of getting into one of the Oxbridge natural sciences courses are not bad at all. Oxford's Biochemistry course admits 42 per cent of all applicants and its Biological Sciences one 38 per cent. The Cambridge Natural Science course admits around 33 per cent.

In view of these facts, it seems strange that relatively few students choose to apply. For a brainy sixth former wishing to both do good and do well, one of these science options seems an obvious choice.

CHEATING DEATH IN THE LAB

Students' reluctance to apply is often rooted in popular culture. While scientists are highly respected in much of the world, their image in Britain has often been that of dangerous madmen or unworldly boffins, engaged in weird, pointless experiments. So, if you are still wondering what kind of contribution these people have made to our lives, here is a brief list.

Take our ability to explore a patient's insides without surgery. This was first made possible by Marie Curie, whose research into radioactivity led to the development of the X-ray machine. Curie, then went on to discover two medically useful new chemical elements, Polonium and Radium.

Magnetic resonance imaging (MRI) has given us a safer, more detailed way of looking inside the body, avoiding even harmful x-rays or dyes. The MRI scanner, which uses magnetism and radio waves, is now a standard medical tool. It is based on research by Peter Mansfield, a physicist, and Paul Lauterbur, a chemist.

Even non-scientists have heard about the decoding of the double helix, the structure of the molecule which determines DNA. Carried out by the physicist Francis Crick and the zoologist James Watson, it has had a huge impact on medical progress. Genetic research is based on it and keeps moving forward: by revealing the structure of large complex molecules such as insulin, penicillin and vitamin B12, the crystallographer Dorothy Hodgkin made possible the development of drugs that have saved countless lives.

Aids research was much advanced by the work of Kary Mullis, a chemist and champion surfer, whose discovery of the PCR test made possible viral load counting. Chemists Sydney Brenner and Robert Horvitz, together with molecular biologist John Sulston, subsequently discovered the key genes that regulate organ development and programme cell death. This, too, has proved crucial to the study of Aids.

By discovering RNA interference (RNAi), a naturally occurring process for switching off specific genes, mathematician Andrew Fire and Craig Mello, a biochemist, pioneered a genetic technique making possible radical new treatments for incurable disorders from blindness to heart disease and diabetes. The research findings of Paul Nurse have given doctors a way to understand, and hopefully alter, the deadly process of cell division in cancer.

You might also like to know is that the reward all those hard-working scientists reaped has not just been moral satisfaction. There is also celebrity status: almost every single one of them won a Nobel Prize for their work. The exception is Marie Curie, who won two, one for Physics and the other for Chemistry.

Research success can have further attractive benefits. Paul Nurse, a London-born biologist who was the first person in his family to attend university, told reporters in 2001 that he had spent some of his £800,000 Nobel Prize money on a 500cc Kawasaki motorbike. As he also received a knighthood, its parking space outside his Cambridge lab is labelled Sir Paul Nurse.

CREATING A HEALTHIER EARTH

Chemists, biologists and physicists might even be able to heal our sick planet. Not only are they steadily increasing their grasp of what is causing ecological change, but they are identifying cures that can be administered with a very large spoon. Research done on ozone depletion by Nobel Prize winner Sherwood Rowland, an expert in atmospheric chemistry, led to the 1995 world ban on the use of CFCs in aerosol sprays.

Rowland is one of several hundred world experts who form part of the Intergovernmental Panel on Climate Change, the UN body which released the first comprehensive report on the problem in February 2007. Global warming, it concluded, was 90 per cent likely to be due to human activity. The consequences would be higher temperatures, a rise in sea levels, hurricanes, droughts and famines. Having named the guilty and spelled out the world's dire prospects, the IPCC scientists will next look at options for adaptation and mitigation.

In other words, the survival of humanity (as well as that of the world's luxury motor cycle industry) may depend on experts like these. With an Oxbridge degree in one of the natural sciences, you could be joining them.

17

Aftershocks

What comes after the admissions process is another long wait. Only in early January will most offers and rejections arrive and your daughter needs to keep up her spirits until them. Even if she left her interview in tears (a sure sign that her interviewer was an amateur) she might well find an offer in the post.

If she does, it is time to go into top gear for A-level study. Oxbridge is not very flexible once a grade offer is made, and the admissions tutors I spoke to could only recall two recent cases in which a candidate had been accepted although he had not come up to the offer level: the first was a girl who had fallen seriously ill. The second candidate had been evicted from the hostel in which he lived, and the grades accepted were ABB rather than AAB.

So, it is time for the study plan, revision course, and a (partial) withdrawal from the endless social whirl that is teenage life. It is also time to withdraw from paid work. If you are a totally penniless, self-supporting A-level student, Oxbridge might be able to help. There is a handful of small study grants for disadvantaged candidates, which the college bursar can tell you about. Cambridge Special Access offers things like accommodation assistance in very exceptional cases.

Let us next assume that the bright girl actually got in. What this means is that you can look forward to several months of mutual incomprehension. Dropping in after her first term, she will confuse you by talking about mysterious things like formal hall, mods and prelims, and you will shock her by failing to understand the basics of existentialist philosophy. Her school friends will wonder who gave her the haircut from hell. When she tries to talk about her new life, her brother is likely to tell the poor girl that her accent stinks and her sister might accuse her of being stuck up.

Unlike students at many other universities, she will rarely come home at weekends. Oxbridge workloads and college social life do not allow for it. Those who see their parents every Sunday are perceived as odd.

After the first giddy year, though, an Oxbridge student and her family usually rediscover their common humanity, or at least a shared liking for Becks. By now, the dizzy girl might have learnt to appreciate your cooking and the fact that money does not grow on trees. She will also have become bilingual: she might still talk posh for a day or so, but will then switch out of it. Knowing that she managed to cope with an initially terrifying study schedule will have calmed her. She'll be smug but sympathetic. She might even go bowling with the younger kids. Holidays will no longer feel like a battle zone. This is the moment for you to rejoice in your Oxbridge work, and for her to help repaint the flat.

AMONG ALIENS

The bad news is that even if your teenager has got in, the Oxbridge dream can still go wrong. What if your visiting daughter confesses that she has not really unpacked anything more than her teddy bear after three weeks of Oxbridge life, because she does not feel she fits in? She hates the whole place, made a terrible mistake and is planning to drop out as soon as she can find someone who will promise to feed the tame rat adopted by the lonely little soul.

That Valium suddenly seems a good idea, after all. What are you supposed to do? Offer to drive up so she can collect her stuff? Or should you just tell her that the feeling will pass and that she ought to pull herself together?

The answer is that it would be a good idea to first know more. The first sight of student life anywhere can be exhilarating for some and terrifying for others, and student life at Oxbridge comes with added medieval pomp. Most students adjust fast, often by doing all the things you warned them against. This may not happen if they encounter situations which they had not expected to find and are not equipped to handle alone. A student in this predicament might become depressed, feel unable to study or decide to drop out. Some Oxbridge students in every year do. (Mercifully, student suicides are rare; they also occur mainly at the final degree stage.)

Given these frightening possibilities, you should try and get your daughter to explain what exactly bothers her. Sometimes the mere act of pouring out all her small initial failures or disappointments will make everything all right.

Chances are, your fears will prove unjustified. The problem is, more often than not, a disappointing grade, a tutor who speaks too fast or the discovery that nobody else in her year likes Jamie

Theakston. The best thing is to let her go on uninterruptedly about those, even if that means having your roast burn to cinders. After three to four hours of woes, she might suddenly jump up, grab her backpack and run for the next bus back because she has just remembered that there is a college entz (club night) at ten thirty.

The girl has just been letting off steam, which is normal behaviour among students. So, don't rush in with advice, or agree that going to Oxbridge was perhaps a mistake for someone from a background like hers.

Still there are areas of Oxbridge life that can give rise to real grievances, and students and their parents need to know about them.

18

Women's troubles

"When I walk home through the quad at 2 a.m. and see the moon rise above the college battlements I can't believe how lucky I am, and I really hate the idea that just two years from now I got to leave again," one girl from a South London housing estate last year wrote to a cousin she was encouraging to apply to Oxford. She is not alone. Female students of all backgrounds often fall in love at first sight with their beautiful old university.

This love has not always been reciprocated. For the first six hundred years of Oxford and Cambridge, women were banned from both universities. Their sheer presence was deemed unacceptable. College fellows (researchers and lecturers) were not allowed to marry until the end of the 19th century, and while a man could do so once he had reached the status of professor, many had lost interest by that stage, wrote Vera Britten in her history *The Women at Oxford*.

Women's attempts to gain at least partial access to higher learning were greeted with contempt. Even liberal figures like John Ruskin, who served as Oxford Professor of Art, declared in 1871: "I cannot let the bonnets in, on any conditions, this term. The three public lectures will chiefly be on angles, degrees of colour-prisms (without any prunes) and other such things, of no use to the female mind and they would occupy the seats in mere disappointed puzzlement."

After the first female students were admitted to Oxford in 1879, the Canon of Christ Church, Professor Edward Pusey, described women's colleges as "one of the greatest misfortunes that have happened even in our own time in Oxford".

In order to save male students from distraction, female students could not initially attend lectures or enter any of the men's junior common rooms in which much of the university's intellectual life took place.

Even when the lecture halls were opened to women, it was not in order to enable them to qualify. They were still denied access to the all-important degree at the end of their course. Without this document, of course, the few dozen exceptionally bright and determined women who had been accepted could contribute to society only as volunteers. Eleanor Rathbone became an outstanding social reformer, while Gertrude Bell joined her ambassador uncle as an unpaid assistant and went on to create the new state of Iraq out of various tribal territories.

Another graduate, Margery Fry, fought to improve the conditions for prisoners in British gaols, organised war relief for Europe during WW1, founded the National Council for the Abolition of the Death Penalty and became a governor of the BBC.

Those who needed the official qualification in order to get paid work had a very long wait. Oxford only started to issue degrees to its women graduates in 1920, Cambridge in 1947.

Women students remained outsiders for decades. They were banished to colleges far from the main university facilities, which initially lacked all basic amenities, from bathrooms to libraries. They were also condemned to an almost prison-like existence. Female students were not allowed out, even to the shops, without being chaperoned by "a respectable, elderly woman". During lectures, the chaperone would sit in the back of the hall knitting until she could take her charge home again.

The female principals who ran the women's colleges tried hard to gain acceptance by being as unfeminine as possible in their meetings with male academic colleagues. "Not a word was wasted, not a charm nor a wile exercised," a biographer approvingly wrote of Emily Penrose, the first principal of the Oxford women's college, Somerville.

Students too were expected to conform to almost unearthly standards of perfection. Elizabeth Wordsworth, who founded Lady Margaret Hall, suggested that it should be named after Lady Margaret Beaufort, the mother of Henry VII: "She was a gentlewoman, a scholar, and a saint, and after having been three times married she took a vow of celibacy. What more could be expected of a woman?"

None of this was enough to change male students' preference for someone who could shoot grouse. Public misogyny was rampant. In 1926, the majority of Oxford Union members voted in favour of a resolution which stated: "The women's colleges should be levelled to the ground."

Widely reported, the resolution caused some embarrassment to Oxford in the outside world. The university's male students were perceived as having gone too far, as being out of touch with the modern world.

Things improved gradually for women students after that, though not to everybody's satisfaction. "The presence of women at Oxford was now a deterrent for friendships between men," the head of one of the town's men's colleges recalled peevishly in his 1940s memoirs. Lest this deterrent should completely scupper the chances of the lonely male don, the number of women students at Oxford and Cambridge was formally restricted to one sixth of all students until 1957.

MODERN TIMES

But all that is history now. Oxbridge is about learning and this could not be restricted to academic fields. The universities gradually came to agree with the anonymous don who had warned in the Oxford Magazine: "The young men and young women are not going to spend their lives here, and we make it difficult for them to learn a very important part of human behaviour, how to conduct oneself in relation to the opposite sex. We isolate the problem, give it more thought than it is worth, enact regulations which, if they are effective, postpone till a later age adjustments which have to be made some time and somehow. The world is not a world of chaperones, of perfect vigilance..."

Equal opportunities legislation did the rest to turn both Oxford and Cambridge into something other than the rowdy boys' towns of yore. Today, numbers are equal, and all colleges and facilities are open to both women and men. Even more importantly, it's fun to be a young woman at Oxbridge, as all the female students I spoke to made absolutely clear.

For a start, living in a smallish town dominated by students can make young women feel very safe. Although neither Cambridge nor Oxford are crime-free, many praised the physical mobility they enjoyed by being able to cycle or walk almost everywhere, day and night. "I really love working my way through a pile of books until I have totally grasped something, and here I can stay in the library all night and walk home at 3 a.m.," one girl said enthusiastically.

There are other advantages, especially for those who have other plans for 3 a.m. The academic atmosphere, plus the presence of so many bright young male students can create new rules of attraction. Elsewhere, talking to a really clever girl can make quite a few men nervous, but at Oxbridge female brains qualify as a definite turn-on.

And, when it comes to careers, not just paid but highly paid employment today beckons after graduation. Oxbridge women do notably better than women from other universities, just like Oxbridge men do.

SIX FOOT IRRITATIONS

This is not to say that Oxbridge is a gender-equal utopia. While most academics are very careful to observe equality legislation and some can seem positively delighted at the progress of an especially bright female student, this is not a universal rule. Some very elderly dons can be awkward or subtly dismissive when forced to tutor a girl. After all, these strange creatures have been wandering among the college walls for a mere thirty years.

Even male fellow students can be irritating. Girls from single sex grammar schools, which are very brainy places, often complain that far less bright boys will hog the conversation in a tutorial, seminar or burger bar. As a result, getting into Oxbridge can be the beginning of a new kind of battle if you are a girl.

Oxford's 2002–3 Student Union Vice President (Women), Melanie Marshall, points out that there are considerable inequalities when it comes to university and college spending on sport. Women's sports are invariably under-funded. Far more money goes on facilities for cricket and rowing than on those for aerobics or yoga. There is also an assumption that what women do in sport is less important; the men's boat race and its outcome are reported in the national press. The women's boat race, an equally annual event, rarely ever gets a mention in the college rag.

The imbalance, Melanie explains, is a leftover from the university's men-only days, and it helps to make male students feel a sense of ownership of the place. This sounds terribly abstract until you look around and see a few young men happily throw about a ball on a manicured college lawn, while two or three girls stand around awkwardly as if someone still needs to hand them a script.

When asked to recall a case of individual discrimination, though, Melanie couldn't come up with one, however hard she tried. What there is of gender injustice is clearly not grave enough to leave any indelible trauma. We parted following her promise that she would consult her archives, in case they contained any striking cases, and that was the last I heard.

THE BRAIN RACE

Academic inequality is a different matter. In 2002, 26.2 per cent of men, but only 16.6 per cent of women studying at Cambridge got

Firsts in their final exams. The gap is similar each year, but rather puzzling. After all, female pupils do as well, or slightly better than male ones in each year's A-levels. One key factor pointed to has been the level of encouragement received from a student's academic supervisor. This, apparently, is more easily given to young men whose aggressive "intellectual muscle flexing" is often taken as a sign of excellence.

What actual discrimination there is at Oxbridge mainly affects female staff. Career prospects for women are limited at the two universities. At both Oxford and Cambridge, women in 2002 constituted about 20 per cent of academic staff, mostly in the lower ranks. By 2007 that figure had risen to just 23 per cent, despite an active women's academic network and the introduction of career development support. Less than 10 per cent of Oxford's professors are female.

This has financial, as well status consequences. In 2006, the pay gap between full time male and female academics was 16.5 per cent at Oxford and 19.7 per cent at Cambridge. While women academics earn less everywhere, such gaps are among the highest in the country. At Bolton University the pay differential is 1.5 per cent.

Women have been more successful at gaining top administration posts. Cambridge has had a female Vice Chancellor, Professor Alison Richard, since 2003 and three of the university's five Pro-Vice Chancellors (deputies) are female. At Oxford the figure for this group is four out of twelve. Oxford by 2007 also had seven female college heads, but this leaves nearly thirty colleges headed by men.

Generally, most female academics still work in the current or former women's colleges, especially in St. Hilda's at Oxford and Newnham and New Hall at Cambridge. Oxbridge is an ambitious world in which men are often that little bit more ambitious, but at least if there are only women to fill the jobs, women get them.

Even the honorary jobs held by students, much contested because they will look good on future job applications, fall to the more pushy, namely men. Take the role of the president of the junior common room (the college union). Despite there being as many female as male students at Oxford, only six of 36 such positions went to women in 2002. Somerville, one of the old Oxford women's colleges which admitted men in 1995, has not had a single woman in the post since.

This matters because female staff might pick students by more women-friendly criteria. Interviewed about sexism at Cambridge a few years ago, the feminist writer and English don Germaine Greer complained that whenever a women's college had taken on male staff, they had shown a worrying interview preference for admitting "fluffy blondes", rather than earnest and sometimes plainer girls with an obvious academic bent.

Equally, female academics can be more sympathetic to women-centred projects. A female student who proposes to do her degree research on, say, maternal needs in public housing, is likely to elicit more support from a female don than from her male equivalent.

WOMEN'S WORLDS

As a result of such differences, current students, old girls and the female staff at the remaining women's colleges have made sure to protect their single-sex status whenever a change was put to the vote. After all, they can offer a roll call of successful women.

St. Hilda's College, Oxford, which educated prize-winning scientist Susan Greenfield, former Tory Education Secretary Gillian Shephard, poet Wendy Cope and broadcaster Joan Bakewell, decided in 2003 against going co-ed. The defenders of the status quo argued that not only are the opportunities there better for women than in mixed-sex colleges (there are no all-male ones anymore), but that the atmosphere is better. Many female graduates describe it as more collaborative, supportive and conducive to lasting friendships.

So, would your daughter be best off in a place like that? Well, it depends. Those with academic ambitions should know that women at mixed colleges get more Firsts than those at women's colleges. There are several reasons for this. Women's library facilities may have caught up since their foundation stage, but the most high-flying academics tend to be attached to mixed colleges. Also, the old Catch 22 problem remains: as fewer of the women's college staff are eminent enough to be involved in setting the exams, fewer of their students get the best possible exam preparation.

In addition, the students who attend the women's colleges are no longer mainly the bookish, hardworking spinsters of yore. The outcome is that exam results are middling at best. St. Hilda's languishes towards the bottom of the Norrington table, the informal ranking of Oxford colleges by degree results.

There is also the general atmosphere. It is not totally female anymore: male friends come to visit and one women's college, Newnham, now has male lecturers too. The odd boyfriend from another college even stays the night. It is hard to imagine now that all girls from this college had to be tutored in pairs until well into the 20th century, as a female student could not possibly be left alone with a male tutor.

Contemporary female concerns are of a different kind. The Cambridge women's officer proudly talks of the improvements she has made in contraceptive facilities. Female pressure also resulted in the introduction of a university night bus, funded by bankers Goldman Sachs, which takes female students safely home to their colleges after clubbing in town. After a long debate, it was decided that male ones could hop on too.

On the other hand, tutorials and seminars in Newnham, New Hall and St. Hilda's remain women-only. For girls educated at a mixed comprehensive (as are most state school pupils) this can be a hell of a shock. Student life, after all, is not just about doing work. They are young women and most of them fully expect to have torrid love affairs with young men at their own level during their student years.

This can still happen, you might want to reassure your girl: lectures, university societies, voluntary work and (ahem) pub crawls bring the sexes together, but finding a boyfriend could be harder work for the girl who does not knock them out at first sight. She might not relish sitting in the JCR or college bar surrounded mainly (or, depending on the day, only) by other girls. Cycling through the pouring rain into the distant town centre to lectures, the superior main library and one of the livelier pubs does make you envy those more conveniently housed.

So, why do a small majority vote to keep things as they are every time? The main reason, I was repeatedly told, was ambition. You do get to try your hand at more things than you would otherwise. Want to be captain of the football team? Edit the college paper? Be president of the JCR? At a women's college, no bossy, overconfident public school boy will snatch these things from you. Even a small, speccy girl might get her chance.

Students also have fewer temptations to just skive off and do nothing. There is some excellent teaching, notably in Newnham. Girls from very religious or traditionalist backgrounds also find the environment more congenial or at least their parents think they should.

The main reasons why today's women's colleges are not seen in a positive light, though, is that many of their students have arrived there involuntarily. One of the few criticisms I heard from the otherwise terribly positive Student Access volunteers about the entrance system was that it advised girls from "non-traditional backgrounds" to not specify their college choice. Far too often, they said, this resulted in them being shunted off into a women's college.

Was it so bad then? I asked. "No, of course not," was the invariable reply. "They are quite pretty places, less draughty than some of the older mixed and formerly all-male ones. Seminars can be great too. But it's harder to have real fun there." It is arguments like those, I suspect, which made St. Hilda's students recently decide to go co-ed in 2008, after all.

So, if your daughter is at one of the few remaining women's colleges, expect a few complaints, perhaps slightly more than you would get if she was at a mixed one. However, don't accept that this is a good reason for leaving. Inequalities exist at other universities and students at any Oxbridge women's college make great friends, complete interesting projects, obtain Firsts and end up in fabulous jobs.

And, as mentioned before, no student is obliged to drink her nightly glass of Hooch or Perrier in her own college. One girl from a northern grammar school consigned to a women's college spent all her evenings at the bar of the mixed one attended by her older brother. Not surprisingly perhaps, she is now living with his closest university friend. Whether you regard this as a happy ending depends, I suspect, on whether you are a parent or a teenager.

19

Race

The publicity material sent out by Oxford and Cambridge shows young people of all different skin colours studying and hanging out together. The pictures are real enough and so, by all accounts, is the happy student experience. Such jolly images, though, can leave an ethnic minority teenager unprepared for what can be a fairly tough start.

Oxford and Cambridge are among the whitest universities in the country, by far the whitest in Britain's multicultural south. This means that a student who has so far been part of an often large ethnic minority group will take time to adjust. Living among people who don't look like you, don't speak like you or don't eat Ackee can be amazingly stressful, no matter how much you were looking forward to leaving home.

What can make this situation worse are the attitudes of others. The days in which blatant, in-your-face racism was tolerated in Britain are long over. It is hard to imagine now that in the 1960s it was possible for pubs to display signs saying "no Blacks, no Irish", or that some grammar schools would not admit Asian students. Such acts are illegal now and public attitudes have changed well beyond the law.

Ethnic minority students, though, can still feel left out even if there is no conscious intention to do so. Sometimes, this is just an assumption that anyone who is not white must be profoundly different. As Pria, a Muslim Liverpudlian of Pakistani origin told me with a shrug: "The fact that you are wearing a headscarf does not mean you don't want to be asked along when the rest of the girls go shoe shopping."

Chima, an extremely bright and outgoing black first year student from East London, loves her Cambridge course but says with slight exasperation: "It's not that anyone has ever been hostile, just that it is always me who has to start the conversation . . . And not wanting to step on anyone's toes can make people edge around meaning."

Chima was not imagining her problem. Since Oxbridge students tend to come from middle class schools, whether state or private, some have never talked to a black person before. "We do have one Black chap on my course, but he rather keeps to himself," a first year from a rural boy's public school told me in reply to a question, then went on slightly nervously: "S'ppose one should make more of an effort, but I'm just not sure what kind of things he'd be into."

At other times, the assumptions made can be deeply offensive. Jad, a well-dressed black student, was quietly sitting in his JCR, when a passing female college worker threw him a suspicious glance, before inquiring politely: "Are you lost, dear?"

A black civil servant recalls once being mistaken for a cleaner by another student during her first week in college. Apologising that he had only just got up, he beckoned her in so she could get started on his room.

A seemingly funny remark may also sting. The white student who takes his black fellow tutee to a club, but then quips: "I thought you people had dancing in your blood," is not just being silly. He is generalising and so might well believe other lies about blacks.

For some reason, asking someone "do you cheer for the West Indies, then?" is still regarded an OK question over a post-game drink in a few colleges.

Ethnic minority students also often feel irritated by hostile remarks on immigration and asylum. After all, many of their parents arrived in Britain by this painful route as, of course, did the people who founded such very British institutions as Marks and Spencer, ITV, the Glyndebourne Opera Festival and the RSPCA.

As a result, your son may return from college in the first weeks tense and unsure. Black male students, in particular, can react badly to their first encounter with Oxbridge life. They may feel they are not being treated with respect and almost every year a few of them drop out.

If your son is actually considering this, it will not help to remind him of the long-term payoff in terms of opportunities and careers (which can be impossible to focus on if nobody at his college has yet invited him for coffee). Nor will it do much good to say that black students have reported very similar experiences at Britain's other top universities, so a switch will not necessarily make the problem go away. The best thing to do, probably, is to ask the lad to defer judgment a little longer, at least until the end of his first year.

At this point, having struggled to get into Oxbridge and then to fit into life there, everything often suddenly falls into place, at least for those black students willing to persist in their initiatives.

Chima, who had struggled in her first term to even keep a student conversation going, six months later had a rich social life involving students of every colour and background. She was vice president of the Cambridge University English Society, social secretary of her college badminton club, a theatre critic for her college magazine and active in the Target Schools campaign seeking to encourage more black applicants. Despite her earlier experiences, she had no doubts at all that going to Oxbridge had, for her at least, been the right choice.

This is not to say that ethnic minority students should passively accept racist behaviour. All universities, including Oxford and Cambridge, now have strong anti-racism policies and will act on reports of racist incidents. The problem can be, of course, that a student, may not feel that her experience was bad enough to mention. A study by the Cambridge student union, CUSU, suggested that one off the cuff comment in the college bar may be enough to cause tremendous upset but not seen as worth reporting. Besides, how do you react to something that was probably not meant to be a snub?

One way of reacting is by getting support from within your own group, and far more of this is now available than there was even five years ago. Sometimes, this just means a club in which you can meet other ethnic minority students from different colleges. This is often supplemented by events designed to spread information about your minority group.

At Cambridge, for instance, the Caribbean Association seeks to bridge the gap through cook-outs, lectures and what they claim are the best parties in the university. Others, like the Hindu society, organize regular talks but also, as the culmination of their annual events a widely popular, colourful Diwali ball.

Some societies are more overtly political. Oxford Black and Asian Caucus (BAC), which was revived in 2003, targets racism, which it regards as a real problem, through events like Black History Week and showings of black films. In this way it aims to "promote equality and celebrate diversity, helping to make the university a tolerant and supportive place for its dynamic student community".

CUSU puts much of its efforts into campaigning for the same aim, but also insists that the atmosphere in its colleges and faculties is broadly anti-racist. Most incidents reported to its officials involve racial taunting on the football pitch. This is not exactly a practice confined to Oxbridge, but most students find it deeply objectionable and their union is determined to stamp it out.

All these bodies, to which has to be added GEEMA (Group to Encourage Ethnic Minority Applications) at Cambridge, seek to emphasize the positive about their culture and about the university's efforts, so much so that, as one white anti-racist student put it to me, you sometimes wish they would just draw up a checklist of the things they absolutely hate!

These societies often meet more urgent needs. According to one activist, the benefits of membership are that "it gives a sense of security, it motivates you to discuss things and to deal with it. It gives you mutual support and counselling... We are in a white institution, we have to encourage each other to be proud. We are role models."

One such role model is Pav Akhtar, president of Cambridge University's Student Union in 2001–2. Asked to comment on the situation, he said he was optimistic about the future: "I didn't think that it was a place for me, a lower class Asian northerner, but the university has accommodated me... It's by coming here that we will change things here and change perceptions."

OFFICIAL LINES

The social experience of ethnic minority students at Oxbridge is not something the university as a whole used to take much interest in. It was implicitly, and sometimes openly assumed that these people had no right to fuss; they were expected to be just grateful for the opportunities offered to them.

Many present day academics feel very differently and will go to great length to make an individual black student feel at ease. However, when you bring up the subject of race with certain Oxbridge dons, these rugged individualists mysteriously produce an almost identical phrase: "Actually, we have a slight overrepresentation of Asian students in certain courses. Some people, you know, have complained about this." A look at the available statistics for Cambridge really does not justify such complacency. Students of Indian origin, who apply in their hundreds, indeed have a reasonable success rate. Around a fifth of them, or 21 per cent, were admitted in 2005. The success rate of Chinese students in the same year stood at 28 per cent.

However, these are young people from established communities and many of their Oxbridge students, when you meet them, turn out to be privately educated. Quite a few of the others too have been raised in families running small or medium size businesses.

According to a 2001 study, Asians from Bangladesh, a very poor community, had only a 13 per cent success rate.

The picture turns really grim when it comes to blacks. Not all that many Afro-Caribbean students apply, but their success rate is abysmal. In 2001, two(!) out of 23 applicants got in, or 8 per cent.

The obvious reason, and that invariably given by dons, is schooling. Afro-Caribbeans tend to live in the most deprived areas and consequently go to the worst schools. As a result, they may lack the knowledge base required to get in. There is also a cultural factor. Black students often talk in a very direct way and can come across as dogmatic or abrasive.

To see whether the key factors are really just culture and schooling, though, it is worth looking at another statistic from that Cambridge list, that for Black African applicants. This includes students of all classes and income groups with parents (or grandparents) from all over the world. Teachers I spoke to felt that most were probably Nigerian and from comfortably off and educated homes. So, how well did this group do? The answer is, not much better than Afro-Caribbeans. In 2001, only 12 per cent (eight out of 67) were accepted by Cambridge.

The percentage of white applicants accepted by Cambridge, incidentally then was 35 per cent.

When asked for an explanation, dons often point to subject choice. Black African parents strongly encourage their children to apply for Medicine, Economics and Law, the courses most difficult to gain admission to. However, black applicants to other courses do not seem to do very much better.

At Oxford, the situation is fairly similar. In 2001, for example, 38.7 per cent of white students who applied for undergraduate places were successful; 100 black students applied, just 1.3 of the total, and only 18 got in.

Admissions figures have not exactly shot up since. By 2007, the success rate of black students at both Cambridge and Oxford had risen to just over 14 per cent. This has to be measured against a rate of around 28 per cent for white applicants.

TEA FOR TWO

There is, of course, an additional explanation, which has its root in the informal, unwritten structure of the entrance process. Until recently, a high proportion of interviews would take place between two people, the admissions tutor and the applicant. Some admissions tutors may be just a little more gruff, a little less welcoming to an ethnic minority candidate than they would be to a white one. This need not even be a conscious process, but can still lower the quality of a candidate's performance. I certainly found that those accepted are less likely to have had a cold, hostile reception.

The new practice of having almost all interviews conducted by two admissions tutors could have a positive impact on this problem, but there are other ones. Interviewers might also react to the candidate's use of "Black" English, or to his refusal to engage in a mannered but very rapid response dialogue, preferring to instead slowly ponder over an unfamiliar question. As the American psychologist Alexenia Y. Baldwin puts it in her study *The Gifted and Talented: development perspectives*, gifted black teenagers do not necessarily "present the classical intelligence or achievement profile that is equated with giftedness."

None of the above, of course, proves that the races are treated unequally at Oxbridge. However, unless the figures improve soon, there might be a strong argument for inviting observers from the Commission for Racial Equality to sit in on a few interviews.

THE WAY FORWARD

Some sixth form teachers would certainly like to see more scrutiny. Raised in multicultural cities, their pupils are stunned by the whiteness of smaller British towns and villages encountered on school trips. To them, the ethnic make-up of Oxbridge already discourages applications. The more confident black students are in their abilities, the more they insist that they will only consider a university which appreciates minority groups.

Teachers often try to counteract this Catch-22 factor by promoting Oxbridge as a top student's natural home. Whenever they hear a bright black pupil say, "I won't go where I'm not wanted," they try to change this fatalistic maxim to "I deserve to be there". However, this does no good if the applicant then fail to get in.

Chris Bland (not his real name), a Maths teacher, told me how he had, a couple of years ago, sent two of his students for an Oxbridge interview. One, a boy with a white and an Asian parent, was a sound mathematician, good rather than brilliant. The other, an Afro-Caribbean boy, was considered by the school to be absolutely outstanding. Guess who was accepted? The black student's Maths teacher, although prone to cynicism after years of sending out Oxbridge candidates, was still livid at the outcome.

This is not to say that such discrimination happens every year – it does not need to. Faced with students hesitant to go where so few academics seem to want them, and with universities unable to appreciate more than a handful of their students, teachers of black pupils sometimes decide to err on the side of caution. Why expose an already doubting student to the prospect of rejection?

Oxbridge staff are horrified if you suggest that anyone teaching at their university might be racist, but the problem remains. Someone does need to explain how the average don finds it so much easier to see intellectual promise in a polite, blond home counties chap or a delicate, soft-spoken Indian girl than in a hulking Afro-Caribbean boy.

By accepting that talent can be found where genteel white manners are not, the best American universities educate huge numbers of brilliant black students. In Britain too attitudes are changing. Inner city teachers were full of praise for the ability of top universities like Imperial College London, UCL and Manchester to identify top potential in all sorts of different applicants.

The academic powerhouse of Oxbridge, though, trusts to instinct, which means that black students, especially, can spend their first months feeling odd, home-sick and cross.

COPING STRATEGIES

Many black students at Oxbridge are actively trying to improve the situation. Having concluded that their key problem is gross under-representation, they put a lot of effort into Access projects aimed at communities and schools with large black populations.

Asian students, who are only slightly underrepresented, can face a different problem, rooted in British youth culture. This is that the two key student leisure pursuits, in Oxbridge and elsewhere, are drink and sex. For Muslims, the fact that they reject alcohol can be a serious barrier to the initial bonding process. Sipping your coke while others are on their fifth, hilariously funny pint of Grolsh can make you feel an outsider, as well as terribly bored. For Asian girls, Muslim or not, the more casual approach to sex taken by their white fellow students can be quite shocking.

Abstinence can certainly slow down integration, giving rise to comments like "he doesn't pull" or "she's a bit of a prude." Luckily, this stage tends to be short. Even in the face of great cultural differences, shared tutorials and the shared worries about seminar tasks or impossible deadlines create real bonds. Future doctors working long hours in the lab rapidly conclude that they have far more in common with one another than with any of their fellow students outside Medicine, perceived as idle slobs.

And there are other ways of meeting people. One young doctor from a Punjabi family I interviewed recalled that she really enjoyed hanging out with the Christian Union students at her university, who shared her moral stance. A Bengal-born London girl, now a young executive, had a wonderful three years as an active member of the Pakistani Society, the Islamic Society, the Iranian Society and the Oxford Union, all without ever touching a drop of alcohol or uncovering her knees. Two of the male Arab students I spoke to admitted somewhat shamefacedly that they did drink in their first month, "because it helps to get to know people". Once they had bought the required number of rounds, though, both confidently reverted to tonic water. Those awkward first term nights in the pub had brought them into contact with a range of people they could pick their friends from, and those they picked had interests that could be pursued sober.

An Egyptian-born writer, now approaching forty, recalls that he enthusiastically took up football and rowing, but avoided rugby "which was for drunks". Coming from a political family, he spent the rest of his free time arguing about Palestinian rights with fellow students. One of the lifelong friends he made in the course of this is now a London newspaper editor, the other a (Jewish) professor of Politics. If you are confident in your own culture, you can clearly get away without drinking.

To sum up, an ethnic minority student seeking a happy social life often needs to do three things. One is to be aware that the dominant culture among Oxbridge students is anti-racist, another is to take lots of initiatives, and the third is to be reasonably flexible. As one female Indian undergraduate said to me: "We girls get on fine but quite a few Asian men wander around all on their own. And when I ask such a chap whether he has joined any societies or mixed much with people from other colleges, the answer is always no. 'You know, how busy us science students are,' one young man said to me. That's quite true, but most of the white students still belonged to something like the boat club or the film society. You can be too cautious, I think."

A DEGREE OF DIFFERENCE

It would be tempting to stop on this positive note, if there were not another, rather crucial fact worth being aware of. This is the degree results.

A "significant" number of black students are underperforming at Cambridge, according to a four-year study commissioned by the university. Published in February 2003, the study results showed that far fewer black students scored Firsts and many more got third class degrees than their white peers.

While 21 per cent of white students got firsts and only 2.4 per cent Thirds, the proportion of blacks who left the university with a top class degree was just 3.1 per cent, while 15.6 per cent got Thirds.

Students from Indian families got the highest proportion of Firsts – 23.7 per cent – compared with 17.9 per cent of students from Chinese families.

How to explain that disparity? Some of it may be due to the schools which students come from. The "better" the school, the better prepared students will be for Oxbridge in terms of working habits and background knowledge. The main answer, though, probably lies somewhere between the Oxbridge teaching structure and its exam system.

To get a First, a student needs active, sympathetic support from his personal tutor and seminar tutor. Those who do well have often also built up a close rapport with other teaching staff. This creates a circle of people around them which they can ask for help with problems, and who will point them in the direction of suitable reading. Perhaps some of the Oxbridge teaching staff are not quite supportive enough of their black students.

There certainly seems to be a clearer case for greater monitoring, and a compulsory staff training course in racism awareness. These are now routinely run for public sector employees elsewhere. In the course of writing this book, I asked most academics I met whether they had had any form of racism awareness training. I might as well have asked for their favourite sexual position. No reply was ever forthcoming.

Still, Oxbridge is forever changing, also when it comes to race. Some colleges are now forging strong relationships with black community organisations and schools. Others have started to provide general "equal opportunities" training for their dons. The problem is that participation is difficult to enforce across both universities, because of the colleges' self-governing nature.

IS IT WORTH THE HASSLE?

Ethnic minority students who had come for the academic buzz of Oxbridge, for a carefully picked course or for contact with a special academic expert, certainly tend to think so. So did students who were keen to get practical experience in fields like drama, public speaking or journalism. The semi-professional Oxbridge societies offering such experiences not only welcomed them but often encouraged them to take up official posts.

Nor does this mean that you have to pay with loneliness for these benefits. All the ethnic minority students I spoke to had made close friends from different backgrounds at Oxbridge, if sometimes after a very hairy start. Quite a few did not feel totally integrated until the beginning of their second year, unlike most white students, but the college system usually worked its magic in the end. Black and Asian students, if they stay the course, tend to leave Oxbridge not less embedded in the Oxbridge network than the rest.

Oxbridge also remains the place for moving you beyond your own world on the careers ladder. Black Oxbridge graduates, especially, seem to go on to top jobs in the higher civil service, the arts, media and politics more easily than other educated members of their communities.

Academic prospects are a different matter. Should your gifted son stay if he cannot be sure to get a First from Oxford or Cambridge? Well, he should certainly be given a fair chance to. It is important to remember, though, that in the end most students at both universities get Seconds, not Firsts, and that still makes a graduate extremely employable in most fields. In fact, some employers prefer Oxbridge Seconds.

What if they do worse in the exam stakes? Well, Zadie Smith, whose first novel, White Teeth, won just about every literary prize in Britain, got a Third in her Cambridge part-one exams. Her old college, King's, now lists her on its alumni page as one of two prominent contemporary British writers. The other writer listed in its official publicity material is one of its 1960s graduates, Salman Rushdie.

20

Working class heroes

There have always been some working class students at Oxbridge. Hand-picked for truly exceptional ability by the local parson or schoolteacher, sponsored by a gentleman through grammar school and encouraged to sit for the pitifully few full university scholarship places, the son of a skilled, respectable working man occasionally managed to get in. In a good decade, there could even be two such students. Careful not to presume and grateful beyond belief, these young men posed no challenge to Oxbridge.

Tension only arose when workers' aspirations increased. The introduction of free, compulsory schooling in 1870 had created a hunger for more education. Demand for the right to study at university also came from those with political ambitions. Working men now had the vote, and the Labour Party was concerned that its leaders should be men with the best possible education; so should the teachers who would raise up the working class and the trade unionists negotiating with employers.

In 1897, the TUC resolved "that the workers... should not be satisfied until the highest educational advantages which the country affords are within reach of all." This was followed by more concrete demands for access to "the deep draughts of knowledge" which only Britain's two oldest universities, so it was felt, could provide.

Cambridge offered a handful of places, but what many talented workers sought was the opportunity to study history, politics and economics at Oxford. This remained out of their reach, both because they lacked the right schooling and because they could not pay.

"We want Oxford to open wide her doors to the best of our people and take them in," declared J.M. MacTavish, a Labour member of the Portsmouth Town Council, in 1907. If the university only realised what enthusiasm there was amongst ordinary people for this education, it "would sell its plate" to help fund it, he argued, adding that such access would benefit both sides. If workers were admitted, "a true view of social questions would be taught... Although we are supposed to have no recorded history, without us all history was and is impossible."

CLOSED GATES

Gradually, the tone became less conciliatory. When told that Oxford could not accommodate working class students, campaigners angrily asked whether it was the true function of a university "to train the nation's best men, or to sell its gifts to the rich?"

There was some minority support for this stand within Oxford. A handful of dons already travelled for miles once a week to teach extension classes to men who had just completed a ten hour working day. Some of these academics had no doubt that their best pupils ought to be continuing their education at the university. Charles Gore, later Bishop of Birmingham, stated in the 1908 Toynbee Report that he hoped for "a great displacement of rich or well-to-do young men who wanted to have a good time, by serious students who would come from all classes but in large measure from among the workers".

Still, when a few of the 29 Labour MPs who had been elected to Parliament in 1906 suggested that Oxford should admit at least a tiny number of outstanding working men who had prepared for this with infinite patience at the night schools of the Workers Educational Association, the response was hysterical.

Writing in the Fortnightly Review, F.C.S. Schiller, a Philosophy don at Corpus Christi College, Oxford, warned that "the workers know what they want, and what they want is destructive of progress in knowledge... What they want is an education for their purposes, an education specifically adjusted to their needs, to wit, a study of economics, politics and history... Of course, the spokesmen of the workers fail to understand the aesthetic function of Oxford... the athletic aspect of the university is equally unintelligible to them... Work people cannot understand that men whose chief interest seems to be 'play' should be allowed to remain at a University... a demand for social equality is included in their demand for 'equality of opportunity and it would almost seem that they were snobs enough to find a chance of slapping a Lord on the back in their cups one of the indispensable attractions of College life."

In any case, the reputable don argued, all clever men already had access to Oxbridge. For this reason "it is becoming more and more difficult to believe that there exists untapped reservoirs of intellectual ability among the workers. This is not to say, of course that there is no practical ability among them ..."

Where that ability should take itself Schiller had no doubt: "It ought to be much easier for the new universities to satisfy the legitimate educational aspirations of the 'workers' and so to save the lily-likeness of Oxford from the hands of the uprooter."

And thus Oxford was again "saved" from the workers. Only after WW1 were the entry requirements marginally eased. This was too late for many aspiring students, but talent still won out in a few cases. One of the trainees in a 1908 extension class taught by a sympathetic Balliol don was A.P. Wadsworth, who went on to edit *The Manchester Guardian* (now known simply as *The Guardian*) without the benefits of an Oxbridge degree.

PICK A NUMBER

It is the folk memory of that ugly debate which has dogged working class entrance to Oxbridge. Young people from working class homes remain deeply uncertain about whether they can get in and fit in. "It's not for the likes of us," is a common view. Having arranged for the year's best student to attend a day school at Cambridge, a teacher at an inner city sixth form college found himself faced with a cross, miserable lad who kept asking: "What's the point of it? Must I go?"

The point, of course, is that working class pupils do get in. In the course of researching this book, I have talked to one Oxbridge student who was the daughter of a care worker and another who was the son of a cook. I have met young Oxbridge graduates whose fathers were lorry drivers or plumbers and an Oxbridge-educated professor whose father was a tailor. Most found their university life a positive experience and a great help with their careers. "It's wonderful that even someone like me can hope to get a job in the city," a girl whose father was a print-worker told me with shining eyes. Those 19th century campaigners for working class access would turn in their graves at the thought of "their" graduates becoming investment analysts but, heck, times do change.

The question remains how much else has changed. Just how rare a bird must a working class student expect to be once he has unpacked his CDs and bought his cap and gown? The answer matters not just because is suggests how fair the entrance process really is. It also determines how comfortable such students will be at Oxbridge. Oxbridge dons can be remarkably vague about student proportions, as was exposed by a very public spat between Margaret Hodge, the

Lifelong Learning and Education Minister, and the University of Cambridge on 4th February 2003. After Hodge had remarked during a visit that the university ought to do much more to attract youngsters from working class backgrounds, the university's vice chancellor, Sir Alec Broers, responded by issuing a strong statement. "It is simply not true that only 'rich kids' are accepted into Cambridge. Last year, 23 per cent of home students at Cambridge did not pay any tuition fees and were therefore eligible for the full student loans and for the bursaries offered by Cambridge."

The middle class parents of Cambridge students may have nodded assent. Not so people who understand the difference between money and class. Many a self-employed business person's accountant can produce a perfectly legal income-expenditure balance which results in a taxable income of around £17,000. This defines the bread winner as disadvantaged in the university's eyes and qualifies his children for considerable financial help. On the other hand, a working class couple raising two children while doing low-paid PAYE jobs might be earning just a little above that figure. This means they'll have to cover most education expenses. Even if their children go to university at all, they'll probably live at home, not pay rent to a college.

So, the beneficiaries of the funding system are, in practice, often the self-employed or divorced middle class mothers. It's a great help for sure, but not a way of improving the class balance.

Talking about 23 per cent, therefore, merely muddies the water.

DO THEY REALLY EXIST?

Most dons agree that a wider range of backgrounds in the student population would be nice, but they usually refuse to define the issue any further. They certainly don't like to use the "c" word – class. Academics involved in Access projects often proved to be the ones most adamant that there is no longer any such thing as the British working class, though there were, of course, deprived people.

Student Access campaigners employed in university-sponsored projects take a similar line. When I asked one of these how to contact working class undergraduates so I could find out how they felt about being at Oxbridge, the response was a long silence. I might as well have asked the poor girl what sanitary towels she used. When she finally spoke, her embarrassment was so profound I could almost watch her blush over the phone: "We can't actually . . . you see, we don't define it like this . . . how would one measure it really . . . it is really an outdated definition."

Did she not know which students were working class, I asked, trying to relax her. "Well, not really ... you know, it's not that, though," came the nervous reply.

What was it then? "It's just that it would be wrong to single out people as working class, you know, we never ask them anyway, so nobody knows."

Surely, the students themselves would know whether they are working class, and they might want to talk about it," I snapped, getting exasperated.

"Perhaps," was the reply. "But you can't be sure, and I don't really want to go down that route. I'm afraid I cannot help you." Was she unique? Clearly not: another Access campaigner I contacted insisted that even to mention the term working class in her Access group circular would be insulting.

So, what term did Student Access use? The answer, here too, was that vague and all embracing one, "non-traditional", which covered several other areas quite apart from class.

It took a great deal of persistence to get beyond that point and a special appeal to the university's press officer but, a clutch of emails later, I was told that a face-saving category had been found. Although nobody would tell me what it was, students started to email me. This was my chance to add to the sample I had contacted by other means.

The wait proved thoroughly worthwhile. I met yet more outstanding young people who had no regrets about their university choice, but also no doubt about their identity. They were, despite a range of accents that ranged from Estuary to mildly posh, all working class, and proud of it.

One of the most interesting things that emerged from this research was that even their interviewers had not necessarily known this fact. Universities might theoretically strive for "wider participation", but practically they operated in a void. Although UCAS recorded the social class of every applicant's parents, it did not pass that information to the university. Unless mentioned by the school, admissions tutors could only guess at this key fact. It was a bit like trying to hit a target with a sack over your head, and while doubting that the target was actually there.

BEING AN "ONLY"

Still, 10 per cent is a substantial figure, a sizeable chunk of any small town's population, and it was puzzling why working class Freshers were so often uncomfortable at Oxbridge. Surely, their accents would be everywhere, even if they themselves could not be picked out; thanks to youth culture, all classes dress much the same. However, those students I managed to meet who were of clear working class origin, which meant they had strong local accents, fathers who were truck drivers and mothers who did piece work on their sewing machine, were adamant that they were unique.

All recalled how they had looked around for "people like me" at their colleges and on their university course, only to find that there weren't any. Lizzie, a third year student in a small college which had 300 students and a reputation as sympathetic to state school pupils, was adamant that she was the only "real" working class person there. Nobody else came from a housing estate and everybody else had parents who were much more educated than hers.

If Lizzie was right, and given that she had by then spent almost three years in the place I have no reason to believe she was not, then this would make her one in 300, or well below one per cent. Quite a different proportion.

So, where does the official figure of 9 or 10 per cent come from? Detailed research I undertook led to a unexpected discovery. Its sole source is the UCAS form, in which all applicants under 21 are asked to put in the occupation of the highest earner in their household – the very information not passed on to admissions tutors.

Using this figure can lead to considerable inaccuracies, as a friendly UCAS statistician explained to me. The first of these is due to the fact that 19 per cent of student applicants (almost one in five) leave this section blank. Others give an occupation that cannot later be classified.

A specific job title too is not enough to ensure a correct statistical outcome. An engineer, for instance, can be either a skilled worker or a middle class graduate.

Even if accurately defined, one parent's occupation is not enough to define a family's class. The "highest earner" in today's Britain may well be married to a low-earning middle class partner, an electrician to a teacher, or a carpenter to a writer.

To complicate matters further, there is no category called "working class". Instead, UCAS divides householders into eight categories. In place of the three old categories of "skilled manual," "partly skilled" and "unskilled", there are now four at the bottom of the list, called "lower supervisory," "technical occupations," "semiroutine" and "routine". It is from these data that the Higher

Education Funding Council (HEFC) deduces the number of working class students at Oxbridge.

In other words, your teenage Fresher may well be in more of a minority than he expected to be, and as a result feel out of sorts. So, don't just tell the poor lad he should count himself lucky for getting in. Show some sympathy. He is in an unexpectedly alien environment and this can spell trouble.

SPECIAL HURDLES

Vaguely recalling that Oxbridge used not to want working class students and definitely finding himself in a minority, the lost lad may respond by withdrawing – mentally at first. Why bother to speak up? Students like him, he may have concluded, are expected to lie low, put up with what they are offered and hat-check their culture at the college gates. Such beliefs can affect not just his social life but also his studies.

What can make this worse is the likely discovery that his course is not pitched at comprehensive school level, and even less so at the level of even the brightest students from disadvantaged schools. Some of this can just be a matter of cultural references. The frequent use of classical imagery in science, as well as arts courses, often stumps those who grew up without any mention of Greek gods. Luckily, this is an obstacle fairly easily overcome. One Hackney student finally ended three months of unhappy puzzlement over references to Zeus by buying an encyclopaedia of classical myths.

The generous use of Latin proverbs by dons may also grate. So can being unable to understand the inscription on one's own college gate. Although no comprehensive student can read Latin, those with educated parents sometimes manage to puzzle out what is meant and, if they can't, seem remarkably unbothered. A working class student often worries far more and needs to understand, as they do, that his education is not threatened by this.

Another handicap can be not knowing that academic help is often available as long as you ask. Paul, a working class student keen to do a course option involving European History in his second year abandoned the idea when he realised that this required a knowledge of German. A middle class student fancying the same course just discussed the problem with her supervisor, who revealed that the girl could acquire the basics of the missing language at the university language lab. There was even the possibility of a vacation grant that would enable her to get some practical language experience.

Other solutions can sometimes be found if a poor student faces what may seem like an insolvable problem. June, a very able English student, found it impossible to study in the holidays, as her family lived in one of Britain's urban war zones. When she explained to her tutor that "it's a bit difficult to read Paradise Lost when people are committing GBH outside," he suggested she should stay in college next time. Told that she could not possibly afford the £8 per night it charged outside term, he just nodded.

A week later, June's tutor mentioned that some funds might be available. When she pressed him for details at the next tutorial, he told her where to go. In the end, June got a hardship grant and spent most of the next holiday in college.

So, much can be done to smooth a working class student's study problems, but that student really needs to be clear about her needs and quite persistent. The more eminent her tutor, the more vague he might be about the basic facilities available. Requests may have to be put to other dons, or the bursar. Another useful starting point can be the college JCR. In fact, Oxbridge is so well equipped that almost any course-related request can usually be met, at least if put forward well in advance.

THE MANY AND THE FEW

With only (perhaps) 10 per cent of new undergraduates being working class, social life for them can still be tough, at least at the beginning. Several students I met revealed that they had hated Fresher's week, because they felt everybody talked so much posher than they did and seemed so much more confident. While public school pupils all seemed to know one another and even many middle class kids from comprehensives formed little groups, a working class student from a struggling school had usually arrived alone.

Even the getting to know you chitchat in class can make a poorer working class student feel different from the norm. One girl said that what she found hardest at first were those endless questions about "what did you do in your gap year?" Another added that she just wished people wouldn't talk so much about their foreign holidays. Her family did not travel abroad and before coming to Oxbridge she had never even been outside London.

Having less experience of academic work can cause insecurity too. Dave, a shop worker's son, accepted by Cambridge for his outstanding potential, remembered that when he was given four books to read for his first Geography essay, the task was so terrifying he could hardly open them. There had not been any books in his home and he was unused to writing long essays or to reading outside the syllabus. He was convinced that all the privately educated students were far cleverer than him. Only after the first term did he accept that he might be any good.

By the time I met Dave, he had become a quite outstanding student, but he still worked extremely hard, sometimes to the extent of making himself ill. He admitted that he was worried that he might not impress otherwise. He knew several other working class students who behaved in the same way. Most of the time, he said, "they all think they are impostors."

This is not to say that Dave has any regrets. As he put it: "Studying elsewhere is probably less stressed, there is more balance in one's life. Cambridge is very competitive. But then other universities would not have challenged me so much. It is harder to excel elsewhere. Here there is so much opportunity and such good expert supervision which develops you. I know that if I can cope with demands here, I can cope with anything."

There is no doubt that many of the working class students were not just bright, but far brighter and more resourceful than others at Oxbridge. One girl worked out all there was to know about the Oxbridge application process herself, after her teacher warned her that it might be too complicated. Another responded to the problem of being asked at her interview about knowledge she did not have by firing back lots of intelligent questions. Her interviewers were suitably impressed.

THE HOME FRONT

Yet another disadvantage working class students can face is their family's attitude. One girl I spoke to had been warned by her mother not to tell any other relatives that she was sitting for Oxbridge, in case she was mocked.

Often, even a well-meaning working class family was unable to offer support to a student coming home after a stressful term. This was the case even if there were no external problems, such as crime. Parents and sibling might find it hard to talk to her and tend to watch for any signs of "uppertiness". On visits, the student might be expected to constantly play down her "other life", except when put in front of relatives to show off. Ruth, a SPS student with particular interest in sociology, commented that working class families often seemed unaware that a young person who moves away from home will change, wherever she might go, and might indeed develop opinions and ideas different from their own. As a result, the student's new identity is sometimes taken as a personal insult. The result can be serious family fall outs. This is a price not exacted from middle class students.

Still, none of the students wished they had made a different choice. June remarked how wonderful it was to live without the TV blazing away, to discuss issues and develop theories, all things she had never done at home. At Oxbridge, she said with a smile, nobody gets angry if they disagree.

The main problem, though, was living in quite such a middle class set-up, in which your behaviour and speech patterns always stuck out. Unlike ethnic minority students, white working class boys, in particular, seemed initially stunned by this. They had had some concerns, but nothing in their lives had prepared them for being outsiders. On the other hand, many did, thanks to time and obvious effort, completely blend it.

Those white working class students I spoke to certainly still loved Oxbridge, usually for its intellectual buzz and the opportunities it had given them, rather than for its social customs. All of them also wished that there would be more people like them, so they could feel more at home.

WHO'S A POSH KID, THEN?

Having said this, it is important to realise that the gap is not always as big as it may seem. Those who come across as "posh" on first sight are often, as the student gradually discovers, young people from all sorts of unrich homes who went to Britain's handful of remaining grammar schools. This group makes up almost 17 per cent of state school students. Many of the privately educated students at Oxbridge are not even the sons of gentlemen farmers anymore. They are more likely to have fathers who are shopkeepers, lawyers or managers and mothers who work in an office to pay the fees. Quite a few Oxbridge parents are said to be self-employed builders.

These people are not sending their bright kids to public school so that they can look down on others, but in order to ensure that they are taught for longer hours, by more qualified teachers and with more attention to their ability, in short, to give them the kind of education which is free and taken for granted in much of Europe.

THE ETONIANS

There are, of course, some very posh students at Oxbridge. There was one question to which all working class students I eventually met responded in exactly the same way. Asked what they found strangest at Oxbridge, the answer was invariably: the Etonians. There seemed to be a huge number of them about, roaming the place in tightly knit, well-spoken groups, utterly at ease there from day one.

This was slightly puzzling since there are, in fact, relatively few Etonians at Oxbridge today. Britain's most exclusive boarding school, whose intake, in any given year, includes one third landed gentry and at least a dozen boys with aristocratic titles, sends most of its trust-funded pupils to slightly less demanding places. The most popular destinations are Durham, Bristol, Exeter or a nearby agricultural college. Still, Eton is a big school with a big scholarship form and at any moment there can indeed be over 200 Etonians at Oxbridge. All of them too seem to know one another or at least someone's younger brother. Most of them are found at Christ Church, Oxford, the college which the school has centuries-old links with, so you can, as said earlier, always avoid it.

On the other hand, why should you? Eton does not actually produce monsters of snobbery, but polite, charming young men who wear their privilege lightly. Despite what you have seen in the movies, they don't ever line up to bray at northern lads for wearing elasticated bow ties. They are all male and, when sober, sweetly polite with the female sex, which they have before mainly known as matron. When drunk, they go in for strange tribal sing-songs, and tend to monopolise the universities wine societies, where they can be rather less charming to outsiders. As the wine societies are almost the only university societies that charge, knowing this can save you lots of money.

However, nearly half of the Oxbridge British student intake does come from various private schools, and it eventually dawned on me that state school students tended to use "Etonian" as a generic term for any male students from a private school. This view can be daunting, as well as misleading. What Oxbridge has, in fact, is a quickly formed fraternity or sorority of people who have never met, but play squash and know what Rugby or Teddy's are (they're boarding schools). Most also live in the same part of the home counties or green belt areas around London.

Once at Oxbridge, all these students indeed stand out by the relaxed way in which they move around their strange new home.

There are good reasons for this. The oak beams, stained glass windows and coats of arms on the wall of the college dining hall will be familiar to them from their school, even if that establishment was only launched after the Beatles' first LP. Their teachers too are likely to have worn black gowns over their M & S suits, at least at formal occasions. The Latin names of various obscure Oxbridge practices and sites are no mystery to those who survived a decade of compulsory Classics.

Most importantly, perhaps, pupils from the private sector do not arrive at Oxbridge alone. Even the smallest rural establishment which will take anyone who pays expects to send a bunch of pupils to Oxbridge a year. What parent would pay some £10,000 per year without at least the distant prospect of a place? The handful of schools that pick (and expel) pupils on the basis of academic achievement alone might each send up to 40 students each autumn. This begets the little groups of first years with the plummy voices.

But do they want to stay among themselves? Well, initially they do, I suspect. In a new place, it is reassuring to be among friends, and so you find clusters of new students swapping fond memories of their housemaster, Mr. Chips, in some distant corner of an Oxbridge playing field. If you went to a comprehensive, this can make you feel excluded, but I wouldn't jump to conclusions just yet. Usually, it's nothing more than a bit of childish nostalgia and the boys will soon drift back into grown-up life.

Asked whether they think it is best to stay among one's own kind, the numerous private schools students I have met over the years certainly responded with an emphatic no. They are at university to meet exciting new people, and some would go as far as drop their h's to that end. There is even a better reason that few will admit to: private schools tend to be single sex, so getting to university is at least partly about escaping this hellish state.

DIFFERENT COPING STRATEGIES

Still, being working class at Oxbridge can often be harder than expected at the earlier stages, and there are problems which do not go away. Having less spending money than others is one of those. When you first arrive, it can often seem as if all the interesting people go out for a restaurant dinner every night, rather than eat in college. Fortunately, this is not actually true.

Drink is a more serious issue. Binge drinking is now so deeply rooted in student culture that it threatens to not just destroy a whole generation's livers, but also all efforts towards integration. Student leaders who are serious about Access must, I feel, confront the reality that if the normal student is spending every night at the bar, then many poorer, working class student will invariably be excluded. So, of course, will all Muslim students. Could this be the moment for a bit of creative lifestyle change?

Meanwhile, working class students need to be prepared for the fact that Oxbridge is a very middle class world, albeit not one necessarily hostile to outsiders. Many of those I spoke to were quite thrown at first by the extent to which they stuck out. Each one also recalled, without prompting, one thoughtless, hurtful remark. When you are 18 and new to a place, being referred to in jest as "our Prole" can really upset you. Of course it's a joke and you should joke back, but that does take confidence.

The most common advice working class students gave was to relax: everybody experiences a bad response once, so there is no point in letting this confirm your insecurity. You are in the modern world, among fellow students. It is crucial to realize that you are not constantly being snubbed. Don't let anyone intimidate you, but don't be too easily slighted.

You also need to reach out. As Ruth, the SPS student I met, put it: "Working class students sometimes don't understand that the way of mixing at Oxbridge is not necessarily by finding similar people, but by doing similar things. They wait for someone congenial to turn up in their year or course, rather than join societies to develop joint interests."

Some students adjust by completely losing their working class manners and accent. "You'd never know he was working class," one girl said of a passing young man with flowing locks, dressed in pure Brideshead. Others play the wide boy for all it's worth, even claiming to be related to the Krays. A few spend far more money than they can afford and have to take a college job to pay their debts. Others again just look ahead and seize the opportunities with both hands. Some, to their own surprise, simply enjoy the terrific features of the place.

It is easier to do the last thing if your parents told you that everybody is an equally worthy human being, and if you are blessed with a sharp wit. It would be even easier if more middle class people taught the young that good manners are not really about gripping a wine glass with three fingers at the stem; they are about making the person opposite you feel at ease. The truth, though, is that in the end both sides adapt a little. Middle class students learn to play darts, working class ones become experts on vintage dry sherry. The bad old days when Oxbridge was a lily that needed protection from the workers are over. If you can persuade yourself that you deserve to be there, you should have three or four great student years.

21

What if he didn't get in?

However, talented your teenager, and however good the preparations he made, the fact remains that more people apply for Oxbridge than get in. There are between three and five applicants for every place. Readers can massively improve the odds by following the advice in this book, but in the end candidates and their parents must also accept that there is an element of luck involved. Young people of equal ability, suitability and amiability compete for the same places every year. It is, therefore, possible that the lad will suffer the disappointment of not getting an offer, or of not getting the grades required to take up the offer made.

Being told that the university you chose has not chosen you can come as a nasty shock, even to those who thought they had allowed for it. So, if you don't want your son's self-esteem to be damaged, don't wait until the rejection letter is in his clenched fist. Instead, think ahead and positively consider other options when you are first looking at university prospectuses, or when he tells you about his teachers' recommendations.

This means that you should say good, constructive things about the second and (if possible) third place he is thinking of applying to. You do not need to be a university expert for this. Just point out that the course in University B looks interesting, the staff friendly and young. Talk with genuine warmth about the location of University C even if your own memories of the bleak East Anglian landscape or crowded central London make your heart sink.

None of this makes you a hypocrite. Students can be deliriously happy in a concrete jungle, as long as it offers them good teaching and a lively campus. Encourage the lad to find out more and perhaps visit the place. Encourage him also to check where his own role models have studied; it may well not be Oxbridge.

What you want is for your son to feel that all the choices he has made are good ones, that he can look forward to his university education, whatever happens. True, Oxbridge particularly suits some students, being more theoretical and more intense than other places. It is also so much better funded. If the lad goes elsewhere, though, he will reap other benefits, not least the skills to survive in the real world and he'll learn about much the same academic subjects.

Again, you need not feel that you are dishonest by telling him this. Britain's world class experts studied at all sorts of universities and many still lecture there. Top careers are made by people who have graduated from all sorts of degree courses or none at all. A great university experience is determined not just by the status of the institution: it can come from the friendships formed and the infectious enthusiasm of one single staff member, plus the kind of bands which the student union gets in for gigs. And this experience, in turn, generates the kind of self-confidence that bolsters careers.

So, do make your son feel from the start that he has a range of attractive options ahead of him. Don't be afraid that unless you turn his getting into Oxbridge into a life or death matter he will rush off to Skate City or the pub, rather than cram for his exams. Firstly, this is not true and, secondly, such brinkmanship will not do him any good. By now he will know from his teachers, his environment and everything said at home that he needs to work to the max. Those with a clutch of strong university choices do so in better spirits and with a lighter heart.

If you follow this advice, the lad will still have something to look forward to, should the Oxbridge offer not materialise. Being rejected always hurts. Without other attractive prospects, your son may well feel cast out into limbo, or appalled at the prospect of studying at a place he has taken absolutely no interest in or treated with scorn.

Nor is being positive about other options merely a fall-back position, as you might think. It is also a great way of enabling your son to impress his first choice. Oxbridge, like the perfect lover, comes to him who is cool – not desperate.

HANDLING THE BAD NEWS
Faced with a glum boy who picked up the courage to apply to Oxbridge or a tear-stained girl who fell in love with the medieval quads on her school's Outreach visit, the temptation is nevertheless to curse that stupid, snobbish place. Or you might want to mumble something about playing the game being more important than winning.

My advice is to do neither. All is not lost yet. If there is real talent here and not just parental pushiness, and if your teenager remains determined, there is always the option of reapplying in the next academic year. The cobblestones of Oxbridge are trodden by a surprising number of students who did just that. However, the steps a student must take depend on the precise situation.

WHAT IF SHE DIDN'T GET AN OFFER?

Let's say your daughter was expected to get above-average grades relevant to the degree subject she had hoped to do at Cambridge. However, as a result of her interview and/or exam not going as well as expected, or of some other mysterious factor, perhaps a tepid reference from her school, she was not offered a place.

If she does not want to go to another university instead, she will have no choice but to wait. Her first wait will have to be for her A-level results. If these are in the top range, meaning three or more As, Oxbridge is still an option the following year. Anastasia Fedotova, a Manchester pupil rejected in 2001 by Brasenose College, Oxford, although she was sitting six A-levels, dealt with this by taking a year out. After receiving her exam results, which were six A-grades, five of them in the sciences, she then applied to Trinity College, Cambridge, and went on to happily read Maths there.

But where should your daughter try next? Theoretically, students can just reapply to another college in the same university, but the dirt among the private Oxbridge tutors is that your chances in these circumstances are vastly better if you try "the other place" instead. In other words, if your very bright daughter was turned down by Cambridge, she should try Oxford next. Apparently, there is a mild form of one-upmanship in taking a good candidate rejected by the competition.

WHAT IF HE DIDN'T GET THE RIGHT GRADES?

This is quite a different situation. Grades well below those specified in the Oxbridge offer obviously mean that another university offer should be accepted. However, if your son missed the required grades by a hare's breath, he needn't give up.

You must both accept that there is no prospect of the college reconsidering its specifications, unless there are documented reasons for the lad's poor showing. A serious illness suffered during the exam period and backed by a doctor's certificate will be taken into consideration. A bog standard, self-treated, runny nose will not.

If your son's results were due to a clear factor such as emigration or bereavement it may very occasionally pay off to resit. But if it is just that one of his grades was a B, rather than the required A, the lad might be wiser to obtain further qualifications for the desired course instead. This could mean taking a third science A-level (Cambridge is less keen on applicants with a mix of arts and science subjects than Oxford) or a course-related AEA. What might also be worthwhile is learning an extra language or, in the case of Law applicants, working for a solicitor.

The student may want to pick a different college to apply to, which can be at the same university. All Oxbridge colleges accept the occasional retry student, but your son's chances are better if he now lowers his expectations. The top colleges, generally those in the centre of town, will be less interested than those at the edge.

This is also the time to target another, slightly less competitive Oxbridge course. Determined students now tend to shift from English Lit. to Modern Languages, or from Medicine to Chemistry. It is too late to make the more drastic switch from arts to sciences or the other way round.

Before considering such a route, though, look carefully at all the facts. First, be sure that your son is capable of getting the right grades. Look at the precise marks he obtained in every part of the A-level exam, which are detailed in the certificate. B-grades and A-grades may seem close, but if the document shows that the lad only just scraped his three B's, despite good teaching at a school which regularly sends other pupils to Oxbridge, then you should probably encourage him to take up her second offer. Cambridge is unlikely to consider an Oxford reject with middling grades and the prospect of much the same.

PREPARING FOR THE RESIT

Even if your son's grade results were a narrow miss, you need to make very sure he really wants to time-travel back to the classroom. Students usually prepare for resits at a local authority (or private) sixth form college, a place without pack drill or uniforms, but we are still talking about 30 hours of schooling per week, plus homework. Much of the work will not be exactly new to the resit student, even though the syllabus changes slightly every year.

Oxbridge is now an option again, and if your son knuckles down to the work, this is the time to cook him his favourite meal or go fishing with him. You can also help him achieve his goal by insisting he takes a part-time job or finds a work-experience placement related to his course. Either could give him an extra edge in the Oxbridge race.

Don't be put off by claims that he can't possibly find the time: even resit students have evenings, weekends and summer holidays; ample time to practice your foreign languages in some tourist hotel, or to scrub hospital corridors in preparation for Medicine. Such activities show that you are a determined, eager young person and might even give you something to talk about at your interview.

What a student hoping for a second Oxbridge chance must do alongside all this, though, is work out where else he and his vast DVD collection could be happy. With the number of Oxbridge applicants steadily growing, second-timers do not stand half as good an admission chance as they did a decade ago.

LAST CHANCE SALOON

Even those who've failed to get into an Oxbridge undergraduate course at all, and this includes some of the brightest and most successful people I know, need not completely give up. If you excel at another good university, there is always the option of doing a higher degree. You might even want to read for a third quali-fication, the doctorate (known as a PhD or DPhil.), at Oxbridge.

This is not a second-rate choice. The Russell Group universities, and especially Imperial College, London, and the London School of Economics, rank right up there with Oxford and Cambridge in the academic world. Other universities may have less famous staff, but their approach may be more modern or more down to earth, and this can make their lecturers the academic stars of the future. Also, some students feel more inspired by younger staff, and these are less common at Oxbridge.

If you want to continue an academic career started elsewhere at Oxbridge, all you need is a First and a good recommendation. You will not be looked down upon. After all, many of the great discoveries that constitute the glory of Oxford and Cambridge were made by people who had studied first at less fussy, more accessible universities.

For a student in need of a reassuring example (beyond that of the outsiders who developed Penicillin at Oxford) there is always Professor Bob Edwards of Cambridge. Edwards who, together with the late Patrick Steptoe, invented the fertility treatment which has so far created a million test tube babies, initially studied at Edinburgh.

IF ONLY

It may be too late for this but you should be aware of another, some-what devious route into Oxbridge. The advice given to pupils at more than one private tutorial college has been to concentrate on getting into the course in which there was least competition from outstanding applicants, no matter what course the candidate actually wanted to do. This could mean, for instance, applying for Materials Science, even if you were really an engineer at heart. A week or so after starting his course, so the student is advised, all he needs to do is to confide in his supervisor that he feels he has made a terrible mistake. Materials Science, however worthy a calling, does not suit him. Would it therefore be possible for him to change to his true passion, Engineering?

He is likely to discover that a college can be remarkably flexible once it has accepted a student. While there are no guarantees, and while switching is most easily accepted between different language courses, the request will be considered. Assuming the waverer has the right A-levels and passed the right test, he might even be found a place on the coveted course.

There are, however, three points to remember if your son might wish to adopt this underhand, but not unknown, strategy. One is that the change of mind really has to take place within the first two weeks of starting the course. The second is that the student might find it rather hard to keep up academically with those who managed to get in the conventional way. Thirdly, and most crucially, it is pointless to try this as a bypass road into Medicine. It never works.

22

Best in show

What I have tried to show in the preceding chapters is that Oxbridge students come in all shapes and sizes. It's a miracle some of them don't bang their heads on those low medieval doorways.

There is one group, though, which does have an amazing success rate. What I discovered after interviewing dozens of state school students who had gone to Oxbridge was that the majority had one key trait in common. This had nothing to do with their individual character or type of ability. Instead, what linked them was their parents' workplace. To stand a fair chance of getting into Oxbridge from a private school all you need is a parent who can pay (or a scholarship). To get in from elsewhere, a pupil needs a parent who is employed by a school.

To some people this will seem an obvious matter. After all, a teacher is likely to know which areas of the syllabus his son needs to cover to get good grades and will be able to help with homework and projects. That sort of parent will also stress the value of studying, although the poor little swot forced to stay at home and study nonstop by his ogre of a teacher–parent is a figure of the past.

Many of the successful Oxbridge entrants I talked to, whether they were white, Asian or Black, had a strong school connection. The majority of those had mothers trained as schoolteachers. A few had fathers who taught at university, but had started their careers in schools. This factor was so common that after interviewing my first three dozen Oxbridge students (past and present) I had to resist the temptation of asking "What does your mother teach?" rather than "What does your mother do?"

But beyond this common feature my interviewees varied tremendously. Some were chatty, others quiet. Some had the kind of curiosity that even an Oxbridge course could not satisfy, while others seemed very focused. Some had well-off middle class fathers and their mothers taught only a few hours a week. Others were raised by a single parent, who barely managed to pay the mortgage with the help of her full-time classroom job.

The story, though, does not end here. Lots of these parents taught at primary schools. This meant they were not equipped to explain the A-level syllabus or help with school work. Nor were they in touch with Oxbridge requirements.

Quite a few parents, moreover, did not teach at all. The mother of a young Oxbridge-educated doctor had given up teaching years before her daughter's birth and had, in any case, only ever taught in Pakistan. Another girl, one of very few "real" working class students, had a mother who had been a school dinner lady. Yet another student's mother was a special needs assistant at a junior school. These mothers were in no position to tutor anybody, yet their bright children still made it into Oxbridge.

By the time the proportion of interviewees with school connection had reached around two thirds of my largely random sample, this became deeply puzzling.

BEING SUSSED

By refining my questions, gradually I discovered that there were important contributions even a non-teacher parent working at a school could make. Often this had to do with realising that not all schools were equally good. Even the dinner lady, it turned out, had heard enough staff room talk to move her daughter out of a poorly performing school and into a more highly rated sixth form college.

Such parents were also often remarkably clued up about the different career paths pupils could take, or the timetable involved. Words like resit did not flummox them. If the school had certain problems, they would hear about it. They had a positive attitude to teachers, but were not overawed by them.

One former student, the daughter of a school caretaker, recalled that she had received a sympathetic but not actually helpful response from her class teacher when she mentioned an Oxbridge course. Her father, who worked at a different school, advised her to consult another teacher before giving up; and this swung it for her. As she put it to me, her father, although not an educated man, was "very sussed" about anything to do with school.

"LIKE A CONVERSATION WITH A TEACHER"

Perhaps the main clue lies in the phrase used by one highly success-ful Oxbridge graduate, now a research scientist with a big pharmaceutical firm. I had expected the London-born daughter of a South Indian junior school teacher to describe her interview as a highly intimidating experience. After all, many others had done.

Instead the young woman thought for a moment, then smiled. "My interview was alright," she said. "It was like a conversation with a teacher." In other words, neither the setup nor the adults asking tough questions had felt alien enough to scare her.

The result is, if my impressions are correct, that teachers' children constitute a staggering proportion of Oxbridge students, far beyond their proportion in the general population.

FINDING OUT MORE

So what is wrong about this? Given that these students seemed as talented, varied and likeable a group as one could wish for, it took me a little while to pinpoint the cause of my unease about my – however provisional – findings. The problem is, in fact, pretty obvious. If the Oxbridge Entrance process is working best for one specific group, students whose parents have school-related jobs, then "widening participation" has some way to go.

It is, of course, possible that my findings were a fluke; that actually the majority of state school students at Oxbridge do not share this common trait. Even the fact that many students themselves had noticed the high proportion of teacher's kids in their year or college may still be an accident.

It would take a much larger and more scientifically structured survey (ideally one based on the entire student population) to reach any definite conclusion. I would, however, be very surprised if I was wrong. There is certainly an argument for Oxbridge commissioning such research. While the bright young people I met clearly deserved their university places, we need to understand why students from their backgrounds, more easily than others, negotiate the Oxbridge maze.

My suspicion is that ability is not always enough. Even the brightest students need in-crowd knowledge to succeed in a system not primarily based on scientific testing but on un-standardised verbal interviews. Meanwhile, I suspect that the range of backgrounds within the Oxbridge student body is somewhat narrower than the statistics suggest and the bright "non-traditional" student who gets in is quite often the daughter of a teacher and an engineer.

BE A COPYCAT

But what, you may ask, does this rather provisional insight do for the student whose mother or father is a bus conductor, cellist or IT manager? The answer is quite a lot: it enables them to improve their Oxbridge chances by copying the strategies that work for teachers' kids.

The most obvious strategy is that of studying hard but in a well-focused way; but there are other, less obvious ones. Among these is keeping up with a school's changing reputation. The retirement of a good headteacher can send a school into tail spin, while its upgrading to specialist status can dramatically improve results. As parents are unlikely to find out about these consequences from the staff, their local paper can be a great source of information.

What also matters is being aware that information about university entrance, and Oxbridge entrance in particular, can be spread out among a number of people in a school. So, if you cannot work out the course requirements, or don't understand the vocabulary, ask around. If you are a pupil, this can mean consulting not just your subject teacher or careers advisor, but also perhaps your head of department. Write out a list of things you want to know and take it with you, in case you get nervous.

If you are a parent, don't be shy about asking "stupid" questions at parents' meetings, or to make a special appointment with one of your teenager's teachers to clarify a point. Not only do entry rules periodically change, but this really is a specialized field. Even the scraps of information you picked up could be out of date. Many parents, for instance, still assume that to get into Oxbridge a pupil needs to stay an extra term at school.

On the other hand, it is important not to be overawed by a teacher's opinion. This is especially true if it conflicts with a student's own. If your dream is to study Chinese (as part of Oriental Studies) but your teacher feels you ought to do a degree in Geography, you need to ask why. If it is because she thinks more highly of her own subject, you might want to stick to your guns assuming you are doing the right A-levels.

Don't assume that teachers are infallible when it comes to picking Oxbridge candidates. If your son wants to apply, has very good GCSEs and is blessed with some of the key qualities outlined earlier, do encourage him to go ahead, even if his teacher is not so sure. Unfortunately, a few teachers identify only the well-behaved, mature pupil as an Oxbridge candidate. You may, therefore, have to consult other staff, or just trust you own instincts before both of you decide. A renowned science writer I know recalled with a chuckle that he had (successfully) applied to Oxbridge against all his teachers' advice.

Teachers have a lot of knowledge at their fingertips and the best interest of their pupils at heart, so take advantage of this, just like their own children do. However, not all of them have the time to keep up with Oxbridge rules, especially the unwritten ones. Fortunately, reading this book gives you the best of both worlds.

23

Nailing down the Oxbridge dream

The road to Oxbridge, as you will have concluded by now, is more open than most people believe and can sometimes be opened up further. However, it is equally true that access remains far from equal. So, how can real progress be made? The good news is that further change is not directly up to you, the parent or potential Oxbridge student. You just need to play the ball where it lies. The bad news is that action needs to be taken by two monoliths, Oxbridge and the Government.

Having said this, it is worth pointing out that there is periodic progress anyway, though not always as a result of deliberate action. When the makers of the Harry Potter films decided to shoot part of the first sequel in Oxford, they had no idea of what they were doing for British education. Visiting pupils, who would once have been intimidated by its venerable sites, now squealed with delight as they recognised the Hogwarts library (the Bodleian) and Hogwarts hall (the dining room of Christ Church). The university town with its crenellated walls and medieval towers had suddenly become a familiar, inviting place. Applications followed.

Other changes, previously unthinkable, suddenly become possible if enough fuss is made. An example of this is the saga of the Oxford medical entry procedure, centred on an exam set by the university's own medical staff. It was this exam which had resulted in the rejection of Laura Spence in January 2000. Known to work best for articulate middle class entrants who already knew a great deal about medicine, it was crammed for at almost every private school in small groups.

Despite this well known fact, Oxbridge academics defended the outcome to the hilt. They were backed up by the President of the Oxford Student Union, Will Straw, who wrote in *The Guardian* as late as 4th July 2003, "there was no prejudice in the procedure... Spence had applied for a particularly difficult course with very few spaces. Tutors at Magdalen College had interviewed over 40 applicants for five places all with similarly outstanding predicted A-level grades. According to the college principal, Anthony Smith, she had come tenth..."

While Straw still blithely argued that there was nothing wrong with the procedure, Oxford had already ditched it in embarrassment. As already mentioned, medical candidates aiming for Oxford, Cambridge and University College London were by November 2003 sitting a completely different exam, devised by experts in ability testing, rather than by medics. The new exam is still combined with a college interview, but the procedure is designed to ensure that cramming and cultural factors play less of a role in medical selection.

Oxbridge, as said before, is ever changing, and those too eager to defend current practices can end up with egg on their face.

IS THE WHOLE ENTRANCE PROCESS GOING TO IMPROVE?

Despite the examples given above, I would not bet my child's higher education savings on this. The Government intervention threats described in Chapter One ended with a hasty retreat and even the new OFFA powers to check the fairness of each university's admissions process announced in 2008 do not mean it can punish offenders. At Oxford at least, University Chancellor Chris Patten is taking a robustly anti-interventionist line.

In an interview with *The Times* immediately after his March 2003 appointment, Patten argued that if too few state school and especially working class students are entering Oxbridge, the blame lies with the schools' "spectacular failure in the past 30 years to raise standards ... It is outrageous for politicians to blame universities over access." In his investiture speech on 25th June 2003, Patten spelt out his stand further: "It is insulting to the able, and damaging to the universities that seek to educate them, to make the issue of access a crowbar for social engineers rather than a challenge for educationalists, and it is downright vulgar to allow it to become a populist political slogan."

While many dons (and parents) might agree that teaching standards have fallen and that basic skills are sometimes absent, the problem with this position is that it implies Oxbridge has a "right" to teach only pupils who have already been taught very well. This, in turn, implies that what it is really looking for is not talent but a candidate who has already been taken through much of their first year university course at school as pupils from the best private school indeed are.

What this approach disregards, say its critics, especially among teachers, is that the state school standard happens to be the national norm. Even the top national universities, therefore, should really teach upwards from it. After all, the education that state school pupils receive is meant to equip them for university and so it does. Those who get in cope. More than that, quite a few excel, even at Oxbridge.

This is not to say that there are no problems. It would clearly be desirable for state school entrants to know rather more grammar or more science. However, eighteen year olds are still capable of learning anything, and in amazingly short time. It is hard to see why a week's transition course, for instance, could not be offered either just before university entrance or in the first Christmas holidays. Devised to bridge the most damaging gaps, it could also point students towards further reading. Such a course could even be devised in website form. Alternatively, a few transitional texts could at least be included in students' pre-Oxbridge reading lists. Encouragingly, some of this already happens in Maths and a couple of other subjects.

Still, dons to whom I have put these bridging proposals have, on the whole, been less than enthusiastic. "Surely, we cannot now also be expected to teach remedial courses," one scientist remarked, his facial expression implying that I might as well have suggested a spot of child abuse. Others politely said that if the Government really wanted to safe-guard their world-famous research standards, a smaller teaching burden, rather than an even bigger one, would be very nice, thank you.

While it is hard not to sympathise with the latter point, too many bright state school students have not been taught up to Oxbridge entrance standard, and it is hard to see how student proportions can change if the private sector, or rather the top of the private sector, continues to set the pace.

A FEW MODEST PROPOSALS

All this suggests that at least part of official Oxbridge might be happy to passively wait until state education improves, thereby punishing at least some bright pupils for their local authority's failures. As mentioned earlier in this book, the situation at both Oxford and Cambridge is, in fact, slightly better. Many dons seek to bring in able student from a wider range than before and try to modify their entrance procedures accordingly. New standardized, subject-specific entrance tests have been introduced in five Oxford subjects; Cambridge has experimented with a broader aptitude test, the TSA, though fears that cramming can distort the result means it is only used by some colleges. Admissions tutors now often trust more in a student's carefully dissected GCSE and AS-level marks. The new A*A-level grade may reliably pinpoint braininess in all kinds of students, at least if all kinds of schools teach towards it.

Change, in fact, has become a feature of the entrance process. University admissions departments have revised some unhelpful entrance procedures and are reconsidering others. Colleges now share information about candidates and quite a few dons are improving their interview techniques to reassure non-traditional students.

The Department of Higher and Further Education has sunk money into a myriad of new initiatives, aimed at students, teachers, parents and universities.

Unfortunately, this is not the same as having an effective strategy. Even worse, there are no binding targets. It seems, therefore, important to list some specific measures which could at least create a more level playing field, preferably before the Harry Potter craze fades. Below are the most urgent ones.

WHAT THE GOVERNMENT SHOULD DO:

1. Reform access

The most urgent thing the Government must do, without doubt, is to end the funding of Access type projects in their current form. Not only has Access swallowed millions of pounds in funding over the last five years without really changing student proportions at Oxbridge; it is also in danger of setting teachers, parents and pupils at different types of state schools against one another.

Access funding, as described earlier in this book, is based on the assumption that the under-representation of state school pupils at Oxbridge is primarily due to low self-esteem. By telling them to visit the two universities and to apply, the problem is expected to go away. Unfortunately, application does not equal acceptance. Those active in Access have no real influence on acceptance policies, and so the balance has essentially remained unchanged.

In the meantime, Access policies are having another, rather unpleasant effect. As much of the funding depends on inventing new types of projects, efforts are increasingly fragmented. There are now Access projects directed at mining areas and rural schools, at further education colleges and at schools which have never sent a pupil to Oxbridge, at ethnic minorities and children in low income groups. Oxbridge sends out videos and email messages. Young people all over the country are told that if they work hard and attend an Oxbridge event, they stand a fair chance of getting in.

Given that the part of the cake allocated to the state school sector has remained the same size, though, this inevitably multiplies disappointment and not just among pupils. To illustrate what this means, let me give an example from a very mixed area of London.

The story starts at a comprehensive, renowned for the quality of its teaching and its excellent Ofsted reports. It is also part of a sixth form consortium which achieves some of the inner city's best state school exam results. Proud of its orderly atmosphere, anti-bullying policy and highly qualified teachers, the school attracts a wide range of pupils. Some, including children from ethnic minorities and asylum seekers, come from the poor neighbouring housing estates. Many others come from the opposite end of the spectrum; they are the children of doctors, lawyers, university lecturers, journalists and civil servants.

In this top-university orientated school, pupils are helped to prepare by teachers who regularly attended Oxbridge staff seminars and are encouraged to participate in every sort of Access project. Usually, out of a sixth form of some 370 pupils, five to eight succeeded in getting in.

In 2002, the school confidently sent off twelve of its pupils to be interviewed. The results were unexpected. Only one pupil, a middle class boy whom the school had not actually picked as a high flyer, received an offer. As the head of sixth form put it: "There is not really much point in our overworked staff putting weeks of effort into encouraging, persuading and preparing pupils for Oxbridge, just to see a single one getting in. All Access has done to build up our kids' expectations, only to dash them again."

Meanwhile, a few miles away in the same area, the staff of the area's largest sixth form college were equally bewildered. The college, whose devoted, well qualified teachers have changed lives, had thought that their pupils were just what Oxbridge wanted now. Most of them were, after all, working class, or from particularly disadvantaged ethnic minorities.

Not that the teachers had ever relied on such assumptions. Over the years, they had instead built up links with a total of six colleges, two in Oxford and four in Cambridge. They also ran enrichment activities which gave pupils experience in journalism, photography and poetry. The college had invested time and expertise in Oxbridge preparation, and this seemed to pay off. Out of a sixth form of 280 pupils, it would annually send up to a dozen interviewees. Between three and five of these would be offered a place. The grades stipulated in the offers remained inappropriately high, but two to three pupils a year were getting in.

When the replies to the 2002 applications dropped through the doors in January 2003, though, the news was really bad. Not one college pupil had even received an offer. Some of the teachers' comments were not printable, but a veteran Maths teacher expressed what many others clearly felt: "It's back to the same old thing. The ones we send are really exceptional, but Oxbridge won't see that."

The college teacher also got on the phone to colleagues in order to find out where "their" Oxbridge places had gone. A chat with a friend teaching in a well-known private school situated between the college and the area's comprehensive revealed that they had not gone there. The private school, which has a sixth form of 90 pupils and prides itself on accepting pupils of widely varying abilities, had received the same number of offers as usual – fourteen(!).

It was a teacher whose sister taught in a small town with a high unemployment rate who finally came up with an answer. For the first time ever, her school had received an offer from Oxbridge. So had another school in the same town, targeted by Access under the "Widening Participation" scheme.

In other words, Access had "worked", but not as most people naively thought it was meant to. Faced with an unprecedented number of "good" state school candidates, an outcome Oxbridge had mysteriously not foreseen, it had decided to redistribute its places within the state school group.

The college teacher, who has an English degree from a good university, found no difficulty in expressing how he felt. "Perhaps they should rename 'Widening Participation' something more appropriate. How about 'Thinning the Soup?'" he said.

On the parents days of some urban comprehensives, the talk can be uglier than that. "Just as our school got itself sorted out, they take it all away and give it to the kids of people who don't even pay taxes," said the mother of a girl put on her school's gifted and talented list, but rejected by Oxbridge.

Unless Access has been created to sow despondency and discord, the Government really needs to restructure it now. The bulk of its money needs to go on learning projects which raise acceptance chances, rather than on aspirations.

Perhaps a few seminars for admissions tutors on the way to communicate with inner city pupils would be a start. Or perhaps funding for all Access projects should initially come from Oxbridge itself, which would be repaid pro rata by the Government if a specific project resulted in an acceptance rate of, say, 30 per cent.

2. Balance the scales

There is, of course, an alternative. The government could simply enforce the 77 per cent quota for state school students announced in 2006. Half-heartedly set and never enforced, it has been whole-heartedly ignored by Oxbridge. More active government inter-vention would certainly please the teachers and parents of the 90 per cent of British children attending state schools.

However, such suggestions do not go down well at Oxbridge. Jane Minto, the director of the Oxford admissions office, spoke for many of its academics when she told journalists on 6th March 2003: "We don't subscribe to quotas at Oxford... Students should be selected purely on academic merit." At Cambridge, her counter-part Susan Stobbs took a similar line.

This would be a convincing argument if only it did not leave the listener with a nagging question. How come academic merit mani-fests itself in quite such a static way among Oxbridge applicants, and among them alone? Surely, different young people from different schools should produce different proportional intakes? Alas, it doesn't and none of my academic interviewees was prepared to comment on this staggering coincidence. In fact, cooperation often dried up at this point.

Nevertheless, the matter remains puzzling for those who under-stand the rules of mathematical probability, which I am sure includes many Oxbridge academics. It is as if a roulette wheel, once spun, would always land on one of the same narrow range of numbers between 49 and 58. Magic, or what? Please don't try this at your nearest casino.

The reality, of course, is different. There is a quota already. In fact, there are several. Most Oxbridge colleges seem to divide the univer-sity places they can offer almost 50/50 between state school and private school pupils, no matter how many applications they receive from each group. On the other hand, some faculties, notably Oxford medicine, accept the same proportion of candidates from each group, usually 20 per cent. Since the state school group is larger, this results in rather more of its pupils getting in.

A few colleges specifically aim for a much higher state school intake, something between 60 and 75 per cent, and reach their precise target every year.

In the end, though, all these decisions are coordinated at Oxford and Cambridge during post-interview meetings of admissions tutors and other university staff. The result is an overall result for each university which is just above 55 per cent of state school and just below 45 per cent of private school students, year after year after year.

There is what some people may regard as a benevolent explanation for this process. Several dons I spoke to hinted that they made allowances for state school candidates. If they were to go purely by evidence of ability alone, so they suggested, their proportion would be even lower than it is now. Instead, the number of state school candidates accepted was regularly rounded upwards, up to a point.

There are two not so small problems with this explanation. One, as already suggested, is the implicit assumption that state school candidates are not only less intelligent than private school ones, but also that all of them are less intelligent year after year. The other problem is that this intellectual difference is assumed to exist despite the fact that both types of candidates obtain very similar A-level grades. It is, of course, possible that the interview, which has at its centre a certain type of highly educated middle class discourse, does not work as well for applicants from other backgrounds, as suggested earlier on, and this would be a strong argument for its abolition.

On the other hand, the whole differential ability claim can just be dismissed as nonsense. Wadham College, which has the second highest state school intake in Oxford, has consistently been in the top half of the Norrington table: in fact, it came second out of 29 colleges in 2003. Clearly, state school pupils can do as well as the rest if given the chance.

It certainly seems hard to think of a convincing argument against the implementation of a representative quota. The only real question is how high it should be. The Government figure of 77 per cent is one option. The benchmark of 62 per cent, a figure which the two universities have in the past said they hoped to reach within five years but are not progressing towards, is another. Given that the Government funds 70 per cent of Oxbridge university expenditure, the proportion of students Oxbridge accepts from the public education sector should perhaps be identical. This would leave the private sector, which educates 8 per cent of pupils, with 30 per cent, still a high proportion but one that acknowledges that it does educate many talented young people, often as sixth form scholars.

3. Make schools more equal

One major obstacle to a more representative Oxbridge intake remains the inequality among state schools themselves. Rather than creating ever-new categories of secondaries, the government must now close the gap among the existing ones. A sixth former doing science A-levels should be taught by someone who has a degree in Chemistry, Physics or Maths, irrespective of whether she is attending a state grammar, specialist school, city academy or bog-standard comprehensive. The current situation, in which a third of all of Physics teachers in state secondary schools (and 70 per cent of all those teaching Physics) are unqualified in the subject, is a real outrage.

So are Britain's class sizes, which are the largest in the developed world. How can a pupil taught in a state sixth form of twenty-eight possibly compete with someone from a private A-level class of twelve? While government funding for education has been sharply raised, much of the record education budget of £36bn. announced in 2006 was earmarked for capital expenditure; it will pay for the construction or refurbishment of some 12,000 schools. It might be nice for every school to have a shiny new steel-and-glass atrium, but having a large, fully qualified teaching staff is more urgent.

Nor should the location of a school make a difference. Merely living in a British city can condemn you to an inferior education. London's state schools hardly feature among the country's top 500. In Birmingham and Liverpool things are even worse. Given that our famous cities attract the most motivated, able people, the fact that their children achieve educationally less than those in small farming towns should not be blamed on the parents. True, some urban areas are struggling with the loss of manufacturing jobs, but this is surely yet another argument for sending in more, better qualified teachers. Creating a larger teaching staff, moreover, can mean shorter working hours for teachers, which should reduce drop-out rates. The government's determination to spend much of the education budget on grand, staggeringly costly new school buildings instead helps nobody.

The current situation does tempt at least some Oxbridge admissions tutors to pick their state school students from a small range of academically strong schools in cosy suburbs. According to a 2007 study by the Institute for Public Policy Research, one hundred elite schools, constituting less than 3 per cent of 3,700 schools with sixth forms and sixth form colleges in the UK, accounted for a third of admissions to Oxbridge during the last five years. The group is composed of 80 independent schools, 18 grammar schools, and two comprehensives.

While Oxbridge really should not get away with making its dons' lives quite so easy, government does have a duty to prepare our brightest students for the most appropriate universities.

4. Modernise

Lastly, the Government must take the lead in defining what the Oxbridge debate fiercely fought already within Government departments, in the media and among parents is really about.

Those who wish to preserve the Oxbridge entrance structure largely unchanged define this, in the words of Anthony Smith, the President of Magdalen College, Oxford, as "a matter of autonomy". The two universities, from this angle, must be allowed to stick with their current system if they so wish. Nobody else is allowed to impose anything on them because they are autonomous bodies in law.

The problem with this argument is that the autonomy enjoyed by all British universities is essentially designed to cover what they teach and nobody is suggesting that this should change. Admissions is a different matter. Legislation, or the threat of it, gradually compelled the universities over the last 130 years to accept Jews and Catholics, Dissenters and women. A-levels too became a universal entrance requirement only because Government wished it, although the pupils of Britain's seven top public schools (Eton, Harrow, Westminster, Rugby, Winchester, Charterhouse and Shrewsbury) were exempted until the mid 1960s.

Usually, such changes are imposed by means of the carrot and the stick. Government, or the Department of Education, states what it would like, and Oxbridge refuses until threatened with sharp cuts in funding. At this point, internal reform kicks in. There is no reason why the same should not happen now, though there are few signs that the current Labour Government has any desire to wave a stick.

Another way of defining the Oxbridge debate was offered by the President of the National Students Union, Mandy Telford, when she stated that the universities needed to reform their entrance process for the sake of opportunity. In a modern society, she argued, a small group of society should not be allowed a disproportionate hold over this.

In the end, though, it would be easiest if the Government looked at Oxbridge entrance in terms of simple justice. If this is indeed the best place to develop certain types of knowledge and to acquire certain skills, then those who can be scientifically shown to be most suited for this endeavour should be allowed in.

This might, of course, require the introduction of universal tests, already pioneered by a few faculties, but need not change much else.

College places could be allocated on the basis of results, and if colleges wished to preserve their individual characteristics, this would be fine, as long as the nature of those characteristics was spelt out.

In other words, Oxbridge could remain the impressive, unusual place it always was, but also embody more of the values of our age.

WHAT OXBRIDGE SHOULD DO:

1. Reconsider the interview

The change that would have the greatest impact would be for dons to acknowledge that the interview, which is central to the admissions procedure, is not an effective ability test. This is not to question the good intentions of those administering it. Contrary to the widespread impression that dons just seek to pick out posh students, Oxbridge is almost obsessed with finding the most able ones.

One elderly science don, determined to get more gifted working class students into his renowned college, confidently told me that he had solved the problem. "The way is to dive straight into the subject questions at the interview, if you want to get the measure of their abilities. Being talked to about this and that for the first few minutes only confuses them," he told me in a firm voice clearly used to imparting universal wisdom.

For a moment I wondered if I should also ask him to tell me also the secret of composing music or of writing a great novel. Clearly a man so certain about his expertise in a field not his own could provide the answer to everything. He had certainly created a new scientific truth: all working class candidates were alike and those who didn't sparkle in response to his majestic, well-spoken approach were just not bright.

The scientist was not alone. Other tutors seemed equally certain that they had found the philosopher's stone, albeit a different one. A mathematician sought to relax all male candidates by discussing sport. One engineering don seemed certain that only through dis-orientating a candidate completely by remaining silent could he identify brains, while another relied on discussing a subject miles from the one which a student had applied for. A historian would confess, after defending the interview process, that she spent a lot of her time thinking up ways of further perfecting it, of making it even more fair.

Listening to this as I was doing my initial research in 2001–2, I some-times felt as if I was in the presence of a very bright young child who knew nothing of the real world. After all, the question of how to iden-tify gifted candidates, a relatively new concern for Oxbridge, has been professionally pondered for decades. The people who administer detailed scientific tests in order to pinpoint abilities are called educa-tional psychologists. Their research has given us ways of spotting talent irrespective of class and methods which reduce cultural bias. They have worked out which background data can be relevant and how to weigh the results accordingly. These experts produce journal pieces and books which, as their authors tend to be non-Oxbridge, never seemed to impact on the two universities.

However, new selection methods are now emerging. Oxford is putting its applicants for their Law and Medicine courses through the same, externally devised ability tests as other top universities. Cambridge has created a new Law test for all its colleges with the help of external advice. Between them, the two universities have also introduced detailed written tests of their own for half a dozen other courses.

That they embarked on much of this shortly after the Govern-ment-commissioned Schwartz report criticized the university entrance process (and just as the first edition of this book appeared) was pure coincidence – perhaps.

2. Watch its language

While standardised, written tests undoubtedly constitute progress, they are not, as yet problem-free. Comprehensive school heads bitterly complain about their terminology and phrasing. Too much of this, they feel, favours students from genteel, educated homes. "Students from working class backgrounds" one London head told *The Oxbridge Student*, "need to learn the language as well as the skill. Maybe a few less Latinate terms and a few more rooted in Anglo-Saxon?"

This mirrors teachers' complaints about the verbal interview. Good talk, like a good test, requires comprehension. University speak is normally learned at university; you cannot pick it up by walking into a don's room. Some interviewers are able to conduct an intellectual cross-examination in colloquial English, but others have communicated in upper middle class, academic language all their lives and are unable to change. So, a student unfamiliar with elaborate wording or vague, open-ended questions may not come across well.

Moreover, the precise role of the tests has been left open. Neither Oxford nor Cambridge will say how much even a top result in the BMAT, LNAT, TSA or the Oxford exams in History, English and Maths actually count for. Teachers have been shocked to discover that a 90 per cent test score may not compensate for a stumbling interview performance by a nervous inner city student. Verbal performance still seems decisive.

Test were apparently introduced to resolve this, but they cannot do so if they are obscurely worded or accorded no weight. True, testing for brains has not yet been perfected and intensive coaching can produce misleadingly good test results, but education experts can usually refine the questions to minimize this. Oxbridge should act to ensure this is done, since written tests are at least familiar to most students. As the warden of New College Oxford, Alan Ryan, has pointed out, they also more accurately reflect academic reality: "What students do at university is write."

3. Join the youth club
The recent, official renunciation of extra-curricular activities as a selection factor will improve many students' admissions prospects. A sign of the commitment to widening participation by Oxbridge, it also reflects the changing social origins of its dons. Around half of them now come from state schools and so know more than their predecessors about how ordinary people live. They are aware that most families don't go to church, that teenagers often hate school sports and that modern music lovers tend to indulge this passion by listening to a CD.

We can glimpse just how resourceful many past state school candidates really were from the fact that they managed to assemble that old, slightly sad parcel of spare time activities. Not only was it a century removed from today's youth culture, but it was also so much easier to fill if you had cash.

Moreover, what sixth formers do determines how they speak and what they understand. This means not just that interview questions should not be worded in ways that are hopelessly incomprehensible to them. It also means that bright students who use every-day or youth culture language ought not be lightly dismissed as unacademic. As long as they have a library card, they too might be "interesting young people".

It might even be useful for dons to know more about applicants' general background. The Universities and Colleges Admissions Service (UCAS) has been trying to help: from 2008, it will tell universities whether either of an applicant's parents is a university graduate. There is no longer any need to blindly guess about this pivotal fact. Knowing it could enable Oxbridge to make allowances for educational disadvantage, even in the case of students not quite poor enough to qualify for special support.

Sadly, both Oxford and Cambridge have announced that they will disregard this information as "uncorroborated data". Some admissions tutors openly say that they fear applicants might lie. The new post UCAS questionnaires Oxbridge now sends to applicants, while useful, do not supply quite the same type of information. A more constructive approach seems essential if the Oxbridge intake balance is to change.

Failing that, there may be a clamour for a more structured solution. Since the introduction of tuition fees, students look at educational provisions with a rather critical eye. They see themselves as consumers and want to know precisely how things work. What might satisfy them are universal entrance exams, a solution already quietly discussed and favoured by a few dons.

Meanwhile, though, it would be nice if the existing entrance criteria were applied with more care. Before insisting, yet again, that "we're just not getting the applicants" as almost every admissions tutor I spoke to did, it may be an idea for Oxbridge to look at the characteristics of those it rejects. Returning from an Oxbridge day school to his inner city comprehensive, one frustrated teacher summed up his feelings to me: "Now that we've learnt all we can about the admissions process, maybe their admissions tutors should get some training. We need to train Oxbridge; our students cannot conform to their criteria, but they are bright young people and will achieve."

Anyone doubting his words only needs to look at the final twist in the Laura Spence saga. The working class school girl who was rejected by Oxford in 2000 went on to excel in the Harvard entrance test, winning not just a place but a £37,000 scholarship. At Harvard, Laura became one of only five women named "All-Ivy" for her academic achievements. Returning to Britain with a top Biochemistry degree, she then applied to the tiny, hugely contested Cambridge postgraduate medical course. She got in, you will be glad to hear, but there must be a faster, easier way of proving your worth.

4. Learn to love teachers

One of the most important things which a university that wants to be sent lots of good, enthusiastic candidates does is to cultivate their teachers. This is a relationship that Oxbridge has yet to build, at least with regard to state school teachers. Quite a few Oxbridge dons seem to regard them as unreliable suppliers of goods: they don't answer Access circulars, I was told; they don't send enough candidates or send the wrong ones. There was a distinct sense of impatience, almost a feeling that the teachers were not really doing their job.

The most serious crime, and indeed one I often heard state school teachers accused of, was anti-elitism. Pushed a little further, some dons spelt out to me what they meant. "There's a lot of left-wingers, of course, among the teaching profession. People thinking that Oxbridge is a posh place, so one mustn't encourage pupils to go there," I was told by an elderly male don, educated at a famous school, in the quiet, confidential tone used by gentlemen to imply that one's butler may have been at the gin.

In the course of writing this book, I went to great lengths to examine this assertion. That there are many left-wingers among state school teachers is undoubtedly true. The kind of people who opt to develop the potential of children whose family has never earned more than the minimum wage tend not to be on the right in their political sympathies. Neither are those who see potential in a scruffy boy with battered trainers.

But does this mean left-wing teachers are against Oxbridge? To find out, I deliberately arranged in-depth interviews about Oxbridge entrance with sixth form and careers teachers I knew not just to be vaguely on the left, but politically committed. Some were active in leftwing branches of the Labour Party. Several were Trotskyites, members of Britain's Socialist Workers Party. Others defined themselves as Communists.

They had a lot in common. All were fully clued up about the technical requirements for Oxbridge entry. Most had read the piles of special bumph emanating from there, on top of other university entrance publications. Some had been on college visits; others were booked on yet another Oxbridge teachers day. This required massive form-filling and a rearrangement of the school's timetable, because their kind of schools was always short-staffed. They would have to take home papers for marking to compensate for the time lost. All had sent pupils up for interviews after preparing them to the best of their abilities. By January 2003, almost all of them also had failed to get even a single Oxbridge offer for a pupil. You might have expected them to proclaim that, as enemies of the people, the two universities should be burnt down, or at least picketed. Instead, the teachers were downcast as well as fearful that I might identify them or their schools.

"It's not an effective use of my time if nobody gets into Oxbridge, yet I don't send a student who I don't think is really good," one teacher in a battered leather jacket sighed. A colleague wearing a Stop-the-War badge nodded, adding with quiet understatement: "We despair a little after having spent so much time and effort on Oxbridge, yet middle class applicants still do much better."

These teachers were, nevertheless, prepared to soldier on. Next year things might improve, was the hope if the Government intervened. What set them apart from others was not any hostility to Oxbridge, though they were scathing about its selection criteria.

These were not people who thought of the two universities as precious national heritage institutions with mysterious, unfathomable ways, unlike quite a few other teachers I had met. Oxbridge, to them, was just top of the Russell Group, to whose universities they directed their very best pupils.

But that's left-wing teachers. What my research suggested is that Oxbridge is doing no better with teachers holding more mainstream political views or none at all. These are people who unreservedly admire the two universities, yet would wistfully say: "We thought we had built a relationship with Oxbridge." Usually, this meant with one of the universities and two or three of its colleges. These teachers had talked to dons, trying to explain their students' back-grounds and strengths. They'd had tea, dinner at high table, promises of consideration.

The problem, so they told me, is that most of this relationship does not bear fruit, at least not on an annual basis. A college which used to take two or three students out of a sixth form of almost 400 kids suddenly stops doing so. Another college keeps taking one student every other year, but the applicant mustn't be too black, it seems, whatever his other qualities. Or there is a sudden, unexplained, several year long gap.

Somehow, an Oxbridge college's relationship with a private school never breaks down. The school may only have a sixth form of 80, and may admit students on the strength of parental paying ability, not student's talent, but it will be going steady with the college.

The state school, on the other hand, can have quite a different experience. It may only find itself taken out for a whirl ever so often if the Government has recently made a fuss; if priorities have not shifted to another part of the state sector, say rural comprehen-sives; if it is compatible with the quota which is blatantly there but never admitted to. The state school is like the girl you can take for granted, the girl who will put out even if you won't elevate her to girlfriend status or show her respect. No wonder state school teachers feel hurt.

To make things harder still, all those teachers were, by choice, working in large urban schools, and this created constant dilemmas. As one sixth form head put it: "You know, it can take up to 20 hours to prepare a kid for Oxbridge, but we do it. Sometimes it's really hard to decide. I had a student living on a really bad estate. He was not a genius, but still a capable kid with a potential for higher education. I could either spend lots of time getting him into some former Poly in another town, away from his criminal environment. Or I could concentrate on getting a kid from a safer, more stable home background into Oxbridge. What would you have done?"

In the event, the committed professional did a bit of both. Unless such efforts are regularly rewarded at the Oxbridge end, it would be hard to blame him if he slackened.

5. Stop the nostalgia
When discussing student proportions at Oxbridge, dons almost invariably launch into a nostalgic account of how much better

things were when the grammar school system was still in force all over Britain.

Despite the heartfelt emotion, the statement is factual nonsense. There never was any golden age in which Oxbridge threw open its gates to those outside its traditional catchment area. In 1955, the number of students who had fathers in manual work was 9 per cent in Cambridge (the same as in 2002) and 13 per cent in Oxford (compared to 10 per cent in 2002). In 1963, the heyday of the grammar schools, 25 per cent of Cambridge students and 39 per cent of Oxford ones came from state schools (compared to 55 per cent now).

In fact, the pre-comprehensive school figures are even worse than they look, because the proportion of manual workers among the public was far higher than today. Also, the number of children at private schools was half what it is now. Meanwhile, the vast majority of children were attending secondary moderns, schools that led nowhere in educational terms. Still, the nostalgia persists because among those bright youngsters fortunate enough to then enter Oxbridge were many of today's dons. Ultimately, there is something cranky about the way in which today's top educators go on about a system that was abolished 30 years ago. It is as if they feel no duty to relate to current reality, which is that most children in Britain are schooled in comprehensives.

There is indeed a great deal wrong with comprehensives: they are shamefully under-funded and short of teachers and equipment. They also often cater poorly for both slow and fast learners. There could even be a strong argument for educating very able children separately from a certain age, if there was a way of identifying ability irrespective of class – not something the old grammar schools did well. Such a change would certainly be welcomed by the parents of such children. Among those, I am sure, would be thousands of middle class couples crippled by school fees.

Meanwhile, though, the comprehensives are our main national secondary schools, and therefore the nation's top universities really must pick more of their bright students. That many dons would genuinely like to do so I have no doubt. That they often don't because they've failed to grasp just how bright and resourceful a state school applicant needs to be in order to merely get interviewed is equally true. Fortunately, the detailed preparation offered to pupils by this book should make the two universities' selection job much easier.

24

At the gates

If you have been able to put your video games, or the housekeeping, or your employer's demands on standby for long enough to read through this book, then your family dream of Oxbridge has become an actual possibility. You now know the real rules of the entrance process, a prerequisite for effectively competing in this snakes and ladders game. Knowledge, in turn, tends to raise a person's confidence, and confidence is another ingredient of Oxbridge success.

You will also be able to distinguish between the two universities' present reality and their past. No longer are talented young people automatically excluded just because they didn't go to public school, or don't have middle class parents, or are not white. Nor need such students expect three years of humiliation if they do get in. True, all those things were a feature of Oxbridge history for hundreds of years, but so were outside lavatories. Government reforms, internal restructuring and new types of schools have changed Oxbridge so much it would be unrecognisable to those fighting over its "lily-whiteness".

This is not to say that today's entrance rules are equally fair to all bright students, and this book has no magic formula to offer which would alter this. What it can do, primarily, is to provide you with the tools to achieve the best possible outcome. It can also point out which aspects require further change.

Many self-help books give the impression that everything desirable will come to those ready to take a few easy steps. "Everyone can be a millionaire," "Think yourself thin," or "Be the person you want to be" are the mantras of their optimistic authors.

Unfortunately, the real world can be less flexible than these books imply. Powerful forces may thwart even the most determined. There are still Oxbridge rules which prevent some of the best students from getting in. Hardly ever talked about, they remain in place alongside all those friendly invitations, worthy proclamations and jolly Access booklets produced with the taxpayer's help.

Some of the obstacles created by these rules are unintentional, I am sure. Others are based on surprisingly sloppy thinking by academics paid to do rather better than that. Lastly, there are a few obstacles whose continued existence can only be due to a determination to keep student proportions roughly as they are, often by people who have invested much money to gain a lifelong advantage for their family or group.

On the other hand, my research showed that not all dons are happy with the present situation. Younger, state-educated ones would like to see the Oxbridge intake reflect the modern world. Quite a few older academics feel that, in the age of the human genome, Oxbridge will miss out on its intellectual lead if too many fine minds are snapped up by Imperial College, the LSE, UMIST or Harvard. Lastly, the fear of Government sanctions in the form of lower per capita allowances concentrates many a don's mind.

Student intake proportions, though, will not change because of some academics' good will. Nor can a young person's talent alone turn an obstacle course into a level playing field. This would require either more ability-test based entrance rules by Oxbridge or a new, quota-based higher education policy by the Government or both. The new aptitude exams added in certain subjects are a big step forward, but not necessarily one that will solve the problem.

More changes are needed and none of these will come about simply because they would make life fairer for bright students. They depend on strong, long-term pressure from several directions. If you're a potential candidate, a parent or a teacher at a school whose best pupils fail to get in, this can be done in the standard ways: badger the media, the Government, public bodies like your union and your MP. State school pupils who made it through Oxbridge might also consider forming a lobby group.

Meanwhile, though, you must be willing to take the emotional risk of applying or to encourage your teenager to apply. If he is bright and hard-working, if she is focused and original, the process, despite its flaws, could well result in success.

All this is hard work, and some of you may be tempted to give up on Oxbridge instead. Together with many of its devoted students and graduates, I would advise you to persist because the rewards are so great. Oxbridge is that rare, amazing thing in today's Britain, a well-funded, high-level, stunningly beautiful public education facility. It is already enjoyed by thousands of state school students every year, and if public opinion can be hitched to individual effort, might yet welcome more.

Contact list

UNIVERSITY OF CAMBRIDGE
Cambridge Admissions Office
Tel. 01223 333 308
Email: admissions@cam.ac.uk
Website: www.cam.ac.uk/admissions/undergraduate/
General website: www.cam.ac.uk

CAMBRIDGE UNIVERSITY STUDENTS UNION
Email: access@cusu.cam.ac.uk
Website: www.cusu.cam.ac.uk

UNIVERSITY OF OXFORD
Oxford Colleges Admissions Office
Tel. 01865 288 000
Email: undergraduate.admissions@admin.ox.ac.uk
Website: www.admissions.ox.ac.uk
General website: www.ox.ac.uk

OXFORD UNIVERSITY STUDENTS UNION
Email: enquiries@ousu.org
Website: www.ousu.org

UCAS
Tel. (0)871 468 0 468
Email: enquiries@ucas.ac.uk
Website: www.ucas.ac.uk

TARGET SCHOOLS CAMBRIDGE
Website: www.cusu.cam.ac.uk/campaigns/target/

TARGET SCHOOLS OXFORD
Website: http://www.targetschoolsoxford.com/

CAMBRIDGE WIDENING PARTICIPATION
Email: access@cao.cam.ac.uk

CAMBRIDGE GROUP TO ENCOURAGE ETHNIC MINORITY APPLICATIONS (GEEMA)
Email: geema@cao.cam.ac.uk

OXFORD ACCESS SCHEMES
Website: http://www.ox.ac.uk/admissions/undergraduate_courses/working_with_schools_and_colleges/

OXFORD SCHOOLS LIAISON & EDUCATION EVENTS
Email: schools.liaison@mpls.ox.ac.uk

CAMBRIDGE OPEN DAYS
Website:
http://www.cam.ac.uk/admissions/undergraduate/opendays/

OXFORD OPEN DAYS
Website: http://www.ox.ac.uk/admissions/undergraduate_courses/open_days/index.html

YOUNG, GIFTED AND TALENTED (Y, G & T)
Tel. 0845 602 1732
Website: http://ygt.dcsf.gov.uk/HomePage.aspx?stakeholder = 14

SUTTON TRUST
Tel. 020 8788 3223
Website: www.suttontrust.com

INSPIRE
Tel. 01344 890126
Website: http://www.inspire-ed.com/